The
SOONER
Story

THE SOONER STORY

The University of Oklahoma

1890–2015

ANNE BARAJAS HARP

Foreword by CAROL J. BURR

UNIVERSITY OF OKLAHOMA PRESS : NORMAN
in cooperation with the
UNIVERSITY OF OKLAHOMA FOUNDATION

Editor in Chief: Charles E. Rankin
Developmental Editor: Alice K. Stanton
Copyeditor: Jo Ann Reece
Design: Julie S. Rushing
Production: Emmy Ezzell
Printing: Edwards Brothers Malloy

ISBN: 978-0-8061-9977-1 (pbk. : alk. paper)

The paper in this book meets the guidelines for permanence and durability of the Committee on Production Guidelines for Book Longevity of the Council on Library Resources, Inc. ∞

1 2 3 4 5 6 7 8 9 10

CONTENTS

FOREWORD

"Tell me a story."

It's the admonition given writers along with their assignments for *Sooner Magazine,* the quarterly publication of the University of Oklahoma Foundation and, before 1980, of the OU Alumni Association. Alumni executive secretary R. Boyd Gunning no doubt said something similar to Charles F. Long, the magazine's associate editor, in sending him out to write a comprehensive history of the university for a special seventy-fifth–anniversary issue in 1965.

Long had his work cut out for him. No one had tackled this task since 1942, when historian-turned–admissions dean Roy Gittinger produced *The University of Oklahoma: A History of Fifty Years, 1892–1942,* a chronicle of OU's first half-century complete with every name, date, vital statistic, and institutional milestone, most of which Gittinger had witnessed personally. Anything but fascinating reading, his book has been the fact-checker's friend whenever that early period is discussed.

Charlie Long was a journalist, not a historian, and he lacked the luxury of time or space required for a book-length treatment. For starters, he dated the university's origin from its official establishment in 1890, rather than the start of classes in 1892, as Gittinger had done. Examining the university through the lens of each presidential administration from the beginning of David Ross Boyd's to the middle of George Lynn Cross's, he completed his highly readable, meticulously researched overview with journalistic efficiency and the help of *Sooner Magazine* editor Paul Galloway. They called their eighty-page "story" *A History of the University of Oklahoma,* never guessing that it would form the basis for two subsequent anniversary updates, both more aptly titled *The Sooner Story,* initially in 1980, and now in 2015.

By the time Gunning commissioned the first *Sooner Story,* both Long and Galloway had departed for Chicago— Long to edit *The Quill* magazine and Galloway to pursue a lengthy career at the *Chicago Tribune.* Carolyn G. Hart was chosen to write this new version, and I became its editor. Hart subsequently went on to great success as an award-winning mystery writer, earning the soubriquet "America's Agatha Christie." I ended thirty-nine years as editor of *Sooner Magazine* in 2015.

Hart revised Long's text, rewrote the Cross chapter, and continued the narrative through subsequent administrations into William S. Banowsky's presidency. Author Anne Barajas Harp carries that organizational scheme forward in this new edition of *The Sooner Story.*

Harp, who also came from the ranks of *Sooner Magazine* writers, was charged with bringing the story up through the first twenty years of the David L. Boren administration in time for the university's 125th anniversary. The task of blending her original post-1980 research with Long's and Hart's material was challenging but skillfully achieved with remarkable seamlessness.

This time, the author had both the advantage and the disadvantage of dealing with living history. On the plus side, seven presidents were available to give her their personal analyses of people, places, and events—Banowsky, Frank E. Horton, Richard L. Van Horn, and Boren and interim presidents Martin C. Jischke, David Swank, and John R. Morris— as well as Paul F. Sharp's widow, Rose, who played a significant role during her husband's tenure. The disadvantage lies in working without a long-term historical perspective. Harp wisely leaves interpretive judgment to future historians.

The Boren chapter, by design more topical than chronological, is noticeably different from its predecessors. Reflecting the personality of its central character—and the fact that it is unfinished—the account of the Boren years deals with big ideas that have dominated his presidency—internationalization, the focus on students, development of fine arts resources, landscaping, and physical plant expansion.

All of the authors who have shaped this project over time have had access to the extensive resources of the OU Western History Collections and its OU Archives. Personal papers, Board of Regents minutes, media reports, and a nearly endless supply of photographs, maps, and other images are to be found there, as well as published works of Harold Keith and others on football; George Cross on integration, World War II, academic freedom, and private support to public education; and numerous departmental and program histories.

The Sooner Story is one of three historically themed publications the OU Foundation and the University of Oklahoma

Press are offering for the 125th anniversary. The long-awaited second volume of OU historian David W. Levy's *The University of Oklahoma: A History*—deeply researched, objective, eloquently written—takes up the story at the end of World War I and ends with the educational explosion after World War II. A more visual treatment can be found in *Path to Excellence,* the coffee-table book of photographs from 1890 to 2015 compiled by the staff of the Western History Collections from their archives.

Whenever books are commissioned, the questions for the publisher are who will buy them, who will want to read them, and with academic publishers, how they will contribute to the educational mission. Histories are niche publications, but what a niche it is with books such as *The Sooner Story*! Long after the older editions have gone out of print, requests for them still come. Interest lingers. Thirty-five years have passed since the last comprehensive look at the University of Oklahoma's history, even as the story continues to unfold with ever-accelerating speed. Just think of the university in 1980 as compared to the university today. It is the responsibility of historians and journalists alike to recharge fading memories and preserve the past in order to better appreciate the present and anticipate the future.

CAROL J. BURR
Norman, Oklahoma

ACKNOWLEDGMENTS

When first asked to write the new edition of *The Sooner Story,* I had no idea how I was going to get the project completed within two years. I discovered that the obvious answer was, "With a whole lot of help."

My job was to update the stellar 1981 edition by Charles Long (OU, 1961) and Carolyn Hart (OU, 1958). Their research and writing provided the foundation for my own, and with permission, some of their 1981 work is carried forward virtually unchanged.

Iconic university figures were incredibly generous in sharing their memories and introspections, especially President David L. Boren; President Emeritus William S. Banowsky; former presidents Frank E. Horton and Richard L. Van Horn; former interim presidents J.R. Morris, Martin C. Jischke, and David Swank; and former OU first lady Rose Sharp. I appreciate their service to the University of Oklahoma.

David Ross Boyd Professor Emeritus David Levy graciously allowed me to lean upon his essential study *The University of Oklahoma: A History, Volume 1: 1890–1917.* I owe much to my first OU journalism professor, William McKeen, now chair of the Boston University Department of Journalism, for the use of his doctoral dissertation, "Field Day: Student Dissent at the University of Oklahoma, May 5–12, 1970." Credit also goes to Bob Burke for his biography of President David L. Boren, *Oklahoma Statesman*; the late OU president George Lynn Cross for *Professors, Presidents, and Politicians*; OU president emeritus William F. Banowsky for *The Malibu Miracle*; distinguished OU professor George Henderson for *Race and the University*; and the late Dean Roy Gittinger for *The University of Oklahoma: A History of Fifty Years, 1892–1942.*

The archives of *Sooner Magazine* were invaluable to my research, as was the work of many an Oklahoma newspaper reporter, with particular thanks to those at the *Oklahoman*. OU Public Affairs, headed by mentor and vice president Catherine Bishop, provided a small mountain of information, as did April Wilkerson, the editor of *OU Medicine* on the Health Sciences Center campus, and Athletic Publications Director Debbie Copp. John Lovett, director of special collections at the Western History Collections, heads a crack team of archivists and student staff members who came to my rescue, and graduate student Bethany Mowry was a writer's-dream photo researcher and caption crafter.

The editorial staff at OU Press led me through alien territory and molded my writing into a book. Sincere appreciation to Director Byron Price, Associate Director and Editor-in-Chief Charles Rankin, developmental editor Alice Stanton, Managing Editor Steven Baker, and editorial assistant Jake Blackwell.

A special note of thanks to OU's chief storyteller Carol Burr, who retired in 2015 after thirty-nine years as editor of *Sooner Magazine.* I am blessed to be among the vast stable of writers Carol mentored and encouraged, and each of us coveted her respect far more than we did a byline or paycheck. Carol put my name forth for this project. For this and every other kindness over twenty-five years, I owe Carol my most heartfelt gratitude.

And finally, this book is dedicated to my husband, Jeff, and my sons, Jack and Sam, who believed I could write *The Sooner Story,* kept me focused on what was truly important, and are far prouder of me than I could ever deserve.

ANNE BARAJAS HARP
Norman, Oklahoma

The
SOONER
Story

DAVID ROSS BOYD
1892-1908

 DAVID ROSS BOYD stepped off the train in Norman, Oklahoma, on August 6, 1892, and looked to the southwest. "There was not a tree or shrub in sight," said the man who had been hired to serve as the University of Oklahoma's first president. "All I could see was the monotonous stillness of prairie grass. . . . Later I was to find out that this prairie grass wasn't so monotonous as it seemed, for its sameness was broken at quite frequent intervals by buffalo wallows. Behind me was a crude little town of 1,500 people, and before me was a stretch of prairie on which my helpers and I were to build an institution of culture.

"Discouraged?" he wrote. "Not a bit. The sight was a challenge."

David Ross Boyd was the son of staunchly religious, hardworking Midwesterners. The Ohio native started teaching at the age of seventeen and worked his way up through the secondary education profession until he became school superintendent at Arkansas City, Kansas, a town that in 1888 was teeming with thousands of people anxiously waiting for the opening of Oklahoma Territory.

In his book *The University of Oklahoma: A History, Volume 1, 1890–1917*, OU professor emeritus and historian David W. Levy relates the impressions of Boyd's wife, Jennie Thompson Boyd, who recalled having fifteen different neighbors in just one year of living in Arkansas City. Jennie Boyd said the town was so crowded that stores could barely keep supplies on the shelves, and strangers would approach townspeople to ask if they could sleep on their porches.

David Ross Boyd was able to form a beneficial plan from this turbulence. He convinced the city to hire men and their teams of horses at $1.50 a day to improve the school grounds and city parks, to grade new streets, and to plant much-needed trees. Boyd met the crews every morning at seven and sent them off to work under supervision. His scheme helped transform Arkansas City. It also burnished Boyd's reputation; he soon was encouraged to run for state superintendent of schools.

Instead an ironic twist of fate and a heater system would bring Boyd to the fledgling University of Oklahoma. Barely a year after the Land Run of 1889, Territorial Governor George W. Steele signed a bill to establish three institutions of higher education. There would be an agricultural and mechanical college in Stillwater, a normal school in Edmond, and a state university in Norman—if, and only if, the residents of Cleveland County came up with forty acres of property and $10,000 to construct a new building. Norman townspeople quickly helped approve a bond issue for the $10,000, but the bonds had to be sold and converted into cash before the State Legislature could accept them. The bonds were sold to an Oklahoma City man for $7,800, which left a $2,200 deficit. The deficit was covered by more bonds, this set sold to Norman businessmen via subscription by Delbert Larsh, an ambitious town father who had partnered in several projects with Norman's first mayor, Tom Waggoner. Both men had put their political acumen behind the push to bring the state university to Norman, and Larsh was able to gather the remaining $2,200 to meet the required $10,000 in cash just five days before the deadline.

The question of where OU should be located in Norman was equally challenging. A contentious debate—the first of many over the next century—erupted between east and west Norman. Democrats tended to live on the east side of town, and Republicans on the west. According to David Levy, an eastern campus was proposed near existing Porter Avenue, on the site of what is now Griffin Memorial Hospital. The suggested western site was owned by Seth "Dad" Moore, who sold the property "bordered today by Boyd Street on the north and Brooks Street on the south, by Elm on the west and Asp on the east" to the territorial government for $1,000. Moore's offer settled the issue.

But OU's new campus sat isolated from Norman's downtown. Delbert Larsh and Tom Waggoner owned abutting properties between downtown and the university site. Each donated a strip of land from the outermost edge of his property, and the conjoined space would become University Boulevard, linking Norman to the campus.

The next important step came when the university's new Board of Regents, all appointed by Governor Steele, awarded a contract to builder C. H. Holcraft for a building to house OU's future students. The cost was not to exceed $15,739. Although Norman had funded the bonds and a building was already in the works, OU's future was still not assured. Territorial Governor Steele had resigned after one year in office and was replaced by Abraham Seay. It was rumored that Seay would move the university to his hometown of Guthrie, the territorial capital, but President Grover Cleveland settled the matter by appointing W. C. Renfrow as territorial governor. Renfrow, with many ties to Norman, chose to leave OU where it was.

Earlier in spring 1892, as Levy explains, two members of the OU Board of Regents had visited David Ross Boyd in Arkansas City. The Regents had traveled to Arkansas City to see the high school's heating system, which was advanced for its time and manufactured by the Smead Company. The system was being considered for OU's campus. Coincidentally one of the Regents was Andrew F. Pentecost, a Civil War veteran whom Boyd had helped to earn a teaching certificate. When Boyd gave the Regents a

tour of the heating system, they asked him to suggest candidates for OU's new president. Boyd offered two names and thought no more of it until much later, when he was en route to Oklahoma City by train on other business. There he had a chance meeting with a Smead Company representative, who asked Boyd to do him the favor of dropping by an OU Board of Regents meeting in Oklahoma City to offer a testimonial about Smead's products. Boyd agreed. He showed up at the meeting and ran into OU Regent Pentecost, who seemed surprised to see him there.

In a 1932 interview between David Ross Boyd and Roscoe Cate, the *Sooner Magazine* editor who later became OU's financial vice president, Boyd said, "When the board convened, they left the [Smead Company] agents and me in an outside room, separated by sliding doors from the room in which the session was held. . . . I could plainly hear the president of the board ask if the special committee on selecting the president was ready to report. I immediately became very much interested, wondering if by chance either of my friends . . . had been selected." Boyd overheard Regent Pentecost talk about his trip to Arkansas City "to make investigations," and then was stunned to hear the Regent close with, "We are, therefore, ready to report recommending the election of Professor David R. Boyd, Superintendent of Schools of Arkansas City, Kansas, to be the first president of the University of Oklahoma."

Boyd was led into the meeting, where he told the Regents that he had never considered himself a candidate for the job. Regardless, he left Oklahoma City with an offer in hand. Several friends urged him to take the challenge of forming a new university, and with further consideration, Boyd accepted the position for a yearly salary of $2,400.

A PRESIDENT COMES TO OU

When Boyd arrived in Norman in August 1892, he had little more than a month to hire a faculty, find space for classrooms and offices, locate and purchase supplies, and arrange student housing before OU's first classes began. As Levy explains, "using a cramped hotel room as an office, with almost no help from anyone else, he had to do everything at once."

Boyd's top priority was hiring a faculty. "I received many applications to teach," Boyd said. "These I first answered by asking them what their motives were in coming here. Too often the reply was that the applicant wanted to do research work or to write. These I didn't even consider. What I wanted was teachers, men and women who would be willing to devote all of their energies to developing fiercely earnest young students."

Boyd had begun hiring before he even left Kansas, employing William N. Rice, a professor of ancient languages and literature from Southwest Kansas College, in July 1892. A month later, Boyd selected Edwin C. DeBarr, a professor at Albion College, as OU's new professor of chemistry and physics. French Amos, a teacher from Lampasas, Texas, would instruct English, history, and civics. At thirty-nine, Boyd was the eldest of the faculty. Taking the title of professor of mental and moral science, he prepared to teach math, grammar, and elementary Latin. "Our first faculty meeting was held on a warm evening out of doors," Boyd recalls, "and the first business we attended to was the cutting of a large watermelon. After we ate the melon, we discussed arrangements of classes."

Because OU's first building would not be completed on time for fall classes, Norman businessmen offered to lease the university the Adkins-Welch building at 12 West Main Street in downtown Norman. OU rented what was known as "The Rock Building" for twenty dollars a month. "In comparison with the magnificent plants of older and wealthier states, it seemed a gross exaggeration to call that stone building and its modest confines a university," said Professor William N. Rice. "Only three rooms without ornament, barely comfortable, cheaply furnished with tables for teachers' desks and chairs for the students; no libraries, laboratories, traditions."

OU's first students were due to arrive in just one week. The territorial government offered free tuition to all potential students and encouraged enrollment through active advertising, promising that "any young man or woman who has finished the course in a good country school may enter the University and find educational work and a welcome." Boyd took an active role in promoting the university and, with the help of French Amos, devised a four-page brochure that was printed at the *Norman Transcript* and mailed to prospective students. Boyd crisscrossed many miles by horse and buggy to recruit students in small towns across the

Oklahoma Territory. His hard work was rewarded when, on the morning of September 15, a crowd of fifty-seven college prospects lined up outside the Rock Building. Most students came from the counties surrounding Norman, and each met with President Boyd and his faculty personally so that his or her readiness for college-level work could be formally assessed. Rice recalled the first group of students as "the unspoiled products of pioneer life, without pretension and without conventionalism. But best of all, they are dead earnest and feel that they are facing a great opportunity."

Most were not yet ready for such an opportunity. High schools in Oklahoma Territory had not been in existence long enough to graduate anyone, and many of OU's first generation were adults who had given up education to work or members of nomadic families who had lost the chance for formal secondary education in the years just before and after the 1889 Land Run. "As there was scarcely a well-organized high school in Oklahoma, it was the policy of the university to take the young people as it found them, to accommodate itself to existing conditions. We were building for a future, and, for the sake of a thereafter, it seemed better to grow up than to blow up," Rice said frankly, adding, "I am not disposed to blush as I record these humble beginnings." Boyd recalled: "It was the hardness of the prairies, the days full of labor, the necessity of facing life in the raw that matured them. . . . And it was this realization that at home, in dugouts and cabins and one-room shanties, mothers and fathers were sacrificing to aid them and dreaming that education would lift their children from the drudgery of the soil."

Boyd began to do his part in that endeavor by placing every one of OU's first students in what was called the "Preparatory College," which offered courses in reading, spelling, grammar, geography, physiology, and U.S. history. Almost all students took beginning Latin, but only the most advanced were prepared for such topics as civics, general

OU's first students at their temporary home in the Rock Building, downtown Norman, 1892. *(Boyd 90)*

history, algebra, or composition. The university's first student class was roughly half male and half female, unusual in higher education at that time. Levy writes that, at its founding, OU likely had the highest enrollment of women among the nation's public institutions. African American students would not be eligible to enter OU until 1949, with the admission of Ada Lois Sipuel Fisher. But Native American students were most likely part of OU's student body from its earliest days.

The Rock Building served as classroom, assembly hall, recitation room, administrative offices, and chapel. Each day started with chapel, and class instruction began immediately thereafter. Small class sizes, sometimes a blessing as male students navigated a clear view around women wearing large hats, resulted in a tightly knit cadre of students who were well known by their teachers. "We were from everywhere, and we had neither customs nor traditions in common," Rice said. "The university was an infant in everything except the hopes and ambitions of its founders."

Those ambitions were furthered by the doubling of OU's student body in the fall of 1893, when 119 students enrolled. The increase was due in part to population growth in the Twin Territories and from the fact that Indian Territory students could now attend OU tuition-free. As in the university's first class, many students lived with family in Norman, and the number of students was still equal by gender. Students who did not have any family in town often lived in "boarding clubs"—houses that offered a cook and housekeeper for a fee. Many of OU's first students were full-grown adults, some as old as forty-five, who had experienced very little formal schooling. As a result, Boyd designed something he called the "Push Class." He would keep a special eye on Push Class students and in attempts to create a cohort, he suggested that four or five adults live together in a rental house and do their own housekeeping. Boyd took it upon himself to visit Push Class members at their rental homes and shared meals with them, which gave him the chance to offer encouragement to the adult students.

Both on campus and off, mature and young students alike dealt with the realities of territory life, where electricity was nonexistent and students studied by candlelight or kerosene lamp. Most walked everywhere they went, since bicycles were rare and could cost as much as $150, roughly equivalent to $3,700 today.

Social events played an important role in college life from OU's earliest days. Informal parties were hosted at local homes, and double and group dating was the norm. Popular outings included light operas, candy pulls, and square dancing. A local religious population, dominated by Southern Methodists and Baptists, frowned upon public dancing, card playing, and smoking. Even with this scrutiny, discipline issues were rare at OU, perhaps because President

Boyd dealt with discipline head-on. In one case, Boyd followed up on rumors that OU minors had been visiting local saloons. He visited the local watering hole in question and asked for the saloonkeeper's help. "Now here is a list of all the students who are not minors," Boyd recalled saying, adding that there were not more than fifteen or twenty people on the list. "You can sell to them. They are old enough to know what they are doing. But I wish you would not sell to minors, and I wish you would get all the other saloon keepers to agree not to sell to minor students." Boyd said the saloonkeeper did as he asked, "and no officer of the law was ever more vigilant in seeing that the law was enforced."

Despite rapid growth during its first few years of operation, OU still faced challenges in recruiting students. Potential candidates were often drawn away by competing private schools. OU's fiercest competitor was High Gate College, a Southern Methodist school that had attracted as many as 130 students per semester since its opening in 1890. High Gate, located where Griffin Memorial Hospital stands today, was on the same site where east Norman residents initially wanted OU to be located. A business school was also operating in Norman, and Epworth College, which would later become Oklahoma City University, was only thirty miles away.

Preconceived ideas and misgivings about the value of an OU education presented another significant challenge. Many territorial settlers traditionally sent their children "back home" to attend college. Boyd served as a member of the territorial school board and strategically tackled the issue from there. "I used this position to preach the gospel of the University of Oklahoma and of culture all over the Territory," he said. "I accepted every invitation to speak, and each speech I concluded with an invitation to come to our school. It was 'educational work and a welcome' which I promised them, and if their means were limited, I aided in finding work for them to do."

Although tuition was free and living expenses seem inexpensive compared to today's costs, at that time most Oklahoma families undoubtedly struggled to come up with $3 per week for student room and board, the equivalent of $78 per week today. Additionally, the young university was fighting its own funding battles. Boyd recalled that the Territorial Legislature was "constantly overdrawn," and OU experienced a budget deficit that the university strived to overcome. Driven by these needs, Boyd devised an ingenious plan that increased OU's funding once and for always.

Typically, primary and secondary education in the territory had received federal funding since 1850 from sales, leases, mineral rights, and other proceeds garnered from landed property. When new townships were drawn up, one land section was always reserved for public schools, and all financial proceeds from that section belonged to the schools.

OU's first building was brand-new when this photograph was taken in 1893. Saplings planted by President David Ross Boyd are visible in the foreground. *(Coleman 40)*

With the help of such friends as attorney Henry Asp, Boyd drew up a new proposal: When the Cherokee Strip or any future lands were opened to white settlement, Boyd proposed that the federal government set aside one land section in each township to benefit higher education. A second section would be set aside for financing public buildings. These areas would be numbered Sections 13 and 33, respectively.

"I talked the matter over with Governor Renfrow," Boyd said, "and he advised me that, because of the prevalence of political red tape, the surest way of obtaining some grant was to go myself to see President Cleveland." In a move that seems impossible today, Boyd went to Washington to meet the president. He first had to get past Cleveland's new secretary of the interior, Hoke Smith, who was being inundated by people seeking political office in Washington. President Boyd anxiously assured Smith that he was not in Washington to lobby for work. "When he [Smith] summoned me, he told his secretary 'to bring in that fellow who doesn't want an office,'" Boyd remembered. Smith arranged the meeting with President Cleveland, and Boyd soon found himself in the Oval Office, watching the president of the United States balance a chair on one leg and twirl it around while they talked.

"He listened to my suggestion. . . . When I had finished, he told me to write up the provisions as I had suggested them to him and gave me a note to Hoke Smith saying that he approved of this move. When the proclamation for opening the [Cherokee] strip was read by the President, it included the clause, just as I had framed it."

But perhaps the happiest, most highly anticipated news of the year was the completion of OU's first building. On September 6, 1893, students finally left the Rock Building behind for their new academic home on the university campus. "The first building. Do you realize what it meant to us?" Boyd recalled. "Can you understand the promise which this mound of brick and mortar, upreared on the flat red sand and clay, gave us? I'm afraid you cannot. You, with your splendid campus of today . . . will never be able to appreciate the fact that such a building meant to us comfortable quarters, classrooms which could hold our already increasing enrollment, a library which was a rarity in the territory, and always, always, the opportunity for learning and more learning."

The completion of what would later come to be called "Building One" also served as a signal to all those watching that OU was a legitimate university. Students in the Twin Territories had a future awaiting them.

THE UNIVERSITY GROWS ROOTS

Building One soon would be surrounded by a grove of trees. Norman founders had worked to forest OU's campus as early as 1892, when then–territorial governor Seay proclaimed the first Arbor Day. The OU Board of Regents had allocated funds for the purchase of one thousand trees that same year. But their combined efforts paled in comparison to those of President Boyd beginning in the spring of 1893.

Historian David Levy points out that Boyd believed the transformation of OU's campus through landscaping was "at the heart of his vision for the future." A variety of stories and urban legends about Boyd's mission to forest OU have been told and retold. It is difficult to sift through the various myths and legends; nonetheless the most well-known story has Boyd buying out a nursery, personally planting and watering the trees on OU's campus, and donating many trees to Norman citizens. According to Levy, "[Boyd] gave the trees free of charge if they lived for at least a year; but if they died, the recipient was required to pay." In another story, OU's first saplings were nearly lost to drought. Boyd had left campus in July to attend an educational conference in Denver, Colorado. Heavy rains pelted the prairie during his absence, and when the OU president arrived home a month later, he saw the new trees "sprouting with foliage in the August moonlight" and described the day as "the happiest of his life." Regardless of which stories are true, Levy confirms that Boyd sold or gave away as many as fifteen thousand trees throughout the Norman area and to several Oklahoma colleges.

Students returned to the new building and a budding campus in the fall of 1893, when 142 students enrolled, including OU's first college (not high school) student, Nahum E. Butcher. "Dr. Boyd himself enrolled me and looked over my grades and qualifications," Butcher said in a 1957 interview with *Sooner Magazine*. "And he said, 'Well, I'm going to enter you in the college department.' I didn't know when he said that that I was going to be the first one to enter that department, but later on I found out that when he printed the first catalog, my name was in the college department all by itself." Butcher became OU's first librarian and earned ten dollars a month. Most of the library's books had been given to the university by ministers and others who shared their personal collections. However, few were appropriate for college-level work. As librarian, Butcher only had a five hundred dollar budget to purchase all the books needed for OU classes.

The 1893 academic year was also noteworthy for the founding of OU's School of Pharmacy. Oklahoma Territory pharmacists had pushed for the new school, which was to be overseen by Professor DeBarr, the chair of OU's Chemistry Department. The pharmacy program would soon produce a high percentage of OU graduates, and these graduates were automatically registered as pharmacists without undergoing any state accreditation exams, which added to the popularity of the program.

The university also witnessed the end of competition for student enrollment from one rival college that year. Enrollment at High Gate College had been steadily waning since its healthy start, and the college finally closed in an agreement between the Methodist Episcopal Church and OU in 1893. The agreement included a clause that OU would donate five acres of land to build a dormitory specifically for Methodist students. The dormitory would include a chapel and serve as "an annex to the University but under the control of the Church, where students could be as well cared for as in a denominational school," Levy writes. The new dormitory was built at the corner of Boyd Street and University Boulevard, the current site of Whitehand Hall. High Gate College disappeared from the educational landscape.

David Ross Boyd at his desk in the university's first building. *(Hadsell 13)*

OU was growing, and along with that growth came changes to the inaugural faculty. William Rice left in 1893. French Amos, who had been President Boyd's right-hand man and the founder of the Oklahoma Historical Society at OU in 1894, left to join a private college venture in the Indian Territory town of Vinita in 1895. His replacement was James Shannon Buchanan, a Tennessee native who joined the faculty to teach history and civics and who would one day become OU's fourth president. OU also welcomed Frederick Elder, a Princeton graduate who taught math and was described by Boyd as "the highest type of scholar."

As the 1895 school year began, one particular OU student was worth pointing out. John A. Harts came to OU from Winfield, Kansas, and brought with him a love of football. But, as he said, "To my consternation, I could find no one who had ever seen a football, let alone a football game."

Harold Keith, OU's first sports information director and a legendary author and sports expert, once wrote, "Football was spawned in Bud Risinger's green-front barber shop on Norman's West Main Street where Harts . . . organized a team at the University, spiking it with Fred Perry, who drove the prancing steeds that drew the Norman fire wagon and other non-students." Harts became the team's coach and captain and taught the members everything they knew about the sport. The OU football team's only game that year occurred December 14, 1895, on a field that the players had laid out themselves in front of present-day Holmberg Hall. Their opponent was the Oklahoma City Town Team, a group of big and rough players that soundly beat OU 34 to 0.

"Many problems confronted us," Harts said of the early OU team. "The most important was lack of capital. We had only one football; in fact, when we put in a substitute, we had to wait until the substitute changed clothes with the regular player, because we only had twelve suits."

Baseball wasn't far behind in developing at OU, and Harts again served a key role in the team's formation. The baseball team played on a meadow about a half-mile west of campus and enjoyed a significant win of 20 to 7 during their first game.

With the continued development of collegiate sports in 1895 came new traditions, including OU's first school yell, "Hi Rickety Whoop Te-Do, Boomer, Sooner, Okla. U," which was adapted from the Sigma Nu fraternity at Southwestern College in Winfield, Kansas. Levy writes that a faculty committee selected OU's colors as crimson and corn. The colors soon were featured on a wide variety of merchandise so popular that stores could barely keep items on their shelves. However, merchants had a difficult time finding materials with the correct shade of "corn," and the school colors gradually evolved into the well-known crimson and cream.

The OU football team was in its second year and had its first victorious "season" after winning two games against Norman High School. Even more impressive, the team won without a coach, since John Harts had departed.

Attention turned from sports to academics in the spring of 1896 when OU's four-year degree students disputed the ease with which the university's first two pharmaceutical graduates had received their degrees. President Boyd had other issues on his hands, as hordes of borer insects attacked his beloved trees. Boyd concluded the problem was cyclical—since there were no mature trees in Norman, there were no birds to nest in the trees and eat insects. According to urban legend, Boyd's solution was to have driftwood logs hauled onto campus from the Canadian River. Woodpeckers discovered the new habitats and eliminated the insect problem. Oklahoma's first bird protection law may have its origins in this tale, as Boyd was said to have faced down a local telephone or electricity manager who was paying boys to kill woodpeckers. Boyd and Professor Buchanan, who also served as a Norman city council member, reportedly drafted an appeal that became the bird protection law.

But along with minor troubles came good fortune. Boyd hired Grace King, an eighteen-year-old musical prodigy, who joined OU's faculty only after gaining her mother's permission. As head of OU's music school King primarily taught students older than herself, and she also formed the university's first glee club, which she toured throughout Territory communities each year via train and stagecoach. King was lively and popular. She was known for leading songs at football games and playing the piano at noon for anyone wishing to dance the latest waltz, schottische, or "risqué" two-step. These dances soon caught the attention of town ladies who were opposed to dancing for religious reasons and expressed horror that the dances took place in OU's chapel. They demanded that the practice cease. In

response, President Boyd pointed out that the chapel held OU's only piano and insisted that the dances were "wholesome entertainment."

King took center stage at a banquet held annually to impress territorial legislators and encourage them to increase OU's territorial appropriation. "We began with many toasts and gave them beaten biscuits, baked ham and roast pig," she recalled. A musical program featuring King ended with the Territory's house speaker requesting a song called "Just One Girl," which was then thought mildly inappropriate for public consumption. Everyone watched to see if King would honor the request. "Well, I sang the song and received the largest applause I had ever heard," King said. "The legislators then sang the song, and the appropriation was in the bag."

King also helped OU land one of its most important and influential faculty members, Vernon Louis Parrington. According to Levy, the two knew each other as children in their hometown of Emporia, Kansas. King recommended Parrington as an addition to OU's faculty, and Parrington agreed to organize and head the university's first English department.

Parrington was a Harvard graduate. The Ivy Leaguer was less than impressed when he arrived in Norman in time for the 1897 school year. "As I came onto the campus, I stopped. This was the University? The word had always meant—well, something very different to me. A single small red brick building—ugly in its lines and with a wart atop—a short misshapen cross between a cupola and a dome—stood in a grove of tiny elms. Across the front and especially about the door, some ivy had made fine growth and was the one restful thing that met my eye." But the new professor was not deterred. Within five weeks, he had started the *Umpire*, OU's first student publication. Parrington quickly established a reputation as an exacting and inspired teacher of English who would have a deep, lasting impact on an entire generation of OU students.

"How can I tell you all it meant to us to have him for a teacher?" Adelaide Loomis Parker wrote in the 1929 *Sooner Magazine*. "When we went into this man's room, for an hour, at least, we lived in a different world . . . we forgot the dry sun and the never-ending wind, and the painful and pressing problem of how to make a living, and while we were there, we lived."

The twenty-six-year-old Parrington was also drafted to serve as OU's baseball and football coach. He had played football at Harvard, and he managed to infuse OU's version of the game with Ivy League atmosphere by organizing cheering, as well as a dance for the visiting team after each game. Parrington's football teams won thirteen games and lost only two from 1897 to 1900. Those were impressive statistics, given that the Rough Riders—OU's team name

OU's 1899 football team, the Rough Riders, plays against an Arkansas City, Kansas, squad. *(Dunn 15)*

until 1908—owned little to no real equipment, including headgear, for the first two years.

Other advances were coming to campus, including a new wooden boardwalk along the length of University Boulevard that linked the campus to Norman's downtown. The wooden path was advertised as "the way to college," and each morning the sounds of student feet drumming across post oak announced the beginning of the class schedule. "It was an improvement to be talked about," said student and future OU geology faculty member S. Roy Hadsell. "It was for 10 years the center of University life. Every student walked on it. It was high and dry and wide, better than some of the cement walks we have today."

One unforeseen problem with the elevated walk was that its underside made a good home for rabbit warrens. An enterprising student decided to solve the problem by introducing the basics of biology in the form of a bull snake, which then resulted in female students refusing to use the boardwalk for some time.

A more academic form of biology had its official start at OU in 1898 with the hiring of Albert Heald Van Vleet, who had met President Boyd at a national education meeting in Washington, D.C. Van Vleet received his doctorate from the University of Leipzig in Germany and was doing postgraduate work at Johns Hopkins University when Boyd lured him away. Boyd effused that OU had "secured a teacher who was little short of a genius."

Van Vleet soon began working with the Board of Regents president and attorney Henry Asp to form a legislative bill for a geological survey of Oklahoma Territory. The bill was approved, and four hundred dollars was allocated from the Territorial Legislature. Van Vleet purchased a wagon and team of horses and began to make a series of trips across Oklahoma, collecting native animals, rocks and minerals, and botanical samples. He also created what was perhaps the first real topographical map of the future state and laid the groundwork for OU's entry into the field of geology.

OU was experiencing change in other ways as well. The university held its first full-scale commencement exercises on June 9, 1898. The *Umpire* called the event "a milestone in the progress and growth of the territory; an epoch in the history of educational institutions of Oklahoma." The "epoch" involved only two graduates, Carleton Ross Hume and Roy Philston Stoops, both of whom received bachelor of art degrees. "In honor of the occasion and as a distinctive mark of progression, the president, faculty and graduates donned

Seven years after "Building One" first opened, the elms that David Ross Boyd planted had grown into a full grove, and ivy covered portions of the brick, lending OU's one and only academic building a collegiate feel. *(Class of 1900)*

University Boulevard ran south past President Boyd's original home, which was nearly obscured by saplings planted on either side of the wooden boardwalk that linked OU to downtown Norman. Tracks in the street were made by bicyclists traveling to and from OU's campus. *(Hadsell 31)*

caps and gowns, the garb of the Collegian the world over, thus emphasizing the fact that the University was entering the ranks of the real colleges of the land and that the first fruits were about to be given."

Student life was still very simple at OU, where the most serious concern was the rivalry between preparatory and college students. Secret dances continued to raise the ire of town matrons. Boyd listened to their concerns but did not take them very seriously, which earned him the respect of his students but may have laid the foundation for future "town versus gown" trouble. Students showed their affection for President Boyd through annual Halloween pranks. One prank featured placing a donkey on the chapel stage. "I told them afterwards to do something original," Boyd said, "and they surely did." The next Halloween, Boyd was summoned to receive a call in downtown Norman, which had the town's one and only telephone. En route, he was waylaid by a group of students who tackled him and shaved off his mustache. The group's ringleader was a student who had served as Boyd's own secretary, George Bucklin. Boyd laughed the event off as harmless fun. If student discipline ever became a problem, Boyd simply wrote home to ask the student's parents to either convince their child about the importance of an education, or to withdraw him or her from school.

More and more students were finding their way to OU, as enrollment had increased to nearly four hundred. Growing enrollment meant growing pains. As the new century approached, President Boyd realized that OU would need to expand beyond its initial forty acres of campus. The OU Board of Regents requested permission to buy fifty acres north and east of the university; their request, initially turned down by the Territorial Legislature, later became the basis for the legislature's approval of OU's purchase of an additional twenty acres. There was a catch, though, as the City of Norman would need to donate the cost of the land. If whoever owned the land did not wish to sell for a "reasonable" price, the legislature would allow OU to condemn

the property. OU chose to expand east on land that is now between Jenkins and Asp Avenues. The university would not expand again until 1914.

The year 1900 also brought new faculty to campus, including Charles Newton Gould, who was selected to head OU's new geology department. Gould was friends with both Sardis Roy Hadsell and George Bucklin, who had recommended Gould to the president. Gould accepted OU's offer of four hundred dollars per year and joined Professor Van Vleet in his summer geological survey of Oklahoma, during which they camped as far away as the Glass Mountains. When fall arrived, Gould and Van Vleet became office mates, as there was nowhere else for the geologist to work in OU's single academic building. Gould found no books, no labs, and no geology students at OU. But that would change.

"By the time he closed his illustrious career, he was one of the best-known geologists in the United States, the teacher of a generation of distinguished geologists and the founder of perhaps the best-known school of its kind in the nation," Levy writes. "A significant part of Oklahoma's oil industry was to owe its origins to the work of this scientist."

OU would soon welcome another future faculty member, Roy Gittinger. Gittinger had arrived from Iowa to teach in Moore, Oklahoma, the year before, but a smallpox outbreak had shut down the school. Gittinger enrolled at OU and was leading the university's Preparatory Department by 1908. Enrollment in the prep school would gradually decrease as area high schools began to produce students who could enter OU's college courses directly after graduation. In the half-century that followed, Gittinger would fill a variety of OU administrative offices; he was the first to hold the title of Regents Professor and wrote the first comprehensive work on OU's early history, *The University of Oklahoma: A History of Fifty Years, 1892–1942.* Gittinger once said that he came to Oklahoma "to grow up with the country" and considered the university an "outpost of education on a vanishing frontier."

In 1900, OU graduated its first master's degree candidate,

The 1906 Ladies Quartet. Music played an integral role in student life and entertainment from the university's earliest days. Singing groups were used as recruiting tools and traveled to perform in communities across Oklahoma. *(Boyd 128)*

Carleton Ross Hume, OU's first quarterback and one of the university's first two bachelor's degree recipients. OU also recognized its first woman graduate, Fantine Paxton, wife of OU Latin and Greek Professor J. F. Paxton. Both Hume and Paxton would join the university's newly formed alumni association, which had only a handful of members.

Meanwhile, Professor Parrington had become so busy teaching OU's growing student population that he decided in 1901 to give up his football coaching duties. He passed the torch to local football star Fred Roberts, who would pass the job on to OU student Mark McMahan the next year.

Besides enjoying spectator sports, OU students were entertained by debating and oration events, which had been the highlight of student activity prior to football's arrival on campus. Students also organized music clubs and geological outings to the Arbuckle Mountains and went to the Franning Opera House on Norman's Main Street for "gym exhibitions" in which female students performed calisthenics drills and male students performed parallel bar and dumbbell drills, along with tumbling and pyramid acts.

OU would get its own authentic gymnasium in 1903—a gray frame building built just southwest of today's Oklahoma Memorial Union. As many as three hundred people would eventually crowd the gym's balcony and line its walls to watch events such as basketball, a sport which was less than a decade old. Basketball players took aim at the basket by placing one foot against the wall to gain height while shooting. Before being demolished almost forty years later, the gym would go through incarnations as a zoology laboratory, band practice building, liberal arts annex, and elementary school building.

Also in 1903, OU celebrated the groundbreaking of its second classroom building, University Hall. The building had been planned for two years and was envisioned as a grand and imposing example of Renaissance design. University Hall would sit where Evans Hall is located today and was intended to serve as administration headquarters and home to most classes with the exception of the natural and chemical sciences classes, which would stay in Building One.

A PROMISE GOES UP IN FLAMES

On the night of January 6, 1903, all of OU's plans quite literally went up in smoke. At 11 P.M., a watchman saw fire erupt in the southeast basement of Building One. An alarm went out to the Norman Fire Department, but was entirely useless since OU was beyond town limits and the reach of city water. Building One's freshly oiled wood floors added to the fire's fuel.

The biology laboratory in Building One. *(Rader 25)*

"A few buckets were found, and a heroic effort was made to put out the fire with water from the vat at the south corner of the building," news reports in OU's *Umpire* related. "When the fire broke through from the basement into the first floor, all hope of saving the building was given up, and all hands turned to save furniture, records and such stuff as could be carried out. George Bucklin and Walker Field went up a ladder from the front steps into the office and were able to save nearly all of the valuable papers of the office, including the students' grades and credits, the voucher book, insurance papers, the University ledger and some private papers of President Boyd."

At the same time, a student named Tom Tribbey and others went to the chemical laboratory and carried out drawers, balances, and smaller apparatus. "Charles Kirk did some nervy work by saving three of the fine microscopes from the north windows of the biology laboratory. The windows in the history lecture room were broken and a ladder was run through down which Professor Buchanan's desk was slid; all of his books and maps were also saved." Though items from the basement, including hides and mounted animals, could be carried out, other areas and items were unreachable and unsalvageable. "Nothing was saved from the third floor or the chapel; the library was a complete loss except for the few books which were checked out to the students."

According to the *Umpire*, the end came quickly. "Just as midnight neared the dome quivered, groaned with breaking timber, turned gracefully over and with point down, crashed through the chapel into the first floor and basement. Everything possible had been done, so all stood back, watched the floors fall and listened to the explosions in the glowing mass of debris where was once the chemical laboratory."

Among those watching were President Boyd and math Professor Frederick Stanton Elder. "What do you need to keep classes going?" Boyd reportedly asked his faculty member, to which Elder immediately replied, "Two yards of blackboard and a box of chalk."

Levy quotes a report that says President Boyd rounded up the faculty by 9 A.M. the following morning and met with students at a local church that afternoon, where he "spoke briefly of the misfortune that had befallen us" and praised the students for their gallant efforts at the fire. He then called upon the students to be loyal in the difficult days ahead. "Though we were in a church building the [school] 'yell' went up. We had heard it given defiantly in the morning and, after the day was won, triumphantly, but that day it touched a deeper chord of patriotism than it ever had before."

The university had $35,000 worth of insurance policies on Building One, but the damages exceeded $85,000. Worse, OU now had a smoking hulk, one unfinished building, and no usable classrooms. The solution lay a mile away at Norman's Rock Building, which had served OU during its first year of operation. A private dormitory and several churches in town—including the Christian Church, which was headquartered in a former hotel—were also offered for OU's use. The compromise was less than ideal. Students recalled perching on wooden soapboxes in the Rock Building while learning Latin; on the upside, the Rock Building had added iron stoves for heating.

"Evidently, Boyd had found both the time and presence of mind on that first day . . . to place orders for books, chemicals, and apparatus," Levy wrote. "All in all, it was a stunning achievement. Within twenty-four hours of the fire, the University's functions, all housed within a two-block area of downtown Norman, were again in operation."

President Boyd had good reason to hurry. Other towns in Oklahoma Territory had expressed a keen interest in becoming home to the university and sensed a ripe opportunity after OU's only academic building was destroyed. The community of Kingfisher even offered to reimburse the City of Norman for the $10,000 it had initially invested in securing OU if the university could be moved there.

Boyd's response was to build, and build quickly. University Hall was under construction and would not open for another year, so two wooden-frame buildings were thrown up in rapid succession, which relieved some of the pressure for classroom space. Boyd also took the opportunity to plan a smaller, more streamlined facility to replace Building One's role as a science center. Using $30,000 of the insurance money from Building One, he commissioned the new Science Hall. The structure would emulate the growing trend of organic architecture, the "Prairie School" design that had been made popular by Frank Lloyd Wright since the late 1890s.

University Hall was completed and opened in March 1904 with much pomp and circumstance that included a procession of students and faculty walking from Norman's First Baptist Church to enter the new building, a three-story stone structure with a wide flight of steps leading up to its entrance and four Ionic columns marching across the front. A stone balustrade stretched across the roof, which was topped by a pine dome covered with tin. OU's seal, which had been designed by Boyd's secretary George Bucklin, was featured prominently on the building's top pediment. The building's cost had been appropriated by the Territorial Legislature and even became the inspiration for a song titled "$90,000 on the Campus."

Rising immediately to the northwest of University Hall was Science Hall, which is known by current OU students

The graceful University Hall served as a replacement for OU's first building and was completed in 1904 at a cost of $90,000. *(Ray 118)*

and alumni as the Beatrice Carr Wallace Old Science Hall. This new building opened to students when they returned to campus in September 1904 and featured laboratories for geological, biological, chemical, and pharmaceutical studies, office space, lecture rooms, cold storage, and an incubator room. The building also held a natural history museum that would form the basis of today's Sam Noble Oklahoma Museum of Natural History.

A third new building became home to OU's library, whose 15,000 volumes were lost in the Building One fire. Plans for a new library had already been conceived a year before the fire occurred. According to Levy, President Boyd had sent as many as eight letters to famed industrialist Andrew Carnegie, whose foundation built more than 1,700 municipal libraries across the country. OU made the foundation's first request for a university library and received $30,000 to construct the new structure, which would sit across the campus oval and face Science Hall. By the time

University Hall, seen from the Commons area that would later become OU's North Oval. *(Kraettli 35)*

OU students and faculty walking on the sidewalk in front of University Hall, with the Carnegie Library in the background. *(Rader 15)*

the building opened, OU had cobbled together 1,000 new books; since the facility was far from full, the Carnegie Building temporarily doubled as a women's gymnasium.

While 1904 saw OU literally and figuratively rise from the ashes, the year also marked the beginning of important new traditions. The Pride of Oklahoma Marching Band had its start with a freshman cornet player, Lloyd B. Curtis, who came to OU from St. Louis, Missouri. The accomplished musician offered his services to then–music school director Henry D. Guelich, and soon became director of bands. The first OU band was just sixteen men strong and played at sporting events and campus activities. OU's yearbook, the *Mistletoe*, said with a bit of tongue in cheek, "Not until this year could we boast of a band. But we have one now with real military suits trimmed with crimson and cream and all the other usual paraphernalia. And oh, aren't we proud of them, and aren't they proud of themselves."

November 1904 was the beginning of the Bedlam Series between OU and rival Oklahoma Territorial Agricultural and Mechanical (A&M) College, the future Oklahoma State University. The matchup, which was played in Guthrie's Island Park on a cold day when nearby Cottonwood Creek was flooded and full of ice, became one of the most notorious games in OU football history.

While returning the kick deep in his own territory, the pressured Oklahoma A&M punter misfired. Wind caught the ball, and a melee ensued. "The kick turned out to be a long one," a reporter wrote some years later, "but it traveled in the wrong direction. The breeze carried it back, back, back behind the kicker and far away from the field. This was obviously a loose ball, and in those days it meant something. The rules specified that if the kicking team recovered it, then it was a touchback. If the other team got to it first, a touchdown would be scored for it. Both the players and crowd went wild. Both scampered off the field, following the ball." The ball landed and rolled down an incline into the icy Cottonwood Creek. An A&M player used a stick to try to reach the ball, while a running OU player stumbled into the Aggie and knocked the player into the water before diving in himself after the ball. "Both were desperately treading water toward the floating ball when it occurred to the [OU player] to duck the Aggie." The A&M player gave up and headed for shore while the OU team member, who apparently was not a strong swimmer, was left stranded in the middle of the creek. A laughing crowd watched as three OU players charged into the water and finally captured the ball.

"The next 25 minutes were no laughing matter. Wearing a wet uniform on a wintry day can be painful. At half's end, those in such a predicament gratefully took the uniforms of substitutes who slipped into their street clothes. Somehow, the remainder of the game seemed dull." OU won the game 75 to 0. The next week, the Sooners would play the University of Texas for the very first time. OU lost 40 to 10.

Another OU tradition started in the fall of 1905, when the first Greek letter fraternity, Kappa Alpha, was granted a charter at OU. The fraternity came under sharp scrutiny later that year when it was revealed that the boys had purchased

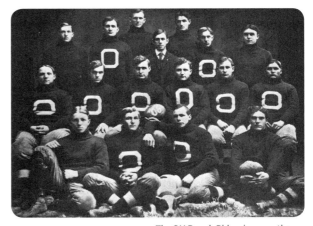

The OU Rough Riders in 1904, the year OU first played against rivals at the University of Texas and Oklahoma A&M, now Oklahoma State University. *(OU 1456)*

a keg of beer during finals week and started a noisy round of barbershop singing that scared off a cow owned by OU's only janitor, Kirby Prickett. President Boyd called Kappa Alpha member Deak Parker, one of the university's most popular and influential students, into his office.

"I have called you to tell you that you are fired from the University," Parker recalled the president saying. Parker protested that he was not even present at the party; in fact, he had been out on a date.

"With whom?"

"Well, I had a date with Alice."

"With whom?" the president raised his voice.

"Your daughter."

Boyd laughed, thought it over, then said, "Nevertheless, the fact that you weren't there was clearly an accident. So, on general principles, don't come back." But Boyd immediately relented, and Parker was back in class.

OU's curriculum expanded that fall when Samuel Watson Reaves came to chair the university's Math Department. Reaves was joined by new faculty member James Huston Felgar, an instructor of mechanical engineering who would become the forefather of OU's College of Engineering.

The true roots of what we recognize today as Sooner football emerged in 1905, as well, with the hiring of Coach Bennie Owen, who would head the team for twenty-two years. Owen had served as head coach at Washburn and Bethany Colleges in Kansas and was an assistant coach at the University of Michigan. He arrived at OU to find only a handful of football players, each wearing uniforms so worn by sweat and use that they were close to rotting. Within a month of arriving, Owen had led the Rough Riders to an 18–12 victory over the Haskell Indians, a Native American team reputed to be intensely physical. Highlighted by fistfights and punches below the belt, the game and OU's

victory gained the Rough Riders even more new fans, who were soon following the team on the road. Owen also led the Sooners to its first victory over Texas in 1905 during a game that ended 2–0.

"Bennie not only made good football teams, he made men of players and students alike. He did this by example, not by preaching," said OU 1913 graduate and former Board of Regents member Charles H. Newell. Newell worked as a student reporter during his college years and "dogged [Owen's] footsteps night after night" during practices. "I never heard him use profanity on or off the field. I never heard him abuse a player for boneheaded playing. And yet he seldom failed to make his men feel their failures and learn valuable lessons from them." When players weren't living up to Owen's expectations, the coach—who would lose his right arm during a 1907 hunting accident—often would jump into a scrimmage to make his point. "It seemed every man of the opposition became animated with the desire to stop Bennie and even undress him in the bargain. They used to throw him pretty hard and pile up on him. But all he did was grin," Newell remembered. During his first two years as coach, Owen left Norman as soon as football season had ended to manage a restaurant in Arkansas City, Kansas; he stayed to train the team year-round once OU could pay him a full salary. The Rough Riders certainly needed his full-time help. Due to travel budget constraints, the team played as many as three games each time they went on the road.

That fall OU laid out Boyd Field just west of today's current McCasland Field House. The site would host OU football, baseball, and track for nearly two decades. OU's fight song debuted when a student named Arthur Alden modified Yale University's "Boola, Boola" to "Boomer Sooner." The "Sooner Born" half of the fight song came along a year later with some judicious borrowing from the University of North Carolina's own fight song.

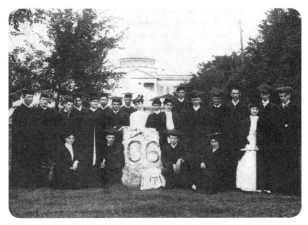

The Class of 1906 with the famed "'06 Rock," the first class gift ever made to the University of Oklahoma. Behind them stands a tent and chairs used for graduation ceremonies on the Commons. *(Class 1906-5)*

Survivors of OU's Class of 1906 reunited at the '06 Rock while celebrating the fiftieth anniversary of their OU graduation. *(Class 1906-7)*

Spirited gatherings aside, 1906 was a relatively quiet time in OU history. However, one notable occurrence that resonates even today was the establishment of class gifts. Each year since 1906, graduating seniors have made a lasting tribute to the university. The custom began with the donation of a waist-high slab of rough stone that was simply engraved "'06." Class members posed around the '06 rock in caps and gowns, standing before the white canvas tent where graduation had just been held and with University Hall looming in the background. It would be the last year that University Hall appeared in any surviving photo.

A "MISERABLE BUSINESS" ALTERS OU

No one could have foreseen how different OU would soon be. The year 1907 would usher in revolutionary, at times cataclysmic, changes and a new era that would reshape the university and the very territory that surrounded it.

The effort to join Oklahoma Territory and Indian Territory into a new state had reached fruition in June 1906, when President Theodore Roosevelt signed the Oklahoma Enabling Act. Delegates, chosen by popular election, attended a constitutional convention that November to establish the state constitution and select leaders for Oklahoma. As Levy writes, the election results were a shock when Oklahomans decided that the vast majority of constitutional convention delegates would be Democrats. All three of Oklahoma's territorial governors had been Republicans. "The rout was far out of proportion to the actual political makeup of the two territories, and a reasonable explanation is that voters were rebelling against the years of Republican rule. . . . The vote revealed a considerable resentment

toward outside appointees, Republicans, and carpetbaggers," Levy notes, adding that the political shakeup meant almost certain change at OU. "David Ross Boyd, after all, was a Republican appointee from the outside; so were many members of his faculty."

Among the constitutional delegates were longtime Boyd supporter and attorney Henry Asp and OU professor James S. Buchanan, who was a Democrat and a member of Norman's city council. The state constitution was written and sent to a vote of the people in September. Newly elected

The inauguration of Oklahoma's first state governor, Charles N. Haskell, was held on Statehood Day, November 17, 1907. The day also marked the beginning of the end for OU President David Ross Boyd's administration. *(Rader 25)*

state officials included Oklahoma's first governor, Democrat Charles N. Haskell, who took his oath of office on Statehood Day, November 16, 1907. Haskell almost immediately dismissed OU's entire Board of Regents and made the board over to his personal satisfaction.

Only a month later, on December 20, OU took a near-fatal blow when it lost the beautiful University Hall at the start of a bitterly cold Christmas Break. Workmen had been repainting University Hall's wooden roof that afternoon, and temperatures were so low that workers heated linseed oil in a gasoline-fueled iron stove. The oil apparently overheated and exploded, and University Hall's iconic dome was quickly engulfed in flames.

A large number of OU students were only a half-mile away at Norman's Santa Fe Depot waiting for trains to take them home for Christmas. "Most of the students who were going home looked out, saw the smoke, and then hurried off in the direction of campus," said Lewis Salter, a music student who would later become an OU professor. The students arrived on campus to find fire dropping through the open space between University Hall's dome and its ground floor. Frenzied, students and townspeople rushed into the building to retrieve as much as they could from classrooms and laboratories. "Many things that were thrown out of the second-floor windows were completely destroyed when they hit the ground, so nothing of great consequence was saved, except for the [paper] records," Salter recalled. "For example, the static electricity machines from the physics department were rescued—and then dropped out of a window. Of course, they were smashed. Those were moments of excitement, so a lot of foolish things were done."

Despite valiant efforts, many OU books and documents were once again destroyed, though not all. Fortunately the one thousand volumes at the Carnegie Library were safe, and OU's most crucial papers were locked in a fireproof vault. As Levy writes, President Boyd had learned invaluable

University Hall, OU's second academic and administration building and the center of campus life, burns on December 20, 1907. The building's roof and trademark dome have already collapsed, and books and papers are strewn across the grass in the foreground. *(Kraettli 36)*

lessons from the 1903 burning of Building One and, ever aware of the unplanned and unforeseen, had taken out as many as sixteen insurance policies on University Hall. OU would receive $67,500, which unfortunately still did not cover the building's $85,000 loss.

It was the second time in just four years that fire had reshaped OU's campus. Once again, faculty and students retreated to Norman's Rock Building. This time, OU had such resources as Science Hall, the Carnegie Library, the gymnasium, and the wooden buildings that had been constructed after the 1903 fire. The Rock Building primarily handled any overflow that could not be accommodated by shuffling spaces on campus. Still, classes were cramped and overcrowded for the university's more than seven hundred students. "Those of us who were on the campus then

The burned ruins of University Hall after the 1907 fire. *(Coleman 36)*

❋ THE SOONER STORY

A 1930s view of the Rock Building in downtown Norman. This simple space provided a haven to OU students during the university's first year of operation and after two separate fires destroyed OU's sole academic buildings. *(Dunn 27)*

remember how crude things were," said former student Robert B. Keenan. "After the fire, wooden shacks were built to house classes temporarily. When the wintry winds began to blow, it was an advantage to attend class early and grab a seat near the radiator." Classes in Science Hall were crammed together anywhere possible, including the attic. "We should have been arrested for holding classes in that attic," said Professor Buchanan. "It was poorly lighted and ventilated, and there was no *fire* escape leading from it."

OU persevered and carried on the best it could. Soon, the university added its first courses in anthropology, social work, business, and sociology. The Oklahoma Geological Society had its genesis during this time, due to a collaboration between OU geology professor Charles Gould and Professor Buchanan. Social fraternity Beta Theta Pi also debuted at OU in 1907, along with a "spirit" group known as the Deep Dark Mystery Club, which was famed for committing campus pranks throughout the 1920s.

But as 1907 passed into 1908, other hardships were coming OU's way, and these trials would prove even more damaging than the December fire that had engulfed University Hall. By all accounts, rumors and complaints had circulated around Norman and throughout the state that OU student life was too frivolous. Many felt OU students had forgotten where they came from, and that the makeup of OU's faculty was not representative of Oklahoma. Only a small handful of OU professors reflected the new state's majority Baptist and Methodist populace. By comparison, most OU faculty members and David Ross Boyd himself belonged to the Presbyterian Church. OU's faculty also held the distinction of being overwhelmingly Republican in a Democrat-controlled state. In addition, there were claims in the Norman community that many members of the OU faculty indulged in behavior that bordered on immoral and enjoyed smoking, dancing, and playing cards. Something of a witch hunt was brewing.

Stories had been circulating as early as December 1907 that David Ross Boyd was going to be replaced. Behind the scenes, an ambitious former OU professor named Ernest Taylor Bynum worked with one of Governor Haskell's new OU Regents, Methodist minister Nathaniel Linebaugh. Their plan to depose President Boyd and install Bynum in his place initially failed in March 1908. Later that same month, the *Norman Transcript* suddenly announced, "BOYD IS DEPOSED," in a bold, red-letter headline. The article's black subheads brought the details into focus: "Oklahoma state university's faculty has been chosen. Dr. Boyd is ousted. Dr. Evans takes his place."

Arthur Grant Evans, a Presbyterian minister who had been born to English missionaries serving in India, had previously been president of Henry Kendall College, today's University of Tulsa. As Levy points out, Evans had become good friends with the future Governor Haskell while both lived in Muskogee. With virtually no warning, OU's faculty and students woke up to learn that they would have a new president on July 1, 1908.

Boyd's job was irrevocably lost. But he fought to save the faculty who he had so carefully recruited during sixteen years as president. It was a fight made necessary in part by a plot revealed in a letter between two OU Regents who were also Methodist ministers, R. E. L. Morgan of Norman and Nathaniel Linebaugh, the Regent who had earlier failed to place his friend Ernest Taylor Bynum in the OU presidency.

"Dear Brother," Morgan wrote to Linebaugh, "The following are the names of the University professors who dance, play cards and who are immoral in their lives." The missive goes on to list nine faculty members, including English Department chair Vernon L. Parrington and music school director H. D. Guelich. The letter labels Cyril M. Jansky, OU's physics and electrical engineering professor, as "an infidel" and goes on to say, "A number of those who dance are also immoral and cigarette fiends." The author suggested that the faculty members he had named should be replaced by friends and church members—some of whom were already on OU's faculty. "Do your best to get as many strong Southern Methodists in the faculty as possible," he concluded.

Morgan's letter came to public light because Linebaugh forgetfully left it behind in a Norman hotel room. The letter was passed on to the *Norman Transcript*, which printed it in its entirety on May 21, 1908. The letter sparked public outrage, but in the end it did little, if any, good. On June 23, every OU faculty member was asked to appear before the Board of Regents to make a case for keeping his or her job. Some two dozen survived the inquiry, but ten faculty members were fired, including Vernon L. Parrington, psychology professor L. W. Cole, pathology and neurology professor E. M. Williams, physics and electrical engineering professor C. M. Jansky, and music school director H. D. Guelich. Three members of the staff were also dismissed; among them was longtime maintenance man and janitor Kirby Prickett.

The Board of Regents announced the appointment of new faculty members at the same meeting. As Levy deduces, many were political patronage appointments or Linebaugh's personal friends.

Following the June 23 meeting, President Boyd graciously granted an interview to the *Norman Transcript*, which reported, "Professedly not filled with malice toward the board of university regents for deposing him from the head of the institution, Dr. David R. Boyd declares that the action of that body in failing to appoint other members of the faculty is describable only by adjectives that are not fit to print."

Boyd defended both himself and his faculty. "Those relieved of their positions are thorough, scholarly and capable and do not deserve to be peremptorily dismissed because of outrageous charges—charges that were so entirely false and improper as to be nothing short of damnable. Politics is all that removed me. I do not believe that anyone has attempted to impugn my character. Certainly the others were not removed for similar charges."

Boyd spent the remainder of his time at OU sending out letters to colleagues and friends in an effort to find the fired faculty members new positions. By August all had new university jobs. Many would go on to illustrious careers, perhaps none so much as Vernon L. Parrington, who joined the University of Washington at Seattle and became one of the nation's most respected literary scholars. His three-volume opus, *Main Currents in American Thought,* is considered a classic in intellectual history and won the 1927 Pulitzer Prize for literature.

The firing of President Boyd and his faculty caught the attention of Lyman Abbott, a Congregational Church minister, theologian, and editor of the widely read weekly opinion and news magazine, *The Outlook*. Abbott had recently visited OU to present a public lecture. Levy writes that Abbott took up Boyd's cause in a series of articles that gained national attention. He accused Oklahoma's governor and the OU Board of Regents of carrying out the firings purely for political and sectarian reasons. "The one essential fact that appears in this whole miserable business," Lyman said in his magazine, "is that the President and a large proportion of the faculty have been summarily removed from office, and that there is no pretense that any question of their scholarly attainments or their competence to teach was involved in the removal."

The firing scandal eventually subsided, but was not forgotten. OU moved on with its newly reformed faculty and president, Arthur Grant Evans, and David Ross Boyd moved on with his new life as head of educational work for the Presbyterian Board of Home Missions. Boyd crisscrossed the country to establish Presbyterian schools in impoverished areas and among Native American communities, and later became president of the University of New Mexico. He and Mrs. Boyd would eventually retire to Glendale, California, to be near their daughter, Alice. Before his death, Boyd reconciled with his successor and made several visits to OU, where he was always warmly welcomed and recognized as an astonishingly gifted administrator, education innovator, and pioneer.

"In a very peculiar sense," said Boyd's former student Deak Parker, who would go on to an acclaimed newspaper career and earn his own Pulitzer Prize, "David R. Boyd had made the University of Oklahoma. It would not be too much of an exaggeration to say that he made it with his bare hands. Every faculty member, every student, every custom, every stick and stone on the campus, was there because of him. Such driving energy, such abundant vitality, such singleness of purpose, such executive genius, are rare on this planet."

"Dr. Boyd was the University, and the University was Dr. Boyd. It will always be," Parker wrote. "He will never be forgotten, nor his work undone."

ARTHUR GRANT EVANS
1908–1911

ARTHUR GRANT EVANS became president of the University of Oklahoma in 1908 following a political upheaval that had pushed aside OU's inaugural president, David Ross Boyd, and many of his handpicked faculty. Evans, a kind and gentle minister who still retained an English accent from his missionary childhood, would fall victim to the same kind of political shifts in loyalty and power just three years later. But during that brief time he would reshape OU's academic structure in important ways and build a campus icon that has served as a symbol of the university's endurance for more than a century.

Within a month of assuming the presidency, President Evans had taken charge of plans to rebuild OU's primary academic space, which had been lost during the 1907 fire. The campus now included the Prairie School–inspired Science Hall and Carnegie Library; between the two were the remnants of blackened rubble that had once been the stately Renaissance building known as University Hall. OU's only other structures were constructed of wood. Evans was determined to build a new academic center and to create an architectural style for the university's future.

Ironically, an architectural master plan had been proposed by none other than Vernon L. Parrington, the acclaimed former professor of English who had been fired in 1908. An architecture aficionado, Parrington had, in the wake of University Hall's destruction, submitted a series of recommendations to the OU Board of Regents only one month prior to his dismissal. He suggested that a new building and all subsequent OU construction should follow a set of guidelines that would develop and maintain a consistent architectural flavor. Parrington recommended that campus expansions be built either in the classical or Gothic style. He also suggested that the buildings be arranged in quadrangles or surrounding an oval. According to David Levy in his book, *The University of Oklahoma: A History, Volume 1, 1890–1917,* Boyd and an associate had followed up on these recommendations by visiting campuses that featured both styles. After the 1908 firings, these plans and Boyd's research were made available to architects hired to design a replacement for University Hall. The board eventually decided that the style of campus architecture should be Gothic, and that any future buildings would be constructed surrounding an oval. Quadrangles were more frequently used at universities nationwide, but executing such a plan would require several buildings to be constructed simultaneously. That was out of the question given OU's fragile financial state.

OU's campus as it appeared in 1910, with the Carnegie Library and Science Hall facing each other across the Oval and the beginnings of Evans Hall in between. *(OU 1825A)*

Evans Hall, with a completed ground floor and girders outlining the second floor. *(OU 345)*

OU's campus bore little resemblance to the "stretch of prairie" that David Ross Boyd had seen when arriving in 1892. Population alone made a difference; there were now more than seven hundred students at OU, and Norman had in excess of three thousand residents. Trees were planted throughout campus and in town, and a row of leafy shade trees lined each side of University Boulevard. Stretching out before the ruined University Hall was a grassy common area that would be enlarged and one day named Parrington Oval.

Construction of OU's new academic center began in September 1909 on the same spot where University Hall had resided. Among the new building's most prominent features would be niches and towers, turrets, and gargoyles. The academic center would rest upon an earthen terrace that lifted it up several feet higher than OU's other buildings; the terrace was to be fronted with salvaged white stones that had once composed the walls of University Hall. Construction would cost $200,000, paid in part through the $67,500 insurance benefit from University Hall and a $132,000 appropriation from the State Legislature.

"President Evans threw himself into the most minute details of the new building, going so far as to help design electrical and water systems and deciding upon the look of furnishings," Levy writes. "The president had a suggestion for every floor, for every room, for every decorative feature of the exterior. It was almost as if Evans knew from the outset that the building was eventually going to bear his name."

INITIATING CHANGE

Evans was also rebuilding the university from the inside out. With many new high schools cropping up across Oklahoma, Evans decided that OU's Preparatory Department had outlived its usefulness and would be dismantled by the end of the 1910 school year. The president also reorganized all of OU's academic programs into colleges and schools and selected deans to head each. The Graduate College was headed by Albert Van Vleet, the School of Fine Arts by Fredrik Holmberg, the College of Medicine by Charles S. Bobo, and the School of Pharmacy by Professor Homer C. Washburn. The College of Arts and Sciences and its satellite School of Teaching was led by James Shannon Buchanan. The new College of Engineering included schools covering Mechanical, Chemical, Electrical, and Civil Engineering, along with a School of Mining Geology. Dean James H. Felgar would oversee each.

Another major change came in 1908 when President Evans established the Senate, a deliberative body composed of faculty members who were empowered to make decisions on behalf of their colleagues. Previously, Levy writes, all OU faculty members had weighed in on important issues. This shift in power proved unpopular with many professors.

OU's library underwent its own changes that year when Milton J. Ferguson, who had served as acting librarian since 1902, handed his post over to recent OU graduate Jesse L. Rader. He would direct OU's libraries for more than four decades and later became director of OU's School of Library Science.

The year 1908 also marked the beginnings of journalism education at OU. The world's first school of journalism had been founded earlier in the year at the University of Missouri. OU Professor T. H. Brewer now offered a course titled "English 33," which enrolled only eight students. It would be five more years before a full program in journalism was available at OU.

The fine arts at OU had a stronger beginning, and Dean Holmberg took his students across the state to perform concerts and plays that helped promote the university to Oklahoma communities. "In older states, some community which happened to be interested in fine arts would form its own school, but in Oklahoma there were none of these," Holmberg later noted. "Here, the College of Fine Arts had grown up with the University as a whole, and, because of

Members of the Sooner yearbook staff "on the job" in 1911. (OU 1301)

this early start, it has had an opportunity to make itself felt both on the campus and throughout the state."

OU football was beginning to have an impact throughout Oklahoma as well. During the 1908 season, the team now known as the Sooners won nine of ten games, losing only to the University of Kansas, and beating Texas 50 to 0. The team's victories added flavor to OU student life and social activities, which were expanding to include Greek letter

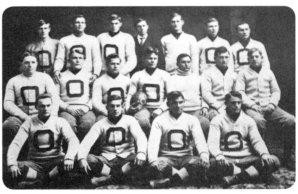

The 1909 OU Sooners football team. (OU 1459)

OU Sooners Coach Bennie Owen, who lost his right arm in an agricultural accident, built the football program and led the team for seventeen years. (OU 164)

This "Yell Card" was made available to OU students in 1910. An early version of "Boomer Sooner" can be seen on the second column. (OU 1152)

fraternities such as Sigma Nu and Sigma Alpha Epsilon.

As the second year of Evans's presidency unfolded, the university's Board of Regents moved to establish the OU College of Law, an idea that had been supported and promoted by Oklahoma attorneys for some time. Levy writes that area lawyers were eager to see their profession protected from amateurs who did not have proper training or certification. But enthusiasm for the new college was missing from one key individual; President Evans was not enthusiastic because he feared spreading OU's resources even thinner. "Given the pressing needs he saw all around him, President Evans probably secretly opposed the creation of a law school; at best he was lukewarm to the whole notion," Levy writes. "But his views were brushed aside, and he was quite effectively marginalized in the search for a dean."

The board conducted its own search and selected Julien C. Monnet of the George Washington University School of Law as the college's first dean. At first sight, Monnet was not impressed with Norman or the university, but, "upon further consideration," he wrote, "in view of the prospects of so excellent a state, I concluded to accept."

Some proposed placing the law college in downtown Norman, but Monnet thought it belonged on the university campus. He accepted a small space in the Science Hall office of geology Professor Charles Gould, whose quarters included a geology collection and the museum of natural history. Pine bookshelves "served as a library," Monnet recalled of his first office at OU. Surrounding the dean's desk were various cases containing such items as geology specimens and stuffed owls. Soon, however, Monnet and his assistant, John B. Cheadle, were teaching forty-seven law students and establishing OU as the state's premier institute for the study of law.

The OU College of Medicine in Oklahoma City in its final stages of completion. (OU 1675)

The OU Spoon Holder, a gift from the 1910 graduating class, served as a romantic spot for "spooning" couples for many years. (OU 175)

The university established its first branch campus for medicine in 1910 after a national study suggested that OU's clinical work should take place in Oklahoma City rather than Norman. Through an agreement between OU and the Epworth College of Medicine, the medical unit of today's Oklahoma City University, Epworth chose to phase out its programs and transfer students to the new OU College of Medicine in Oklahoma City.

On the OU campus 1910 began with seniors designing their class gift to the university in the shape of a circular concrete bench. For decades to come, the bench would serve as a romantic spot for "spooning" couples, which led to it being named the Spoon Holder. Students also had a new spot to congregate off campus with the opening of the Varsity Shop, a small frame building featuring wooden tables that would eventually bear the carved initials of many diners. The Varsity Shop was the first business to open in what became known as Campus Corner.

A SHIFT IN POWER

The year also held political intrigue and drastic change. While students celebrated a football season in which the Sooners had left six out of seven competitors completely scoreless, the eyes of faculty and staff members watched as Oklahomans elected a new governor in Lee Cruce, an OU Regent who had challenged outgoing Governor Charles N. Haskell for the 1907 Democratic nomination. Almost immediately after taking office, Cruce proposed abolishing the individual governing boards that had administered Oklahoma's colleges and universities. In their place he offered up one centralized State Board of Education that would have the power to make decisions for all schools. Approved by the State Legislature, the board met for the

first time on April 8, 1911, and immediately began making high-profile changes.

The board summoned the president of every Oklahoma college and university for review in Oklahoma City. Shortly after, as Levy relates, the announcement came that the board would elect "the heads of several institutions under its jurisdiction, beginning with the President of the University." OU President Arthur Grant Evans was the first of eight education administrators to lose his job. Evans's departure was probably the result of politics and patronage. It did not help that Evans had openly shown little enthusiasm for OU's newly established law school. Also, several State Board of Education members were friends of David Ross Boyd, and they may have sought payback for his dismissal three years earlier. Evans had also supported the wrong candidate when

picking political sides in a hotly contested campaign for superintendent of public instruction; the man Evans championed lost to Robert Wilson, who now chaired Oklahoma's new State Board of Education.

Several other OU faculty and staff lost their jobs as well. Their replacements included Josiah L. Lindsey, who would serve as OU's treasurer and controller until retiring some four decades later. The primary street going east and west through OU's Norman campus would later be named in Lindsey's honor. Other new faces included John Alley, who taught government at OU for many years, and German professor Roy Temple House, who established *Books Abroad*, predecessor of *World Literature Today*, the internationally recognized literary journal that has been published continuously since its founding.

Students strolling and reclining on the Oval in 1911. *(Class 1911-17)*

Also that spring, the State Board of Education offered the OU presidency to law dean Julien Monnet, who stated flatly that he did not want the job but reluctantly agreed to take an interim presidency for one year while a national presidential search was conducted. Evans left OU and returned to the work of a Christian missionary. In time, he would become pastor of El Montecito Presbyterian Church at Santa Barbara, California, where he remained until his death in 1928.

While Monnet carried on as interim president, students went back to their studies, and the newly empowered State Board of Education went to work finding a president for the University of Oklahoma. The job was not easy. The fact that two successive OU presidents had been fired had not escaped national attention. In fact, OU was considered a scandal among the higher education community. According to OU's first historian, the late Regents Professor Roy Gittinger, "The real sufferer was the reputation of the State and the prestige of the University."

Despite hurdles, the State Board of Education succeeded beyond its wildest dreams and hired Stratton Duluth Brooks, who had handled volatility in the cauldron of Boston politics. Brooks would depend upon the hard lessons he had learned to lead OU into its third decade.

STRATTON DULUTH BROOKS
1912–1923

 HAVING EFFECTIVELY RUN OFF the University of Oklahoma's first two presidents, the State Board of Education was now tasked with finding someone willing and able to take the job. They found their match in Boston public school superintendent Stratton D. Brooks.

Brooks, with degrees from the University of Michigan and Harvard, had risen from the post of high school principal to professor at the University of Illinois, where he helped develop the state's secondary school system. He had served as superintendent of Boston schools for six years before taking a six-month sabbatical in 1911 to study vocational education in Europe. Upon returning to Boston, a friend told him, "I declined a state university presidency for you while you were gone."

"Where?" asked a surprised Brooks.

"At the University of Oklahoma," the friend replied. "President Butler [of Columbia University] was asked to recommend a man for president out there, and he asked me if you would be interested. I told him no."

"Thank you!" Brooks said with relief. The Oklahoma State Board of Education's habit of interfering with university operations and the firings of Boyd, Evans, and multiple faculty members had reverberated throughout academia and earned OU a dismal reputation among educators. Brooks forgot about the matter until February 1912 while attending the annual National Educational Association meeting. Several members of the Oklahoma State Board of Education were at the meeting in hopes of successfully recruiting a new OU presidential candidate. Brooks was approached by board member William A. Brandenberg, who introduced him to board president Bob Wilson. Brooks recalled the conversation some thirty years later in an interview with author and OU sports information director Harold Keith. "My train leaves in twenty minutes," Brooks told

the men curtly. "Why do you wish to interview me? Is it not unusual to consider a public school superintendent for the presidency of a state university?"

Wilson explained that the State Legislature had accused the State Board of Education of playing politics, a charge that had attracted the attention of Oklahoma governor Lee Cruce. "We feel that it is desirable that we appoint a president at the university whom none of us has ever seen. Besides, you have a national reputation for freeing the Boston schools from political influence. This might be helpful to our situation."

Brooks expressed interest in moving into higher education, but quickly said he wasn't interested in the OU job. As a courtesy, he gave the state board members two pieces of advice: If the board was serious about shying away from politics, they first must agree not to recommend any OU appointees, whether directly or indirectly. The board must also promise to have nothing to do with the day-to-day administration and operation of OU.

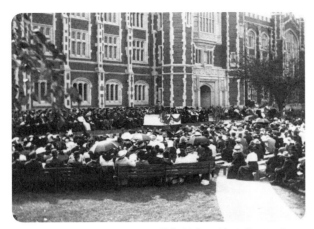

OU's third president, Stratton D. Brooks, speaks to crowds attending his 1912 inauguration in front of Evans Hall. *(Newby 51)*

"Wilson looked at the other board members and then back at Brooks," Keith writes. "That's a big order. It leaves nothing for the board to do."

The following month, the board convinced Brooks to visit OU for a conference. While touring campus with Bob Wilson, Brooks became impressed by the friendly, energetic people he met. "You told me in St. Louis that you wanted to build a great university," Wilson said to Brooks. "Well, this is the only state big enough to have one that hasn't already got one."

"That argument fetched me," Brooks admitted wryly. "I didn't have any answer for it."

BUILDING THE WALLS

Brooks became OU's president in the fall of 1912 and found a mountain of work awaiting him. OU had 723 students and 57 faculty members on the Norman campus, with another 37 faculty teaching medical courses in Oklahoma City. Brooks surveyed neighboring universities and learned that more than 1,500 Oklahoma students had left the state to complete their education, often going to college in states their parents had once called home. Brooks considered this just one more sign that Oklahomans lacked confidence in OU.

"Although Dr. Boyd had things worked out fine until his discharge, the school had gone to pot when he left," Brooks told Keith. "The state had no conception of what a university was, or ought to be." Brooks said many in the state lacked loyalty to or confidence in OU, and some of the university's faculty were incompetent to teach courses. In addition, students coming from Oklahoma's recently established high school system were not well trained. "I was anxious to build a strong graduate school, but you can't put a roof on first," Brooks said.

Brooks could see evidence of political interference nearly everywhere he looked. Democrats and Republicans had battled over OU since its establishment, and many people tried to get whatever they could out of the university. "Everybody seemed to be milking the school," Brooks remarked. "One faculty member even brought his cow to campus with him daily, pasturing her on the university lawn until he finished teaching and went home at night."

One of Brooks's major goals was strengthening OU's faculty. He quickly added five new teaching positions, including hiring noted musician and 1917 OU alumnus Lewis Spencer Salter, who would become dean of OU's College of Fine Arts in the 1930s, and Gayfree Ellison, who was hired to teach bacteriology and later became director of OU's student health service. Brooks called the faculty together and was forthright about his expectations. "I know some of you were sent down here by political friends who are now out of power," he said candidly. "That won't hurt your standing with me. You don't have to please me, nor come to the faculty receptions. You've just got to be good teachers."

Brooks laid out loftier goals for OU's mission during his inaugural address. "A man must not only do something worth doing, but he must be something worth being. The university cannot neglect to perfect him in his doing, nor can it neglect to perfect him in his being." Brooks went on to express his belief that the purpose of education "is to improve both the labor and the leisure of mankind," and stipulated that an education should give students "a taste for all that is best and noblest . . . thus may a man, because of his university education, live more serviceably, enjoy more intensely, die more contentedly. And when all these things

The president's house, now known as Boyd House, as it looked during Stratton Brooks's occupation. The house was commissioned by President Boyd in 1906 and later underwent significant expansion and renovation to achieve its present appearance. *(OU 33)*

The University of Oklahoma Band in 1913. *(OU 2434)*

are done well, the university may feel in some small degree it has fulfilled its mission."

Brooks also focused early on the training of teachers. His many years of experience in public schools gave Brooks a special understanding of OU's role in supplying educators and providing well-trained teachers to the infant state of Oklahoma. At the beginning of the 1912–13 academic year he hired a new director for the School of Teaching, Warren Waverly Phelan, who also would head the university's summer session. Brooks soon renamed the unit the School of Education, but it would remain under the auspices of the College of Arts and Sciences for another eight years until becoming a freestanding college in its own right.

According to Roy Gittinger in *The University of Oklahoma: A History of Fifty Years, 1892–1942,* Brooks arranged with the State Board of Education to reinstate the office of the high school inspector at OU. High school teachers were required to enroll in OU summer session classes annually to maintain their certification. Having the high school inspector, Andrew Clarkson Parsons, on campus gave the university an inside track to help Oklahoma high school students ease their way into higher education. In a way, Brooks's efforts were a continuation of President Boyd's Preparatory College, which ended in 1911 after nearly two decades of transitioning students into college-level work. Historian David Levy found that only eighty-six Oklahoma high schools had been accredited by 1913. Within a year, Parsons offered accreditation to 125 high schools. Parsons's position also gave OU leverage in convincing high schools statewide to hire recent OU education graduates; whereas before, many schools had hired teachers solely from out of state.

Brooks rapidly brought two other major curricular changes to OU academics. In September 1913, OU organized

the School of Journalism and the School of Commerce and Industry, both under the auspices of the College of Arts and Sciences. Previously, OU students had been able to enroll in only a single journalism course taught by Professor T. H. Brewer in the English Department. Now, students could undertake two years of general studies and two years of focused journalism courses. President Brooks recruited Chester C. Wells, a newspaper reporter from Illinois, to establish the new school, which would nominally be directed by T. H. Brewer. In a twist of fate, Wells died before taking the job during a routine tonsillectomy. His childhood friend and fellow journalist, twenty-four-year-old Harold Harvey Herbert, took up the directorship reins and formed OU's journalism school. Five decades later, H. H. Herbert would receive the recognition he deserved when the journalism school was named in his honor. In *The University of Oklahoma: A History, Volume 1, 1890–1917,* David Levy emphasizes the importance of Herbert and his leadership, as attested by the fact that more than 260 of Herbert's students were working in journalism professions across the United States by 1938.

OU's new School of Commerce and Industry, the predecessor of today's Price College of Business, was under the direction of Jerome Dowd, who had served as head of OU's Department of Economics since 1907. Like the new journalism program, the School of Commerce and Industry offered two years of general studies followed by two years of specialized instruction. Dowd helped to recruit Arthur B. Adams as assistant professor of economics; as such, Adams taught all courses in business and in theoretical and applied economics. Adams often fought for his division's success, sometimes in direct opposition to OU's administration, and would prove to be a powerful and divisive force in OU academics for decades to come. A colleague diplomatically described Adams, for whom Adams Hall is named, as "animated by self-reliance, intense energy, love of adventure, and love of combat." As David Levy surmises, "Whether one admired or detested Adams, it was clear that he almost single-handedly laid the groundwork for the stunning expansion in business education."

A MAN IN CONTROL

During Brooks's first year, OU also developed an extension division that provided public information and welfare, public discussion, debate, and correspondence studies. A large part of the division's purpose was to increase awareness about OU across the state.

Brooks helped ensure his continued success by hiring Emil Rudolph Kraettli, one of the university's most enduring and valuable staff members. Kraettli began his career working in the president's office, but would eventually become secretary of the OU Board of Regents and secretary of the university. By the time he retired in 1969, Kraettli was among the most influential and revered staff members ever to serve at OU.

A fitting cap to Brooks's first year as president was the grand opening of Monnet Hall, OU's law building, which provided much-needed space for offices, classrooms, and seventy additional students. Oklahoma Governor Cruce and Harvard law professor Eugene Wambaugh were present for the ceremony.

Brooks had accomplished much and settled in happily at OU; he found that his midwestern upbringing made Oklahoma a comfortable fit. "There was a noticeable difference in the attitude of the people of Oklahoma and those of Boston," Brooks said. "Oklahomans didn't go in for

Emil Rudolph Kraettli, one of OU's longest-serving administrators, served as secretary of the OU Board of Regents and secretary of the university. (OU 814)

precedent. Nobody in Oklahoma was interested in your ancestry. . . . I would say that in Boston everybody was against you if you had a new proposal, but in Oklahoma everybody was against you if you didn't listen to their proposal."

Harold Keith described Brooks as "a frowny, brown-eyed, ruddy-cheeked little man who wore a stubby mustache and walked at a half trot. . . . He was the finest executive the university had ever had. When you went to his office to ask for something, you always knew when you walked out whether you got what you had gone after. Brooks would tell you yes or no in a flash, and he always stood by his decisions."

Brooks's administrative style seemed to suit OU, and the university grew quickly; in 1914 alone, student enrollment rose by 30 percent and the university reached its coveted goal of more than 1,000 students. Among them was law student Huey P. Long, who would go on to become both governor and senator for his home state of Louisiana. Before "The Kingfish" became one of the nation's most notorious political bosses, Long had supported himself by walking miles from Norman to neighboring Noble, Lexington, and Purcell to sell vegetables and fruit.

A growing university needed land. Brooks quickly advocated for OU to expand beyond its original sixty-acre boundaries with the purchase of sixty additional acres north and west of the existing campus. He also brought the practice of academic sabbaticals to OU in those first years, albeit for a unique reason. "When President Brooks came to the university he found several members of the staff whose preparation had perhaps been sufficient for teaching in a small college but who had not the training and perspective needed for members of the faculty of the larger university that he was undertaking to build," Roy Gittinger writes. Sabbaticals would allow faculty members to receive half pay while furthering their own training and education, with the understanding that they would return to OU to teach for a specific number of years.

Several of Brooks's early faculty appointees would spend the bulk of their teaching careers at OU, including 1914 hires Edgar D. Meacham and Paul S. Carpenter. Meacham had recently graduated from OU with multiple academic honors and had been a standout football player. Brooks promptly asked Meacham to join the university's math faculty; he also served as assistant to football coach Bennie Owen. After taking breaks to complete his master's and doctoral degrees, Meacham became OU's assistant dean and then longtime dean of the College of Arts and Sciences. Carpenter, a child prodigy violinist from Philadelphia, took command of OU's symphonies and later became director of OU's School of Music. Gittinger notes that Carpenter's work was important in the development of musical education throughout Oklahoma. Both men are memorialized in today's Meacham Auditorium and Carpenter Hall.

The 1915 OU campus centered on "the Oval," which included University Hall (now known as Evans Hall), the new Monnet Hall, the Carnegie Library, and Science Hall. Rising directly across from Monnet was DeBarr Hall, a four-story chemistry building that would provide laboratories, classrooms, and an auditorium at the cost of $115,000 and be named for OU's first chemistry professor, Edwin DeBarr. At the time, OU's catalog claimed, "In equipment and construction there is no more modern chemistry building in the United States." OU's campus would also include a new landmark, a brick and stone arch presented as a gift from the graduating class of 1915. In time, arches would be placed at each of the Norman campus entrances as gifts from graduating classes.

A LAST TASTE OF INNOCENCE

Across the Atlantic Ocean, Europe was consumed with the beginnings of World War I, while the United States declared its neutrality. OU students were seemingly oblivious to anything other than college life, which now featured the first alumni Homecoming celebration. Some five hundred former students returned to Norman and watched OU continue an undefeated football season that featured Coach Bennie Owen's first All-American player, Park ("Spot") Geyer. Homecoming weekend also included "the peripatetic pajama parade," during which students wore costumes ranging from flannel pajamas to Grecian robes, and the new RUF/NEKS spirit group sported brightly colored silk pajamas. Also new to student life was the first organized student association, led by Leon C. Phillips, who would one day become Oklahoma's governor. The university was stretching its influence statewide and beyond; students hailed from all seventy-seven Oklahoma counties and even as far away as Russia. The growth of the student body was reflected in the newly created office of dean of undergraduates, a position that was filled by none other than Roy Gittinger.

OU's faculty also had a new association in the Administrative Council. Its job was to coordinate OU's various schools, a task made exponentially more difficult by the fact that "each independent school or college that conferred degrees had a separate faculty," Gittinger writes. In 1915, the

A gift from the Class of 1915, the first brick and stone arch at Boyd Street and University Boulevard established an OU landmark that would be replicated by other classes for decades to come. *(OU 1901)*

OU art professor Oscar B. Jacobson mentored the "Kiowa Five," a group whose work brought international attention to Native American art. *(OU 105)*

fine arts faculty welcomed a new art professor named Oscar B. Jacobson. A Yale graduate and former cowboy and policeman, Jacobson had studied at Paris's Louvre and took charge of OU's Art Department and its fledgling art museum. He would later be credited with discovering and mentoring the legendary Native American visual artists known as "The Kiowa Five." Two others who joined OU's faculty during this time would also forever be associated with Oklahoma and western history. Edward Everett Dale grew up farming and ranching and enrolled at OU at the age of twenty-nine after serving as a school superintendent in rural Greer County. He graduated from OU at age thirty-two and was accepted for graduate study at Harvard, where he studied with Frederick Jackson Turner, widely considered the grandfather of western American history. Dale returned to OU as a history instructor and would, in time, become chair of the History Department. He was known as one of OU's most beloved professors and as an internationally recognized expert in western history.

Walter S. Campbell, who had lived in Oklahoma since childhood and was the state's first Rhodes Scholar, came to OU in 1915 to teach English. Previously a high school teacher in Kentucky, Campbell's return to Oklahoma allowed him to delve deeply into the history of Plains Indians. He launched a prolific writing career under the pen name Stanley Vestal. A writer, poet, and historian, Campbell also established OU's acclaimed Professional Writing Program.

"To whatever extent the university has gained national celebrity over the years for its scholarly work on the American West, some of the credit must go to Edward Everett Dale and Walter S. Campbell. . . . They helped to turn the institution in a promising and potentially important and useful new direction," Levy notes.

Medical education at the university also took a new direction in 1915. Previously OU's only medical teaching center had been a privately owned hospital based in a house in Oklahoma City. Professionals viewed the facilities' circumstances as tenuous, which led to OU earning an inferior accreditation rating by the Council on Medical Education. State Education Board leaders and Oklahoma governor Robert Lee Williams felt that the quickest route to recovery was to convince Dr. LeRoy Long to become dean of OU's medical school. Long resisted until May 1915, when, he said, "Appeal was made to my sense of duty to the medical profession. I hesitated and when I hesitated I was lost." Long served as dean of the OU College of Medicine for nearly two decades and helped OU regain its superior accreditation. He also created legislation to acquire land for the future OU Health Sciences Center.

OU's growth would be recorded and reflected in a new student publication, the *Oklahoma Daily,* which had its start at the beginning of the 1916 academic year. OU students had published a newspaper in one form or another since 1897, but the *Daily* offered news coverage five to six days a week, excepting times when war shortages caused printing to be discontinued. A decade later the *Daily* would become the first student newspaper in the nation to be admitted to the Associated Press.

Among topics surely covered in the 1916 *Oklahoma Daily* were the growth of OU's Geology Department, which added several new faculty members who laid the groundwork for OU's preeminence in this field; the steady addition of student social outlets, which now included fourteen Greek letter fraternities and a new University Theater; and the dedication of OU's new DeBarr Hall. OU's more than 1,700 students also enjoyed evenings at a downtown dance hall, which hosted interfraternity dancing clubs with names like Tabasco and Enchiladas. Students could reach the dance clubs more easily now that Norman offered "the jitney," an open-top Ford that could carry as many as five people across town for five cents apiece.

This would be most students' last true taste of innocence, as the United States declared war on Germany on April 6, 1917. When the 1917–18 academic year began OU was a vastly different campus. Student Senate president Josh Lee, who would graduate and go on to a distinguished career in the Oklahoma State Legislature and the U.S. Senate, called a mass meeting of male students and organized voluntary military training within days of the war declaration. Before World War I ended in 1918, more than eighteen hundred OU students and professors would enlist, and three professors and twenty-one enrolled students or recent graduates would die. OU's campus was also transformed. All physically fit male students under the age of twenty-one were required to enlist in the Student Army Training Corps under the direction of chemistry Professor Guy Y. Williams, and some thirteen OU courses were offered to train soldiers and

Officers of the Student Army Training Corps Unit in 1918. *(OU 498)*

civilians in necessary skills. OU also hosted a vocational unit for nonstudents to offer training in general mechanics, auto mechanics, radio operation, and surveying. New wooden buildings were constructed on campus to provide four large mess halls, a guardhouse, an infirmary, a canteen, a bathhouse, three barracks, and a "Y" hut. Several fraternity and sorority houses were commandeered for use as barracks, as were OU's gymnasium and Monnet Hall. Wives of faculty members and female students volunteered their free hours to knit and sew clothing on behalf of the Red Cross.

MOVING PAST A WORLD WAR

Despite the campus having been transformed into a quasi-military base, OU life continued. The university now boasted thirteen buildings and an auditorium, geology building, and a new library were under construction. The library and auditorium would later be named Jacobson and Holmberg Halls, respectively. In Oklahoma City, OU was building University Hospital, which would primarily serve

the state's poor and indigent patients. OU also started its School of Manual Training and School of Social Service that year, and the university's School of Commerce and Industry was renamed the School of Public and Private Business.

On the social side of life, OU women could now enjoy membership in one of six sororities that included Kappa Alpha Theta, Pi Beta Phi, and Alpha Chi Omega, and OU's fraternities would have a new member with the addition of Phi Delta Theta that year. One in four OU students was a member of the Greek system and lived in houses with fewer than forty members. Oratory and debate were still popular pastimes for students, and OU offered a dozen options for participation. But there were difficult moments in student life as well, including a dangerous epidemic of influenza and a student-set fire that burned the wooden-framed journalism school and YMCA. The journalism school was relocated to the basement of Science Hall, where it would stay until 1929.

Perhaps ironically, OU was enjoying stability and growth in the midst of war. "The institution seemed at long

Though World War I had ended, OU still was home to the Student Army Training Corps's three barracks, four large mess halls, guardhouse, infirmary, canteen, and bathhouse. *(Kraettli 50)*

OU students in the 1920s embraced what Roy Gittinger called the "hectic buoyancy" of postwar life, as seen in this image of two couples sharing a horse-drawn buggy on the Oval. *(OU 1305)*

last to be indubitably on the right track," Levy relates. "It was led by an able, incorruptible, and energetic president. Its various academic subdivisions were being efficiently supervised . . . To all appearances, by 1917 the University of Oklahoma had recovered the ground that had been lost by the disastrous events of 1908 and 1911."

Much of that lost ground had been at the hands of Oklahoma's State Board of Education, which was disbanded by the governor in 1919; in its place, each college and university was allowed to reform its own governance board, and the OU Board of Regents reclaimed control of OU, a move that implied more peaceful times in university life.

Military peace had been achieved through the 1918 armistice, yet a military presence remained at OU. The Student Army Training Corps was replaced by the new, national U.S. Army Reserve Officers' Training Corps, and OU soon built the armory that still stands east of the Gaylord Family Oklahoma Memorial Stadium. The war had wrought other, indelible changes upon OU students, who experienced reentry shock. "The successful conclusion of the First World War brought on a hectic buoyancy that made itself felt on the campus," Gittinger observed. Students seemed less serious about their studies, and a raft of new clubs "which proved to be of little advantage either to the university or to the students concerned" cropped up sporting names like Tall Cedars of Lebanon, Battle Axe, and Chi Chi Chi. Student Council dances were held each Saturday night and were among the most popular campus events. Students also enjoyed OU's all-victorious teams in football, basketball, and track.

Although football coach Bennie Owen remained wildly popular on campus, some members of the Oklahoma State Legislature thought his salary of $3,500 per year was too high and found an excuse to get rid of him based upon the firing of a one-handed piano teacher from a small Oklahoma college. "The university has got a one-armed football coach. Why don't we fire him, too?" Harold Keith said in recalling the events. "And presto! It was done. But [President] Brooks

Spectators and players enjoy a football game on Boyd Field, c. 1915. *(OU Centennial 1)*

The OU campus as it appeared during President Brooks's tenure. Visible from the left are Carpenter, Jacobson, Monnet, Evans, DeBarr, Science, and Holmberg Halls. (OU 410)

soon got wind of the action and had it rescinded so quickly and quietly that Owen never learned of his dismissal until one week after he had been rehired."

"Bennie invented football here, owned it, contracted for it, and paid for it," President Brooks later said. "I told him it was his job, and I wanted him to run it."

Brooks supported strong leaders in the classroom as well. In 1919, he hired twenty new faculty members, including such OU notables as Homer Dodge, the professor of physics who would later lead OU's Graduate College; Spanish instructor and recent OU graduate Eugenia Kaufman, for whom Kaufman Hall would be named; and Joseph H. Benton, a voice teacher who was still an OU student and would soon move to Italy to become the admired opera singer Giuseppe Bentonelli. Among Benton's good friends was fellow OU student and future famed playwright Lynn Riggs, whose *Green Grow the Lilacs* would be retold as the musical *Oklahoma!*

For Brooks and OU 1919 was a successful year. The university had its largest enrollment to date with more than 2,600 students and introduced two degree programs in the new School of Home Economics, which was part of the College of Arts and Sciences. OU also launched its first health service. Dr. Gayfree Ellison supervised a rented hospital on East University Place and offered students medical services for $2.50 per semester.

OU's enrollment continued to rise to nearly 3,000 students in 1920, including 128 in the Graduate College and 1,309 during summer session. More academic growth followed when the School of Education earned independence from the College of Arts and Sciences and instituted a degree program for the Bachelor of Science in Education. Only juniors and seniors were permitted to enroll in the curriculum, and space was remodeled in the Carnegie Library to provide classrooms for the new school. The 30,000 volumes in OU's library collections were moved to the "New Library" in

today's Jacobson Hall. Librarian Jesse Rader accomplished the task in a midwinter week with the use of only a few pushcarts.

Student attention in 1920 was focused on OU's fourth undefeated football season, led by Captain Dewey ("Snorter") Luster, and on a growing rivalry between OU law and engineering students that had started in 1914. Friction between the law and engineering students escalated into fights, and President Brooks threatened to abolish the St. Patrick's Day celebration on campus altogether. One year, law students notoriously poured a harsh laxative for cattle into coffee at a College of Engineering banquet. Another time, a group of law students that included Hicks Epton stole three gallons of green paint and vandalized Monnet Hall, carefully leaving drips of paint leading back to the engineering building in hopes of implicating their rivals. The next day, one hundred innocent engineering students were sent to clean the paint from Monnet, then known as the Law Barn.

"Those who did the act were sworn to absolute secrecy, and I'm sure none of them told," Epton said. "Yet, a few days later, I received a firm tap on the shoulder and was invited by the dean [Monnet] himself into his office. . . . There he told me, after allowing me to quake in my boots for the necessary eternity, that we had better be careful that the word never got out who painted the Law Barn."

With time, the rivalry died down, though engineering students occasionally painted the owls adorning the Law Barn a bright color or law students kidnapped the engineering queen or perhaps even the Civil War cannon known as Old Trusty. In 1920, engineering students mobilized to protect the queen and cannon through a secret society named the Loyal Knights of Old Trusty, which endures even today. The original Old Trusty would be destroyed in 1933, reportedly dropped to the bottom of the South Canadian River after an engineering student named Latham Yates lost both hands while loading the cannon.

The last of Stratton Brooks's additions to the OU campus, the Women's Building provided offices for the women's counselor and organizations, a gymnasium, and a swimming pool. *(OU 583)*

Arthur B. Adams, OU's first dean of business and the namesake of today's Adams Hall, led the way for business education in Oklahoma. *(OU 745)*

TROUBLE ON THE HORIZON

Fall 1921 brought more additions to OU's faculty, including longtime medical instructor Dr. Richard Clyde Lowry; law professor Joseph F. Francis; and journalism instructor Fayette Copeland, for whom Copeland Hall would be named. A new Women's Building provided offices for the women's counselor and women's organizations, along with reception rooms, a gymnasium, and a swimming pool. Off-campus facilities for students were growing as well, including the Albert Pike Hall for men, run by the Masonic Lodge, and Agnes More Hall for women, offered by the Methodist Episcopal Church. Fraternity and sorority choices also continued to expand with the addition of such organizations as Delta Tau Delta.

Students returned to OU in 1922 unaware that yet another disruption of university life was on the horizon. Their focus was on fall afternoons crowded around Barbour's Drug Store, where they waited for the Western Union telegraph operator to shout out Sooner football results through a megaphone. So many gathered to hear game results that traffic on Main Street was often blocked. Soon the place of such bulletins would be taken by radio,

which premiered at OU thanks to engineering student Maurice L. Prescott. Prescott formed the Oklahoma Radio Engineering Company and established a 50-watt station, WNAD, from the basement and living room of his home on Eufaula Street, where he provided play-by-play commentary for Sooner sporting events and spun phonograph records.

Enrollment at OU now topped 3,500 students, and the newly renamed School of Business was under the leadership of Dean Arthur Adams. New faculty members included Ellsworth Collings, for whom the College of Education would be named; John Clark Jacobs, a recent OU graduate and physical education instructor whose name is featured on OU's track facilities; and Thomas Marion Beaird, a government professor and future secretary of the OU Association. Beaird Lounge in Oklahoma Memorial Union carries his name.

With the election of Governor John Calloway "Jack" Walton in 1922, Oklahoma had a new leader as well. OU President Brooks had enjoyed an easy and amicable working relationship with Walton's predecessor, Robert L. Williams, and with the Oklahoma State Legislature. "You had to find

President Brooks in his Evans Hall office, circa 1920. Note the telephone with an accordion-style extension arm. *(OU 1835)*

which way the trend was going," Brooks said of working with legislators. "They used to try to get me to ask for one building. I always refused. I told them I wanted six. At the close of the session, I would have found out which of the six buildings we had the best chance to get, and we'd go after it." Brooks often befriended influential legislators and consulted with them about issues of concern. Once, he overlooked a legislator who took offense at being left out of the process. "You have discussed this proposition with everyone but me," the man said angrily. "Now I want to know why." Brooks quickly ended the argument by replying, "Why, I didn't think I needed to explain it to you. A man of your intelligence and influence doesn't need to have a simple matter like this explained to him."

But neither Brooks's political acumen nor quick reflexes could save him from the simple truth that Jack Walton was hostile toward OU and its president. Walton had already gone so far as clearing five members from OU's Board of Regents and reappointing five men of his own. Gittinger writes that Walton "represented the current movement from Wilsonian idealism to 'practical' politics. The growth

of the university and its contributions to the winning of the war were not fully appreciated by all members of the new regime. President Brooks had a strong position in the state and he probably could have continued in the presidency, but he did not feel that it would be advantageous either to him or to the university to try to remain in the face of opposition."

After eleven years at OU, Stratton Brooks resigned the presidency on July 1, 1923. The University of Missouri had made repeated overtures to Brooks to become its president, and he would preside there for eight years before becoming educational director of the Grand Council of the Order of DeMolay in Kansas City, Missouri. "But his heart, and also that of his wife, was back in Oklahoma, where he liked the gracious hospitality of the people, where nobody was interested in your ancestry," Harold Keith writes. When Brooks's wife, Marcia, died in 1941, he chose to have her buried in Norman. OU's former president remained bright and active until his death on January 18, 1949. Brooks is buried alongside his wife, mere miles from the campus he helped to rejuvenate following years of conflict and instability, throughout the world war, and the many changes the university faced in the years before and after.

"Brooks not only had imagination, but was an organizing genius whose plans worked out. He was fearless, aggressive, and had fine intuition. Brooks was a good judge of human nature. [His] campus reforms were legendary," Harold Keith said, pointing out that OU's third president established a permanent faculty salary schedule, sabbatical leave, and permanent tenure. Other lasting legacies include his foresight in starting and being the first contributor to the student loan fund, originating the book exchange, and helping OU to secure more buildings than during any other period in the institution's first fifty years.

"That a man of Brooks's ability and enormous energy should come to the presidency at exactly the time the school was undergoing the difficult expansion from its old territorial order into that of a large, busy, highly specialized state university was the state's good fortune," Keith concluded. "Brooks eventually rebuilt the damage done to the school by the Haskell political hierarchy and restored the state's confidence in it."

JAMES SHANNON BUCHANAN
1923–1925

RECOVERING FROM THE SHOCK of losing yet another president to state politics in 1923, the Board of Regents understood the grave importance of carefully vetting and selecting a new leader for the University Oklahoma. At the same time, they knew OU would benefit from an administrator who was both calm and competent and who could serve as acting president and manage the minutiae of the university's daily business. Without hesitation or second thoughts, the board turned to James Shannon Buchanan, a beloved faculty member and administrator whose professional life was indelibly woven into OU's very fabric.

Buchanan, a native of Franklin, Tennessee, came from a family who had long been among that state's most prominent citizens; his father was related to the founder of Nashville, and Buchanan's brother, John P. Buchanan, had served as governor of Tennessee. A graduate of Cumberland University and a principal of the private Connersville Academy, James Buchanan was appointed by his brother as Tennessee's assistant superintendent of schools. He undertook graduate studies at Vanderbilt University and the University of Chicago before coming to Oklahoma in 1894 as a professor of history at Central Normal School in Edmond.

The following year OU President David Ross Boyd hired the young professor to teach American history, as well as English for the university's Preparatory Department. Buchanan was freed from English instruction when Vernon L. Parrington arrived at OU in 1897, though the historian continued to develop the new Department of Economics in 1899.

When the 1903 fire devoured OU's first administration building, students braved the flames to slide Buchanan's desk and books down a ladder. And it was Buchanan who spoke stirringly on behalf of the faculty at the dedication of OU's second administration building, University Hall, later that same year. Buchanan was invested in the fine details of OU life and even chaired the committee that selected the university's colors as crimson and corn. The OU professor, who had brought his new bride, Vinnie Galbraith, to Norman in 1896, was also deeply involved in Norman's civic and religious life. He was among the lay leadership at First Presbyterian Church and served as a member of the city council, where he helped plan the installation of Norman's first water system and passed the bird protection ordinance that purportedly saved President Boyd's grove of trees. In 1907, Buchanan became a delegate to the Oklahoma Constitutional Convention and contributed to both

Interim President James Shannon Buchanan (*bottom row, center*) in 1925 with fellow faculty members (*from top row, left*) James Wellings Sturgis, Charles N. Gould, Roy Gittinger, Sardis Roy Hadsell, and Charles N. Paxton. *(Dale 134)*

the state preamble and bill of rights. At the urging of OU friend and colleague Charles N. Gould, Buchanan also developed a constitutional provision for the Oklahoma Geological Survey, which made Oklahoma the only state in the nation with such a requirement.

Buchanan was unique among OU's faculty. He was one of only two southerners to serve during Boyd's presidency and his ties to the Deep South may have saved Buchanan during the 1908 firings brought about by Democratic governor Charles N. Haskell and his new Oklahoma State Board

The OU football team in 1923 had only sixteen members. Players of this era wore leather helmets and shoulder pads, and their uniforms often were made of wool. *(OU 1495)*

of Education. When OU's second president, A. Grant Evans, reorganized OU's academic divisions in 1909, Buchanan became dean of the College of Arts and Sciences and also served as chair of the History Department. By 1917 Buchanan was one of only four remaining faculty members hired by President Boyd in the 1890s.

"Each day he attacked the day's job, whether instruction, administration, or research, as it came up, and each day he finished the task in a workmanlike manner," Gould wrote of his friend in a *Sooner Magazine* article. He described Buchanan as "kindly, friendly, jovial," and said that the future OU president offered both a listening ear and sage advice to anyone in need. "One of his outstanding qualities was that of friendship. Everybody liked Professor Buchanan. I presume he never had an enemy." Students were among those who liked Buchanan the best. His nephew, Tom Matthews, came to OU from Tennessee, and soon students across campus had begun referring to the dean of arts and sciences by his family nickname of "Uncle Buck."

CREATING STABILITY

Buchanan's attributes made him the ideal candidate to serve as OU's acting president in 1923, when newly elected Oklahoma Governor John Calloway "Jack" Walton forced Stratton Brooks out of office. Walton continued his criticism of OU and began cutting budget lines he found wasteful; among the casualties was the Oklahoma Geological Survey. But Walton was not governor for long. The Progressive Democrat had won his campaign on the promise of being an

advocate for everyday working people, but he soon alienated the public by exceeding his authority. Walton began a "war" on the Ku Klux Klan and declared martial law in Tulsa and Okmulgee Counties. He later suspended Tulsa County's writ of habeas corpus. Walton's action, in direct violation of the Oklahoma State Constitution, led to his being investigated by a grand jury. His response was to declare "absolute martial law" and place the state capitol complex under his direct command. Less than ten months after his election, he became the first governor to be impeached by the Oklahoma State Legislature.

Ironically, one of OU's founding fathers, longtime chemistry professor and vice president Edwin DeBarr, was brought down in the summer of 1923 for his support of the Ku Klux Klan. DeBarr had been named Grand Dragon of the Klan and was dismissed for "pernicious political activity" in support of Klan-backed gubernatorial candidate Robert H. Wilson and "public utterances attacking certain classes of citizenship of Oklahoma."

Under state law at that time, Lieutenant Governor Martin E. Trapp succeeded Walton, and Buchanan and the OU community breathed a collective sigh of relief. Trapp was far friendlier toward higher education, and Buchanan could concentrate on stabilizing and expanding the university.

He quickly organized the School of Business as an independent unit and named Arthur B. Adams as dean. By September 1923, OU had purchased the privately owned local radio station WNAD and doubled its broadcasting capacity. Buchanan also led construction of two new buildings—for engineering and pharmacy—on OU's Norman campus.

By the end of Buchanan's first year, the OU Board of Regents decided to grant him the full title of president, though he had no intention of staying in the job and was keen to return to teaching and academic administration. The change in title had become necessary only because "An *acting* president just doesn't work," Buchanan acknowledged.

The work of his final year in office included reorganizing the School of Fine Arts into a college with schools in painting and design, dramatic art, and music. Fredrik Holmberg continued to serve as dean of fine arts and became director of the OU School of Music. The School of Petroleum Engineering was also established in 1924 within the College of Engineering with the support of both the OU Board of Regents and Governor Trapp. Former U.S. Bureau of Mines engineer and University of Pittsburgh instructor Harry Coulter George was chosen to lead the school. That year also brought the reinstatement of the Oklahoma Geological Survey, and Charles N. Gould returned to OU after a twelve-year absence to lead the survey as director.

Campus expansion was one of Buchanan's greater challenges during his brief administration. The Oklahoma State Legislature granted $372,000 in funds to build a liberal arts building that would eventually carry Buchanan's name, as well as a physical education building now known as the McCasland Field House. Two women's residence halls were slated for construction, later to be named Hester and Robertson Halls, and plans were in the works for both a student union and a new stadium. In preparation, students and university officials worked jointly on the campaign for a student union, and they traveled to the campuses of Chicago, Purdue, Illinois, and Northwestern universities to examine similar projects. A goal of $350,000 was set for the new union. At the same time, OU athletic director Bennie Owen was trying, after several fruitless attempts, to garner support for a new stadium that would add sixteen thousand seats. Soon, the two efforts combined

An architect's rendering of the future student union bears little resemblance to the building we know today. *(1924 Sooner Yearbook)*

into a $1 million campaign for Oklahoma Memorial Union and Oklahoma Memorial Stadium—OU's first private fund-raising drive.

CHALLENGES AND CHOICES

Students during the "Roaring Twenties" posed separate challenges for the Buchanan administration. Enrollment had grown significantly during the previous two years, and OU's six thousand students enjoyed rowdy new traditions that included the university's first panty raid, aimed at Delta Delta Delta sorority, and a much larger raid on Norman's downtown drug stores, during which students took such items as lipstick and toilet water. Merchants

presented President Buchanan with a bill for nearly one thousand dollars in stolen and damaged goods, and students responded with a self-imposed fee of two dollars per person.

Perhaps this same spirit and discipline helped form the careers of such Class of 1924 luminaries as A. S. "Mike" Monroney and William Franklin "Dixie" Gilmer, both of whom would go on to serve in the U.S. Congress, and Henry G. Bennett, who would become president of Oklahoma A&M (now OSU) and expand that school significantly during two decades of service.

New OU professors included notables Mark R. Everett in biochemistry, Jens Rud Nielsen in physics, and William H. Carson in engineering. Everett would become chair of

Buchanan also helped plan a new football stadium, as seen in this 1925 rendering, which depicts a grand, collegiate bowl topped by a clock tower whose design would eventually be added to the new student union. *(Kraettli 23)*

Hester and Robertson Halls, the first residential housing built on OU's Norman campus, were restricted to women students. The buildings, which shared a large dining room featuring murals and formally set tables, were completed in 1925. *(OU 632, 1346–1348)*

the Biochemistry Department and dean of OU's College of Medicine; he was also among the founders of the Oklahoma Medical Research Foundation. Carson would serve as director of both mechanical and petroleum engineering, and later as dean of the College of Engineering for nearly thirty years. Carson Engineering Center is named in his honor. Nielsen emerged as one of OU's finest research professors. OU recognized his contributions to teaching and research when, in 1946, the university physics building was given Nielsen's name.

Buchanan looked forward to his future as the OU Board of Regents wound down its two-year nationwide presidential

search. After the death of his first wife, Vinnie, in 1921, he had been a single father to their two sons, William and James, and their daughter, Frances. In 1924, Buchanan married Catherine Osterhaus, and together they were raising his children. A newlywed Buchanan was relieved to refocus his attentions on being a teacher, administrator, and family man when, in the summer of 1925, the Board of Regents announced they had chosen William Bennett Bizzell, a seasoned administrator and former Texas A&M and Texas State College for Women president, as OU's fifth president. Bizzell took office on July 1, 1925, and Buchanan happily returned to academic work, where he remained a vital part of OU's daily

James Shannon "Uncle Buck" Buchanan was such a beloved, central member of the university community that his 1930 funeral was held in Holmberg Hall. *(OU 759)*

AN APPRECIATION

OF

JAMES SHANNON BUCHANAN

BY

WILLIAM BENNETT BIZZELL
AND OTHERS

NORMAN
UNIVERSITY OF OKLAHOMA PRESS
1930

"UNCLE BUCK"

by Mary McDougal Axelson

*The tree has fallen upon the hill
Oh mourn for the oak, the great gray oak!
The tree lies broken there, and still—
Oh mourn for the great gray oak!*

*The dug-outs knew the great gray oak,
And the covered wagons rolling west—
But the boys and girls who climbed the hill,
Perhaps they knew it best.*

*The suns swing by, and the rains still fall,
And the winds blow on, across the hill,
And though the great oak is gone,
Our hearts will see it still.*

*In pride and love our hearts will see
The oak still stands where it stood so long,
For Love is great, and has her will,
And Death is not as strong!*

OU Press published a poem in Buchanan's honor.

life, serving as a university vice president and chair of the OU History Department for a cumulative two decades, as well as director of the Oklahoma Historical Society, becoming well known as one of the nation's foremost experts on U.S. President Andrew Jackson.

Buchanan, OU's beloved "Uncle Buck," served the university for thirty years. When he died on March 20, 1930, his passing marked the end of an era for those who had watched the fledgling prairie school grow into a full-fledged university.

Buchanan's death inspired accolades and tributes in newspapers and magazines, a memorial lectureship was quickly established in his name, and the Oklahoma Historical Society passed a resolution honoring Buchanan, calling him "one of the most distinguished citizens of the state." His friend and colleague Charles N. Gould said, "He has been more intimately connected with the internal working of the school and has served in more different capacities in university affairs than has any other single man among us."

WILLIAM BENNETT BIZZELL
1925–1941

THE BOARD OF REGENTS took two long years to select a new president for the University of Oklahoma, and they chose wisely. William Bennett Bizzell's presidency ushered in a fifteen-year era of relative stability and growth that would bring OU to a new maturity and a more reputable status in higher education.

Bizzell was a professor's president, a man of distinguished learning and character who had already experienced great success as president of Texas State College for Women from 1910 to 1914 and Texas A&M College from 1914 to 1925. The native of Independence, Texas, held an armload of degrees, including a bachelor of science from Baylor University; a bachelor of laws, master of arts, and doctor of civil laws from the University of Chicago; and a doctorate from Columbia University. He was also an unapologetic bibliophile who had amassed a book collection ranging into the thousands, many of which bore a bookplate with the Shakespearean quote, "Ignorance is the curse of God; knowledge is the wing wherewith we fly to heaven."

"Here was a president of national prominence; his academic credentials were impeccable, his eloquence as a speaker well known, his integrity unquestioned," wrote Carol Burr in *Centennial: A Portrait of the University of Oklahoma*. "And he was, above all, a gentleman."

Bizzell's character was obvious from the beginning of his presidency on July 1, 1925. "I solemnly pledge my best efforts to so direct the policies of the University as to merit the moral and financial support of all those who believe in the cause of education," he announced at his inaugural address. "My entire time and thought shall be given to the task that has been set before me." The new president announced three major goals during his speech: to develop OU's research and graduate education offerings, to establish a university press, and to

expand OU's extension program into a "statewide campus." Bizzell expressed hope that these collective ideas would raise OU's standards of scholarship.

There were more mundane but crucial issues to be undertaken at the university as well. Roscoe Cate, a 1926 alumnus who became editor of *Sooner Magazine* a decade later, recalled that the southern edge of OU's campus ended immediately south of the Evans Hall administration building. "Behind this beautiful structure there was what amounted to a dump heap," Cate wrote. "Brooks Street was not paved and Asp was poorly surfaced. Classrooms were overcrowded. The teaching load was too heavy. The faculty salary scale was not adequate to keep good men from being lured away to better-paying jobs. The campaign for funds to build a stadium and Union building was lagging. The campus 'utilities department' consisted of a carpenter and a plumber and a few miscellaneous laborers who worked independently and were likely to come to the

President William Bennett Bizzell poses alongside his predecessor, Stratton D. Brooks *(right)*, and OU's first president, David Ross Boyd. *(Bizzell 70)*

oval. Bizzell estimated that the new library would cost $500,000, roughly the equivalent of $6.4 million today. He forwarded a request to the Oklahoma State Legislature, whose members, Cate noted, found the idea "laughable." But Bizzell had found a champion in OU 1914 law alumnus and OU Regent John Rogers, a Tulsa attorney who would later become a member of the State Board of Regents. Rogers worked his connections with the legislature, and Bizzell got an opportunity to make his case for the new library before a legislative committee. Committee members were impressed by what they heard and believed they were being generous by offering $200,000 for the library budget. They expected Bizzell to take the money and run and were shocked when he replied, "It will take at least $500,000, and that will only build the first unit." The OU president held firm to his convictions. Using his formidable speaking skills, Bizzell created a persuasive image of what the library would mean for both OU and the entire state. He won over the committee and soon had secured $500,000 in legislative appropriations.

One of the library's most prominent divisions also got its start that year with two $10,000 gifts from Bartlesville oilman Frank Phillips, founder of Phillips Petroleum Company. Phillips commissioned OU to gather "source material on the history of Oklahoma and the Southwest" in hopes of establishing a western history center near Bartlesville. OU history professor Edward Everett Dale expressed a strong desire to keep the collection in Norman, where he believed the materials would benefit future graduate students, and he enlisted the help of Phillips's friend and attorney Patrick Hurley. Hurley successfully convinced Phillips that the collection should be housed in Norman, where it formed the basis of today's OU Western History Collections.

president's office each morning for instructions as to what to do."

Bizzell received an enthusiastic welcome from OU's faculty, which then included eighty full-time members on the Norman campus and thirty-five on the medical campus in Oklahoma City. OU had little more than six thousand students in 1925, and its budget topped out at $1.1 million.

Cate recalled that the "most distressing" problem facing Bizzell was the state of OU's library, which then was housed in Jacobson Hall on the North Oval. Only sixty-five thousand volumes were available to students, and there was little room for library collections and acquisitions to grow. The university's aspirations to offer graduate degree programs were also hemmed in by the sparse state of the library collections, and OU's book-loving president found the situation unacceptable. "We can't build a great university without a great library," Bizzell told the OU Board of Regents. He quickly formulated plans for a new, grand structure that would fill the unsightly spot behind Evans Hall. He proposed that the building face south toward forty-five acres designated as the site of OU's second

The Great Reading Room of Bizzell Library in its final stages of completion, September 1929. *(OU 1326)*

Statues of Presidents Bizzell and Boyd, 1936. *(OU Photo Services 485)*

The resplendent details of the new library included carved woodwork, such as this intricate arch that framed one of its water fountains. *(OU 1322)*

SPREADING THE WORD

OU also began one of its most successful student loan programs in 1925, with an initial $50,000 gift from oilman Lew Wentz of Ponca City. Wentz's gift was invested and grew to benefit thousands of OU students; in 2011–2012 alone, more than seven hundred students received in excess of $2 million in Lew Wentz education loans. Other familiar touchstones that developed during Bizzell's first year as president include Mortar Board, a national honor fraternity for women that took the place of the Owl and Triangle, which had been in operation at OU since 1912, and the arrival of social fraternities Delta Upsilon and Lambda Chi Alpha. The year also brought the completion of the west wing of OU's stadium.

As for Bizzell, he began a robust travel schedule to speak to high schools, colleges, and civic organizations, often crisscrossing the state in a single weekend, chauffeured and accompanied by his assistant Emil Kraettli. The speaking engagements gave Bizzell the perfect opportunity to promote his concept of OU's Extension Division as an educational outreach serving a "statewide campus."

"The obligations of the state university cannot be completely fulfilled by offering instruction to a few thousand resident students," he had said during his inauguration earlier that year. "The state-supported university must satisfy the intellectual hunger of every man and woman, regardless of age or place of residence within the state," he said. "We must, therefore, think of the state's geographical boundaries as the limits of the university campus and the people of the state should regard the buildings here in Norman merely as the reservoirs of knowledge that they may freely tap whenever they desire."

Soon, the Extension Division advertised correspondence study; in-service training and graduate education for teachers; a Public Information Service that distributed more than 30,000 prepackaged library, literature, and research items to teachers, businesses, students, clubs, and

The aerial shot on the left reveals OU's Norman campus during the early presidency of William Bennett Bizzell. In the center of the photo, the stands, field, and track at Oklahoma Memorial Stadium have been completed. The photo above shows the stadium under construction in 1925. (*Kraettli 7; OU 1112*)

organizations each year; short courses and conferences; and a Forensics League that sponsored speech competitions for more than 150 Oklahoma high schools and junior colleges. The division's Lecture and Entertainment Bureau booked OU student talent programs and lectures, and the Visual Education unit distributed films, slides, and exhibit materials to schools and groups for education and "cultural betterment."

Bizzell's focus on the Norman campus was equally intense. Academic changes in 1926 included the merger of OU's advertising department with the School of Business, and degree programs as diverse as First Aid and Highway Engineering were attracting new students. Residence halls were expanding as well, and Newman Hall opened

at Boyd Street and Chautauqua Avenue to house thirty-five female students. The hall, built by the Catholic Diocese of Oklahoma and administered by the Sisters of Divine Providence, housed both Catholic and non-Catholic students.

Under Bizzell's leadership, 1927 was a year of tremendous growth at OU. Enrollment had increased to seven thousand students, and the president received the promised $500,000 for his new library as part of $1.3 million in state appropriations. The legislature also granted Bizzell $130,000 for a student infirmary, $250,000 for a new College of Medicine building, and $350,000 for the new Hospital for Crippled Children, which would be constructed on OU's medical campus in Oklahoma City. The Oklahoma School

In the "Roaring Twenties" OU's party scene carried on to the rhythm of several dance bands, including the Sooners, who performed such popular tunes as "Down in Old Joe's Barroom." (*1926 Sooner Yearbook*)

Campus Corner in 1927, as seen from Asp Avenue. *(Heffner P264)*

of Religion also started at OU that year, as did the School of Business's Bureau of Business Resources, comparable to today's noted Center for Economic and Management Research. Under the direction of Dean Aute Richards, the Oklahoma Biological Survey was established that June. Subsequently, Richards Hall would be named in the dean's honor. Even more impressive, in one month alone, OU established both the School of Geology and the School of City and Public Affairs.

OU's success was bolstered by another institution's failure. Kingfisher College had been a tiny liberal arts school established in 1895 by the Congregational Church in Kingfisher, Oklahoma; despite its size, Kingfisher College was recognized as a state leader in liberal arts education. The school foundered due to lack of endowment growth, and OU agreed to absorb Kingfisher College's records, degrees, and library holdings, and even granted OU degrees to Kingfisher graduates. In time, $30,000 in Kingfisher endowment funds would come to OU, where they would be used to fund the Kingfisher College Chair of Philosophy of

Religion and Ethics, still considered among OU's most prestigious endowed faculty positions.

In addition to these accomplishments, OU's field house finally opened in 1927. Considered a showcase facility at the time, the field house served as both an athletic venue and gathering spot for the university community even into the present day.

A very different type of showcase premiered that year with the establishment of the international literary journal *Books Abroad,* founded by Professor Roy Temple House and coeditor Kenneth Kaufman. *Books Abroad* was established as a quarterly publication to disseminate literary information on a worldwide scale, with a secondary goal of promoting international understanding. The journal put OU on the literary map and within a year of its publication began changing outside perceptions of Oklahoma and its flagship university. "One day a man from Oklahoma depresses us by yawping about it in such a way as to give the impression that there is nothing in that young state but oil wells and millionaires," wrote Pulitzer Prize–winning historian

Women students photographed in the living room and bedrooms of Hester and Robertson Halls in the late 1920s. *(OU 587, 1308)*

Portions of Oklahoma Memorial Union were finished by the late 1920s, including the Will Rogers Cafeteria, pictured here. *(OU 858)*

James Truslow Adams, "and the next day one gets from the University there its excellent quarterly critical list of all the most recent books published in France, Spain, Germany, and Italy." Renamed *World Literature Today* in 1977, the journal continues to be well regarded in literary circles today.

Perhaps the most significant development of 1927 was a fundamental change in OU's governance. The OU Board of Regents announced that it had come to an agreement with Governor Henry S. Johnston by which board members could only be removed by the Oklahoma State Legislature, and then only after "impeachment and trial," according to Roy Gittinger. Previously, Regents served solely at the pleasure of Oklahoma's governor, and members had been removed and added at whim to further political agendas.

OU continued to build programs and structures. In September 1928, the university consolidated all of its College of Medicine efforts on the Oklahoma City campus, which now enrolled two hundred students under the direction of Dean LeRoy Long. Among those on OU's medical faculty was Dr. James Patton McGee, who would later serve as chair of the Department of Ophthalmology and become the namesake for today's cutting-edge vision institute. On the Norman campus, the Oklahoma Memorial Union opened November 22, despite the fact that several rooms and the bell tower were unfinished. The new facility, featuring a bustling student cafeteria, was named in honor of students, faculty, staff, and alumni who had served and died in World War I. OU students voted to approve a self-imposed fee of $2.50 per semester to pay for the union and stadium. President Bizzell also declared his intent to transform and beautify OU through landscaping and landscape architecture. A sunken garden was installed between Evans Hall and the site of the future library, a rock garden was designed for the South Oval, and a formal garden that still stands today would link the library to Adams Hall.

TURNING TIDES

Unaware of the financial turmoil that would engulf the nation later that year, Bizzell accomplished one of his primary goals in January 1929 with the establishment of the University of Oklahoma Press, devoted to publishing scholarly books not typically considered by commercial publishers and with a special focus on the American Southwest. Until that time, no significant publishing had been done at OU; projects had been limited to brochures and class bulletins. "The press was planned as an agency to further the activities of the university and to complement the work of the classroom," Roy Gittinger wrote. Bizzell recruited Joseph Brandt as the inaugural OU Press director. A 1921 alumnus and Rhodes Scholar, Brandt had worked as city editor of the *Tulsa Tribune*. Little did Bizzell suspect at the time that he had handpicked OU's next president.

Brandt shepherded the OU Press's first book into production within a year, far more quickly than Bizzell had predicted. *Folk-Say* was the first volume in a collection of

The cover of the 1928 inaugural issue of *Sooner Magazine*. *(Courtesy* Sooner Magazine*)*

Classes were canceled for the 1928 funeral of "Mex," the Sooners' beloved mascot. Mex regularly cheered the team on by barking from the sidelines of Owen Field and at away games. *(Heffner P740)*

contemporary folk stories by such authors as Carl Sandburg and Langston Hughes. Series editor and OU English professor Benjamin Albert Botkin would go on to become the nation's most prominent folklorist and change perceptions that folklore was strictly part of America's past. His work and that of other early OU Press authors soon had the university in the national spotlight for such nonfiction titles as *Wah'Kon-Tah: The Osage and the White Man's Road* by John Joseph Mathews, which became the first university press publication selected by the Book of the Month Club. In addition to Press publications, Brandt also created the first issue of *Sooner Magazine*.

Another of Bizzell's goals was reached in 1929 when he awarded the first doctoral degree in OU history to zoology student Mary Jane Brown. OU's School of Library Science was established that same year and directed by head librarian Jesse L. Rader. Among other achievements was the completion of the Petroleum Engineering Lab and Refinery, which was producing up to 250 barrels of crude oil on OU's campus each day.

Growth at OU slowed as the effects of the 1929 stock market crash began to be felt. Although seemingly calm in comparison to the flurry of activities during the first four years under Bizzell's leadership, 1930 had its important moments, such as when OU's first president, David Ross Boyd, was awarded the title of president emeritus and when OU added paleontologist J. Willis Stovall to the faculty. Stovall

would amass a vast collection that formed the basis for today's Sam Noble Museum of Natural History. The former OU library became home to OU's School of Art and was named in recognition of longtime professor, artist, and noted Native American art promoter Oscar B. Jacobson. The year's highlight was the January opening of OU's new library. The facility, with its elaborate gargoyles and cavernous reading room, boasted 110,000 volumes and offered the capacity for 350,000 volumes, making it more than five times the size of the previous space in Jacobson Hall.

The library was Bizzell's greatest triumph, ironically unveiled the same year that he faced his most daunting challenge. In November 1930, Oklahomans elected former U.S. congressman and state Constitutional Convention president William H. "Alfalfa Bill" Murray as governor. Murray promoted himself as a friend of the poor and as a threat to those he felt were taking advantage of average Oklahomans. Unfortunately, he counted OU as such an adversary.

"It was clear that the new state administration would not be favorable to the university," Gittinger wrote, adding that the financial crash of 1929 had "affected public confidence and disrupted the finances of the state. The new governor was determined to reduce expenses wherever possible and especially to curtail appropriations for education institutions."

Historian David Levy is more blunt about Murray's intentions. Murray "had a profound distaste for and suspicion of higher education," Levy argued in a *Sooner Magazine* article, "The Great Ticket Scandal of 1933, or Alfalfa Bill Calls Out the Guard." "To him, colleges and universities were the refuge of the rich and lazy, the drunken and dissolute. He once charged that there were too many college graduates in the state. . . . He seems to have reserved a particular animosity, however, for the University in Norman and a very genuine enmity for William Bennett Bizzell, its president."

Murray's animosity toward Bizzell may have stemmed from the president's friendship and support for OU Regent Frank Buttram, who had run against Murray in the Democratic primary. Or, as Roscoe Cate once said, it may simply have been a clash of two radically different world perspectives. "To discuss President Bizzell's troubles with politicians would require a book in itself," Cate wrote in *Sooner Magazine*. "The difficulty probably can be summed up in the simple statement that he just doesn't talk their language." Whatever the cause, the new governor was a genuine threat to OU.

Almost immediately, Murray targeted items to cut from higher education. He recommended that OU and Oklahoma A&M College conduct internal studies to reveal duplication of programs and consolidate their curricula. The governor also suggested that OU and A&M be reserved for juniors and seniors alone, and that all freshman and sophomore students should be funneled to the state's community colleges. Murray was successful in destroying only one OU program during his tenure, when state appropriations for the Oklahoma Geological Survey were omitted from the state budget. The survey was forced to close on July 1, 1931, and it would not return to the university for four years.

State appropriations to OU steadily decreased, from $1.5 million in 1930 to $1.1 million by 1933, and salary funding sank from $1.1 million to $851,000 during that time. Conversely, OU recorded its highest enrollments to date during the 1930–31 academic year. "Citizens looked to the universities of the country to provide both an outlet and a training ground for the jobless. Many unemployed came to school, bringing with them barely enough resources to carry them through the year," wrote OU 1932 alumnus Ernie Hill. A growing number of students were from outside Oklahoma; some 714 hailed from 37 other states, and 10 foreign countries. OU's 5,400 students struggled to pay their annual tuition and fees, which were $3.50 per credit hour for in-state students and $5 for nonresidents. Such costs were more than reasonable for the time, however. One study showed Oklahoma had the lowest per-capita spending on college students, and that OU had one of the most poorly paid teaching staffs of any state university nationwide. The statistics compiled in 1931 showed that the highest paid public university president was at the University of Wisconsin. He made $20,400 per year compared to President Bizzell's annual salary of $12,500.

A STEADY HAND

Despite these challenges, the university made progress, conferring its first doctorate of education degree to James Henry Hodges and adding Rupel Jones to OU's drama faculty. College of Medicine dean LeRoy Long resigned from his post that year and was replaced by longtime faculty member Dr. Lewis Jefferson Moorman. In addition, OU's College of Engineering added two schools, in general engineering and natural gas engineering. WNAD Radio, originated in a home basement belonging to OU engineering student Maurice Prescott ten years before, opened a grand new studio and broadcast at 500 watts. WNAD was

WNAD Radio, which occupied a studio in the tower of Oklahoma Memorial Union, broadcast educational, cultural, and entertainment programs across the nation. *(Heffner V721A)*

OFFICIAL PROGRAM

TEXAS vs OKLAHOMA
October 10, 1936   Price 25¢

Whether at home or away, OU
Sooner football remained at the
center of student fall activities,
as seen in this 1931 photo of the
student cheering section and the
1936 OU–Texas game program.
(Heffner V545; OU 1532)

Oklahoma's only noncommercial station and was considered among the OU Extension Division's greatest successes. The station's nickname was "The Pride of Soonerland," and it was renowned for its broadcasts of educational, cultural, and entertainment programs for both adults and children that reached forty-one states and as far away as Canada and the Panama Canal. Each year, WNAD broadcast in excess of three hundred hours of academic lectures, plays, and debates in its mission to disseminate education and culture, and to build a better citizenry in Oklahoma.

Gayfree Ellison, a member of the faculty since 1910 who had directed the university's health service since 1919, died in 1932. The Ellison Infirmary had been named in his honor. Joining the University of Oklahoma Press staff that year was 1929 graduate and Rhodes Scholar Savoie Lottinville, who would play a long, meaningful role with the university and especially with the OU Press.

President Bizzell was, as ever, focused on OU's future, yet he was well aware of the challenges facing students enrolled at OU during the Great Depression. Delivering a brief speech to OU's largest graduating class during the 1932 commencement, the president aired his concerns and frankly admitted that the previous decade had been "the hardest ten years of my life."

"World conditions are vastly different today from what they were when you entered college," Bizzell was quoted in *Sooner Magazine.* "I am sure that many of you are wondering today what you will do after you leave this campus," he said, adding optimistically: "Let me remind you that existing conditions will not last forever. When that day comes, you will be prepared to avail yourself of the opportunities that life will offer." Bizzell encouraged graduates to put their hand to any form of meaningful work and to move forward with determination. In answer to Governor Murray, who had criticized OU's very mission, he said: "There are those who believe that college men and women seek a college education because students expect by virtue of their training and experience to secure easy jobs. This is your opportunity to demonstrate that this is not true. Show the world that you are not seeking an easy place but only one of useful service."

Bizzell was right in his estimation of Governor Murray. As historian David Levy notes, the governor had fired five university presidents in his first year. Bizzell had survived, even though Murray charged that corruption and immorality were rampant at OU, and that the university was being mismanaged financially. The governor sought and lost the Democratic Party's presidential nomination to Franklin Delano Roosevelt and was gaining national notoriety for taking extreme measures to achieve his goals; he called out the Oklahoma National Guard twenty-seven times and declared martial law thirty-four times, perhaps most famously during the 1931 "Red River Bridge War" over toll bridges spanning the border between Oklahoma and Texas.

In November 1933 Murray declared the area surrounding OU's Oklahoma Memorial Stadium under martial law during the Thanksgiving Day football game against Oklahoma A&M. According to Levy's *Sooner Magazine* article, "The Great Ticket Scandal of 1933, or Alfalfa Bill Calls Out the

The staff of the *Oklahoma Daily* in the paper's newsroom in 1934. *(Heffner V2232)*

Guard," all tickets were to be collected, counted, and compared to gate receipts while the governor's office investigated allegations of duplication and forgery. The governor reinforced his command by calling out fifty National Guardsmen from Chickasha to staff the stadium gates and collect tickets. Days later, Murray's office admitted that no irregularities had been discovered and claimed that the National Guard's presence had been necessary to combat "public drunkenness." The governor also stated he had been responding to a handful of complaints from OU football fans who said that their stadium seats had already been taken when they arrived at games earlier that fall; Levy says the issue may have been as simple as an usher misreading tickets and sending two guests to the same seat. Regardless of the governor's intent, the *Norman Transcript* accused Murray of "scandalizing the good name of the University and humiliating the athletic officials," who included beloved former football coach and athletic director Bennie Owen.

President Bizzell had won the admiration and devotion of his faculty—if, for nothing else, for standing firm against Governor Murray. "Too much praise cannot be given the faculty for the manner in which it remained loyal to the leadership of Dr. Bizzell as he battled against tremendous odds to keep the University together during these days of despair," Ernie Hill wrote. "And the extent to which his personality was instrumental in keeping a loyal faculty and student body hopeful cannot be overestimated." Bizzell held a sterling reputation within the broader Norman community as well, strengthened by the fact that Boyd House was home to an extended Bizzell family that included the president, his wife Carrie, daughter Elaine, and Bizzell's elderly mother. In future years, townspeople would take delight in seeing the president walk hand-in-hand across campus with his grandchildren.

DECADE OF PROGRESS

In Bizzell's first decade as president, university enrollment had increased to 5,700 students, making OU the nation's tenth largest state university and twenty-fourth largest university overall; in the Southwest, only the University of Texas had a bigger enrollment. More than a dozen buildings had been constructed during the previous ten years, yet classroom space was still so scarce that the west wing of the stadium had been partitioned and turned into classrooms for the College of Education. The bulk of campus construction had slowed and eventually stopped due to the Depression, though OU's South Oval was being readied for new additions. But OU could only grow within the confining bounds of state appropriations, and the university did its best to push through. George Lynn Cross, a new botany professor, was among those added to the university's faculty in 1934, and OU welcomed "The Playhouse," a group of students and faculty offering dramatic productions.

Bizzell also responded humanely that year when Dean Fredrik Holmberg, who had formed OU's School of Music and been a pivotal figure in music education both at the university and across Oklahoma since 1909, asked for help with affording serious medical bills he incurred during his time at the Mayo Clinic. The popular Holmberg returned to Norman but passed away in early 1936. Two years later, Bizzell would lead the OU Board of Regents in naming the university's fine arts building in Holmberg's memory.

There were changes at the medical campus, when OU medical dean Dr. Lewis Jefferson Moorman retired in 1935, to be replaced by former U.S. Army Surgeon General Robert U. Patterson. The OU campus added an Independent Women's Association, which joined the already functioning Independent Men's Association in providing intramural and social activities for non-Greek students. OU also established the William Bennett Bizzell Book Fund and hosted the Southwestern Conference on Higher Education. Faculty gathered to talk frankly about challenges they faced and how to best adapt to contemporary demands on education. Apparently, the conference also served as a tribute to President Bizzell. "During this span of turbulent years, the President of the University has been faced with problems more serious and more difficult to solve than the general public will ever realize," *Sooner Magazine* opined.

Oklahomans showed their displeasure with Governor Murray's shortsighted policies at the ballot box, denying the governor a second term in 1935. In addition to his stand against higher education, Murray fought against New Deal programs implemented by President Roosevelt, thus costing the state millions in federal funding. In his place Oklahomans elected another Democrat, E. W. Marland of Ponca City. Marland continued the state's penchant for populist politics and ran on a platform of bringing the New Deal to Oklahoma. Among his promises was supporting a strong funding package for education.

As 1936 progressed, Bizzell asked the State Legislature for and received $250,000 in state funds to build a new College of Business, and the national Works Progress Administration (WPA) pledged a matching grant to construct a biological sciences building. The tower of Oklahoma Memorial Union was completed and partly occupied by WNAD Radio, and OU's Museum of Art was established as two rooms in the art school building under Director Oscar B. Jacobson. The museum boasted a collection of 1,800 donated items, including

President Bizzell settles onto the running board of a car to enjoy dinner at the annual OU Men's Picnic in 1938. *(OU Photo Services 1778)*

the Lew Wentz Collection. Valued at $250,000, it featured ancient paintings, statues, precious stones, and textiles from the Middle East and Far East. Subsequently OU added the School of Applied Biology and School of Letters, both part of the College of Arts and Sciences, and William H. Carson became dean of the College of Engineering after having been a member of that faculty since 1925. Student crowding was evident in OU's new placement tests, which were required of every student taking courses in English, math, or science at the beginning of the 1938 academic year. Student housing remained in great demand, even as ninety new rooms for

Students share a meal in the central dining facilities of the "cooperative dormitories," built in the west wing of the Oklahoma Memorial Stadium in the late 1930s. *(OU Photo Services 75)*

The 1937 Pride of Oklahoma Marching Band poses in front of Evans Hall. *(OU 1120)*

male students were added to the west wing of the stadium and dubbed the Cooperative Dormitory. Three more of these dorms would be added later for both male and female graduate students.

In summer 1938 Walter S. Campbell and Kenneth Kaufman began the Short Course on Professional Writing, a writers' conference that became a national gathering of writers, editors, and agents for decades to come. When OU Press director Joseph Brandt was lured away from Oklahoma to become the director of Princeton University Press and a Princeton professor in 1938, Savoie Lottinville became director of the OU Press. Within two years, Navy ROTC made its debut on campus, marking the first naval presence at OU since World War I.

In August 1940, OU President Bizzell, citing declining health, said he intended to retire in one year. Thus, in November 1940 the OU Board of Regents announced that former OU Press director Joseph Brandt would become the university's next president. Formally supporting Brandt's appointment, Bizzell stated: "My long years of association with Joe Brandt while he was director of the University of Oklahoma Press made it possible for me to know him intimately. He is a man of excellent ability and fine scholastic attainment."

A TIME OF TRANSITION

As Bizzell wrapped up his presidency, one last major gift made possible the Max Westheimer Flying Field. Ardmore oilman Walter Neustadt, Sr., made a $10,000 gift to purchase

The University of Oklahoma Press on a snowy day in the winter of 1939. *(OU 1354)*

President and Mrs. Bizzell greet students at a reception in the summer of 1941, shortly before he resigned. *(OU Photo Services 11336)*

160 acres north of OU's campus. Made from the estate of Neustadt's father-in-law, Max Westheimer, the gift was expressly to provide an airport and training school for "all lines of aeronautics, including pilots, mechanics, etc." The field would play a major role in shaping OU and Norman in the years to come.

In August 1941 William Bennett Bizzell quietly stepped aside, accepting the titles of president emeritus, professor of sociology, and chairman of the Sociology Department. The preceding year of transition had provided time for friends and colleagues to consider accomplishments during Bizzell's sixteen years as president, years that represented one-third of the university's time of existence thus far.

"In material progress, and in scholastic reputation, the University of Oklahoma has become a vastly different institution than it was when he walked into the president's office in the summer of 1925, hung up his hat, and went to work on a thousand different problems," Roscoe Cate wrote in *Sooner Magazine*. He pointed out that the university had conferred 21,000 degrees since its inception in 1892; an astonishing 16,000 of those degrees were conferred by Bizzell, and all but 400 of OU's graduate degrees had been awarded under his watch.

Bizzell's many contributions included instituting rapid growth at OU, changing the face of the university's educational outreach and service, and seeing the university calmly through a devastating financial era. His devotion to integrity and academic vitality set more rigorous undergraduate standards and developed the role of research and graduate studies. Among his additions to OU's physical campus were the University of Oklahoma Press, Buchanan Hall, the Field House, the student infirmary, and facilities on the medical campus in Oklahoma City. The most prominent and lasting symbol of his legacy, however, will always be OU's library. By the end of his tenure, Bizzell's pet project held more than 225,000 volumes and was equipped to hold in excess of one million books. The library was key in helping OU institute graduate studies and represented the highest ideals that Bizzell had fostered during his sixteen-year administration.

Two years later William Bennett Bizzell suffered a devastating heart attack. He survived, but the former OU president remained ill until his death at age sixty-seven on May 14, 1944. In a touch of poetic justice, Bizzell's funeral was held in Holmberg Hall, the building dedicated to the friend whom he had helped and honored throughout Holmberg's own long illness.

In the days ahead, the university that Bizzell had shaped and steadied would face a period of intense change and turmoil, beset by a world war and the unshakable convictions of a reformist president whom Bizzell himself had chosen for OU.

OU's library would be named in Bizzell's honor in 1949; on the day of its dedication the Bizzell family donated the late president's 650-volume Bible collection to the library, and a statue in Bizzell's image was unveiled facing the building he

"Books were always near him," professor and friend Jewel Wurzbaugh wrote of OU's fifth president, William Bennett Bizzell, who gave the university a library that today has more than five million volumes. *(OU Photo Services 1772)*

had so lovingly conceptualized and seen to fruition against all odds.

"A book was to him 'the precious lifeblood of a master spirit,'" OU English professor and friend Jewel Wurzbaugh wrote for the library dedication program. "Books were near him always, piled on his desk, lining the walls of his study and home, under his arm when he crossed a barren or flowering campus. . . . He dreamed of a legacy to outstrip time, a magnificent treasure-house of books. And he made his dream a reality."

JOSEPH AUGUST BRANDT
1941–1943

JOSEPH AUGUST BRANDT never wanted to be president of the University of Oklahoma, yet for two years he led one of the most turbulent and controversial administrations in OU history. Like the prophet who was not welcome in his hometown, Brandt brought a message of reform whose importance would be recognized only over time.

Brandt was the first alumnus ever to lead OU. The 1921 journalism graduate supported himself during college by washing dishes and stoking furnaces. He served as both editor of the *Oklahoma Daily* and president of Delta Tau Delta social fraternity, whose chapter meetings started at midnight after Brandt had put the paper to bed. He still made time to join OU's Army Reserve Officers' Training Corps and was awarded almost every available student honor, including being inducted into OU's PE-ET Top 10 Senior Honor Society and the Phi Beta Kappa national honor society, and being awarded the Letzeiser Medal for good citizenship and achievement.

Upon graduation, he was named a Rhodes Scholar. At Oxford he took three degrees and rowed crew. His Oxford studies on the political and constitutional history of Spain became the book *Toward the New Spain: The Spanish Revolution of 1868 and the First Republic*, published by the University of Chicago Press in 1932. Brandt returned to Oklahoma to work as a reporter and city editor for the *Ponca City News*. A year later he joined the *Tulsa Tribune* staff, where he was city editor and met his future wife, reporter Sallye Little.

It was during his time at the *Tribune* that he also met OU president William Bennett Bizzell. What began as a brief elevator conversation became a job opportunity when, in 1928, Bizzell picked Brandt to head one of his

leading initiatives, the University of Oklahoma Press. Brandt, ever prepared, had the OU Press's first book in production in less than a year, a feat made even more remarkable by the fact that he also established OU's new alumni publication, *Sooner Magazine*, almost simultaneously.

Under his direction, the OU Press quickly gained a reputation for works dealing with the history, industrial development, and sociological issues of the American Southwest. Brandt drew upon the expertise of such OU faculty as historian Edward Everett Dale to establish the Press's scholarly works, and the academic series The Civilization of the American Indian was, and still is, considered among the nation's best examples of "constructive regional publishing." Brandt also became well versed in international literature and served as managing editor of OU's fledgling *Books Abroad* literary journal, the predecessor of *World Literature Today*. The witty, pipe-smoking editor frequently welcomed

Future OU President Joseph A. Brandt (*third from left*), with members of the *Oklahoma Daily* newspaper staff, posing on a snow-covered Norman campus. (*Brandt 49*)

writers, scholars, and intellectuals into his Norman home for stimulating conversations and was known to have encouraged many literary careers.

"He had a contagious enthusiasm," said Savoie Lottinville, who would succeed Brandt as director of the OU Press. "He took an active, intelligent interest in everything under the sun. Ideas flew from him like sparks from a fast-spinning emery wheel," Lottinville continued. "He was seen to best advantage as he worked at a typewriter, which he hammered furiously, like a city editor two minutes before deadline . . . it is curious but true that he was never able to recognize an obstacle—which is another way of saying that he was an idealist."

WALKING AWAY, COMING HOME

Not everyone admired Brandt. Foreshadowing challenges ahead, members of Bizzell's administration tried to obliterate the OU Press in what Brandt later called an "obstinate reaction" to change. Offering his resignation to the president, Brandt explained why, and Bizzell insisted that the opposition meet with Brandt to hash out their differences. Brandt walked away from the meeting victorious but was hospitalized that same day with stomach ulcers.

During his ten years as director of the OU Press Brandt became known as one of the country's most successful publishers, someone whom even the bibliophile President Bizzell referred to as an "expert in finding authors, in encouraging and directing their work, and in designing and producing beautiful books." All told, Brandt published eighty-five titles at the OU Press, a number considered nearly outlandish at the time.

Brandt left OU in 1938 when he was named director of the highly regarded Princeton University Press, which offered to more than double his salary. OU modern languages professor and friend Kenneth Kaufman heard that Brandt's

boundless energy and casual bearing raised eyebrows among the more staid Ivy League environment at Princeton. "He strides from his office to the staff offices and back, trailing tobacco smoke behind him like clouds of glory, talking like a whirling dervish and he has them all jumping to keep up with his flow of ideas," Kauffman wrote. "When he first came, they wanted to ask him to get an interpreter so they would know what he was talking about. Now they merely ask him to take his pipe out of his mouth."

Joe and Sallye Brandt settled happily in New Jersey and were active in university life, where he continued his practice, begun at OU, of serving on several campus committees. He received offers for better-paying jobs, but Brandt was content to stay at Princeton.

President Bizzell, meanwhile, announced his retirement in August 1940, to be effective the following academic year. Flabbergasted by being asked three separate times to apply for the OU presidency by members of the OU Board of Regents, Brandt refused each time, but board chairman

Joseph Brandt at his typewriter, sporting his trademark pipe. (*Brandt XX*)

President Joseph A. Brandt *(center)* with Board of Regents chairman Lloyd Noble and former president William Bennett Bizzell. *(Brandt 21)*

Lloyd Noble was convinced that Brandt was the man for the job. "The regents wanted a man with a Southwestern background, preferably an Oklahoman and preferably a graduate of the University," said *Sooner Magazine* editor Roscoe Cate. "They wanted a cultured, scholarly man. They wanted a comparatively young man."

Noble visited Princeton twice in pursuit of Brandt and even sent OU faculty members to Brandt's home as emissaries. He finally convinced Brandt and his wife to meet secretly with the board in Dallas on a strictly advisory capacity, a meeting Brandt recalled in his 1950 *Sooner Magazine* article, "A Former President Speaks." "The Regents suggested that if I would not come [to OU as president] I should propose what reforms I thought were needed," he wrote. "The more I outlined what needed to be done, the more determined they were that I should come and help institute those reforms."

On November 4, 1940, the OU Board of Regents elected Joseph Brandt as the university's sixth president with a salary of $10,000 per year. When extending the formal offer to Brandt, the Regents appealed this time to his sense of duty to OU and Oklahoma, which had provided him with a free education and a remarkable career. Brandt finally agreed to take the OU presidency for five years. Both he and Sallye had serious misgivings, but Brandt made it clear to the Regents that he was coming to OU with an agenda of change that they had approved. He also came with one caveat: if the Oklahoma State Legislature cut education funding, he would resign. "It was after a terrible personal struggle and [with] a feeling of great personal sacrifice that I ever agreed to undertake the office," Brandt admitted in 1950. But in the world of 1941,

with congratulatory telegrams and phone calls pouring in, Brandt softened his reaction for the public announcement. "Becoming a university president was about as remote from my mind as anything could be and while I was extremely reluctant to change my career, I have to agree that perhaps it is time for an alumnus to return interest on the state's educational investment," Brandt wrote, "and therefore Mrs. Brandt and I, having made the decision, will bring to task our complete loyalty, imagination, and enthusiasm."

The forty-one-year-old Brandt called his appointment "a great honor," but acknowledged that "honor is merely a synonym for hard work." The hard work was to begin on August 1, 1941, when President Bizzell would step aside. Yet when August 1 came and went, OU still did not have its new president. The delay was partly due to a controversy that erupted six days before Brandt's official appointment. Brandt received a frantic phone call from friend and colleague Maurice Halperin, an OU assistant Spanish professor known to have "leftist leanings." Halperin told Brandt that he had been fired without cause or explanation. Brandt quickly called OU Board of Regents chairman Lloyd Noble, who confirmed that the firing had been recommended to the Regents and approved.

Brandt recalled his reaction. "Well, Lloyd," Brandt told Noble, "you are going to have a telegram in the next hour saying that you have no president, because I don't want to become president of a university where they don't respect academic practices." Noble asked Brandt to give him some time to work out the issue, and Brandt agreed. "So there Sallye and I sat with our furniture packed, waiting for our

Joseph and Sallye Brandt on the steps of the President's Home. *(OUPS 9515)*

moving man. . . . The board had to do something," he wrote.

Board members offered to meet Brandt in Chicago. There they "wrangled all day," and the Regents freely admitted that no formal charges had been brought against Halperin. "I was adamant that you must have the proper hearing before the proper committee," Brandt said. By the end of the meeting, Halperin had been reinstated for one year. Brandt later learned Halperin's troubles started when a local banker unethically revealed that Halperin had sold a Soviet Gold Bond, then considered a good financial investment.

A PRESIDENT ON TRIAL

Joe and Sallye Brandt finally moved to Norman in mid-August 1941. Legislators and reporters, many of whom knew Brandt from his former days as a newsman, attended the new president's welcoming press conference. One asked their former colleague if he intended to become a "lifetime president." Brandt replied: "I may only be here for one year. I'm on trial here," he said, looking around at the collection of journalists and lawmakers. "But the State of Oklahoma also is on trial by me." The room of stunned reporters "nearly dropped their pencils," one observer noted. The Joe Brandt presidency had begun.

Among those with a front-row view of Brandt's administration was future OU president George Lynn Cross. Writing extensively about Brandt's impact in a 1983 *Sooner Magazine* article, Cross said, "He began what, in the long run, would

be the most significant administration supplied by any president from the beginning to the present." Cross, who in 1941 was head of OU's Botany and Microbiology Department, added, "In my opinion, he abruptly changed the course of the institution, headed it toward *university* status." Although Bizzell and his predecessors had made tremendous strides, OU still lacked "most of the characteristics of a true university," Cross said, including real tenure, a policy of academic freedom, and the participation of faculty in policy formation. To that date, OU had been governed by the president, in conjunction with deans, directors, and department heads. Together, these men formed what one writer referred to as an "oligarchy" that controlled the university's academic and fiscal policies. In fact, Cross said, the university's Council of Deans was run by a handful of powerful members serving lifetime terms who "were able to dominate the rest [of the council] and, to a large extent, control the president."

Brandt had heard such concerns directly from friends who served on OU's faculty. He stated publicly that "the president should be a servant of the professors" and followed these words with drastic action at his first OU Board of Regents meeting. Brandt recommended to the board that department leaders should drop the title of "head" and replace it with "chairman." Those presently serving as chairmen would be relieved of their duties at the end of the fiscal year, to be replaced by new members who would serve a three-year term without option of being reappointed.

Brandt also suggested one-year terms for all existing deans and five-year terms for new deans. "This recommendation was designed to curtail the power of the deans and provide a mechanism for bringing about changes that might be needed in the future," Cross wrote. The Board of Regents approved Brandt's recommendations, which had been made without consulting any of the current heads or deans, and OU's faculty learned of the coming changes in the next day's newspaper. "It would be difficult to conceive of a more effective way of antagonizing influential members of the University community," Cross later observed.

"The academic hierarchy of the University began to crumble," he wrote. "It would end at a meeting of the Regents in January 1942" when Brandt approved a plan to form a Faculty Senate, which he and Dean Homer L. Dodge of the Graduate College had devised before Brandt ever left for Princeton. OU had a de facto Faculty Senate briefly during President Evans's administration, but it had been disbanded when Stratton Brooks became president. Brandt's Faculty Senate would be composed of elected faculty representatives. As OU president, Brandt would hold only an ex officio position with no real power. Faculty Senate members would have the right to make their wishes known directly to the administration without going through deans, directors, or departmental chairs; their recommendations would be reviewed solely by the president and the Board of Regents.

This one move "abruptly changed the direction the University had been taking," Cross said. In addition, Brandt stood firm on tenure and academic freedom, which Cross called "of the first importance in the development of a good university." Brandt recommended an appointed faculty committee on grievances and tenure that would be responsible for assembling facts about any charges brought against individual faculty members. Findings would then be presented to the administration and the Board of Regents for action.

In a few swift and deliberate moves, Brandt had transitioned OU firmly from the realm of an oligarchy to a democracy. He later summed up his revolutionary changes by saying, "I tried to put some of the ideas which had been agitating in the minds of the OU faculty for years into reality." But rapid change was not welcomed by everyone. "This much-needed restructuring brought intense opposition, almost overwhelming criticism, from the administrative personnel involved and their followers," Cross observed, "opposition which made life difficult for the Brandts."

Showing no visible reaction to the opposition, Brandt maintained his breezy, energetic persona and was perennially outgoing and helpful, but Sallye Brandt was far less resilient. The former journalist found the life of a president's wife unfulfilling, and the controversy surrounding her husband confirmed her worst fears about returning to OU.

WAR COMES TO OU

Then the world changed when the Japanese attacked Pearl Harbor on December 7, 1941. The following day, thousands of OU students, faculty, and staff filed into the field house to listen to President Franklin Delano Roosevelt's declaration of war to Congress. A recruiting station was set up by the U.S. Army almost immediately after the broadcast to accommodate "scores of students" wishing to enlist. OU's two campuses felt the effects of military recruitment immediately with an abrupt depletion of enrolled male students, a process quickened when the national draft age was lowered from twenty-one to eighteen. Many faculty members also served; their loss was offset by waning enrollment, which dropped from 5,431 in 1941 to 4,609 in 1942. By the end of the

Hundreds of OU students gathered in the field house to listen to President Franklin D. Roosevelt's declaration of war to Congress on December 8, 1941. *(OU Photo Services 12891)*

OU students promote the sale of U.S. Savings Bonds to raise funds for the war effort in 1941. (OU Photo Services 14180)

it was clear that the navy was coming to Norman. Many faculty members and townspeople did not welcome the news. They worried that a student body composed almost solely of females would be an easy target for military men. But Brandt, Lottinville, and others saw past such concerns to longer-term opportunities. As Cross explained: "The Navy would need to acquire a great deal of land adjacent to Westheimer Field and would construct buildings on the land. The war would not last forever . . . and the University would have an excellent opportunity to acquire the property sometime in the future."

Brandt and Lottinville returned to Washington for additional meetings and learned that the navy was seeking a location to train mechanics. Brandt and Lottinville convinced the navy to purchase 2,200 acres south of the Norman campus for its Naval Air Technical Training Center and arranged for the land to revert to OU after the war. In addition, OU contracted with the navy to fill its classrooms with students participating in the V5 technical training program and the V12 program, which offered a baccalaureate education to naval personnel. Many of these personnel became members of OU's athletic teams, whose rosters had been decimated by student enlistments.

Despite the gains in students and the land acquisitions that became known as "North Base" and "South Base," Brandt continued to be criticized harshly on campus. Ironically much of the conflict arose from the fact that Brandt, the same man who had brought democracy to OU's faculty, often made decisions quickly and without discussion. It was not uncommon for Brandt to take an idea directly to the Board of Regents and walk away with a final decision. Faculty and staff members chafed when they continually learned about important campus events and decisions while reading the newspaper.

Popularity aside, Cross believed that Brandt consistently did what was best for OU. "These were exceptionally trying times for the University of Oklahoma, and through it all, Brandt proved to be an exceptionally versatile president," he wrote. He added that Brandt dealt with wartime problems "in such a fashion that his institution made a maximum contribution to the war effort and, in doing so, made it possible for OU to acquire large real estate holdings, housing facilities, and vast quantities of naval equipment after the war ended."

The war also allowed Brandt to introduce OU to the concept of public-private research collaboration. While still director of the OU Press, Brandt's wide range of interests had led him to work with Dean Homer Dodge and President Bizzell to make OU research available to private industry, agriculture, and business. Their concept was to have a centralized agency that could prepare proposals and administer business, grants, and contracts. The idea

war in 1945, only 1,991 students would be enrolled at OU. It was the only time that OU female students outnumbered male students three to one.

Wartime brought "catastrophic burdens on education," Cross wrote, but it also brought tremendous opportunities. In January 1942, OU Press director Savoie Lottinville was traveling by train to New York City on business. He struck up a conversation with K. B. Salisbury, a U.S. Navy captain who was assigned to locate sites for naval flying schools. Lottinville told Salisbury about OU's new Max Westheimer Field, which had been donated to the university by Ardmore oilman Walter Neustadt, Sr., only a year before. The City of Norman had added 128 acres to the field by purchasing adjacent land and leasing it back to OU at the price of one dollar per year. Salisbury asked if OU would be willing to loan the airfield to the navy for the duration of the war. Upon arriving in New York, Lottinville called Brandt, who sent Lottinville to Washington, D.C. There the university publisher was joined by Brandt; together they undertook two weeks of negotiations between OU and the U.S. Bureau of Aeronautics.

Although a contract was not signed until March 1942,

Press director Savoie Lottinville began negotiations between OU and the U.S. Bureau of Aeronautics, which established a naval flying school on the university's new Max Westheimer Field. *(OU 1165)*

Brandt asked the OU Board of Regents to approve a new undergraduate program called University College, which would enroll every freshman and sophomore student in a balanced curriculum of liberal arts courses before students entered one of OU's specialized, degree-granting schools or colleges.

Brandt said the idea stemmed from his years as an OU student, when he witnessed friends starting over after realizing that they were ill-suited for certain degree programs. "We have to find some way in which a student has some time to orient himself, to find what he wants to do, his true inclination," Brandt said, adding that the Regents were "very enthusiastic" about the concept. Once again, Brandt's idea was approved with little or no discussion among administrators and faculty. All OU freshmen and sophomores would be enrolled through University College beginning in fall 1942. The backlash was immediate. Among those opposed, Cross said were deans "who wanted control of their students from the beginning of their enrollment." Cross himself believed the concept was "one of the better ideas for improving higher education that had emerged" and moved OU one step closer to being a full university as OU celebrated its fiftieth anniversary.

A FOCUS ON THE FUTURE

Brandt had other plans to bring OU into full university status, several of which were shelved by the war. Compelled by his own struggles to survive as an OU student, Brandt worked to build student residence halls on campus, but state legislators would not appropriate the funds during wartime. Brandt understood that the Oklahoma State Legislature held much of OU's future hostage. He became a strong proponent of private fund-raising and establishing permanent endowments. Shortly after becoming president, he hired OU advertising alumnus Shelley Tracey as a consultant to develop a mechanism for private giving and investment. War slowed this project as well, but the OU Foundation would be incorporated in 1944 due to Brandt's foresight and commitment.

OU did have some success with legislators in 1943, when $500,000 was allotted to build a Research Institute facility, known today as Nielsen Hall. Still, the university had a total budget of only $1.2 million that year and continued to experience critical shortages in student housing. Many of OU's army and navy students, who numbered more than 1,300, were living in leased fraternity houses that had emptied when members went off to war. Partial relief came when the military constructed the Woodrow Wilson Center, which housed 900 army and navy trainees and featured an activity center. Work also was completed on a residence hall and cafeteria christened Jefferson House that had been funded by

challenged the traditional academic notion that relationships between academia and outside clients were improper. Dodge had pursued the idea after Brandt left for Princeton, and the OU Research Institute was incorporated in 1941. Cross was named acting director of the institute and dean of the Graduate College in 1942, when Dodge left OU to serve as director of the National Research Council's Office of Scientific Personnel.

Among the Research Institute's first contracts was the development of an infrared spectrograph for the Naval Research Laboratory. OU physics professor Jens Rud Nielsen, then considered one of only two men in the nation capable of completing the assignment, led the project. The new spectrograph instrument was delivered to the Naval Research Laboratory only a few months later. It was considered a significant contribution to the war effort and helped establish OU's reputation among research universities.

Other projects begun by Brandt were not as well received among faculty and administrators, although their impact would be just as meaningful. In January 1942,

Among the additions to wartime OU was the Woodrow Wilson Center, which housed nine hundred army and navy trainees and featured the stone-trimmed Wilson Activity Center. Students used portions of the WAC until the 1990s. *(OU 1182)*

the National Youth Administration before the war. Jefferson House remains OU's oldest residence hall.

Another campus addition had its roots in 1943, when the senior class chose to donate funds for a statue of the late President William Bennett Bizzell. Brandt was delighted by the gift and suggested that the statue be placed on the new South Oval, facing the library that Bizzell had conceived and built. Student leaders objected forcefully; one went so far as to call the suggestion a "slight to Dr. Bizzell," because the empty South Oval was considered OU's back door. But Brandt, who owed his entire career in higher education to President Bizzell and had counted him as a close friend, knew better.

"President Bizzell, as a true educator, knew that the library was the front door to learning," Brandt said. He held fast to his conviction that the statue should be placed facing the library. Brandt won the battle although his wish would not be fulfilled for another nine years.

That same year, Brandt began to lose his battle for OU when he learned that preeminent historian Edward Everett Dale had received an offer for a distinguished professorship from Oklahoma A&M College (today's Oklahoma State University). Brandt countered by creating OU's first distinguished professorship at a salary of $5,000, which was then 25 percent more than any other OU professor earned. Dale protested being singled out as "distinguished" from among his peers, but agreed to accept an appointment as a "graduate" professor of history at the same salary. Brandt floated the idea of establishing additional research professorships, hoping that the prestige and increased salary of such positions would help OU to retain outstanding faculty.

Brandt's creation of the research professorships was the final straw for members of OU's disgruntled old guard, and the president soon learned that several deans were working to oust him. A meeting held in the office of business dean Arthur B. Adams included Edgar Meacham, dean of arts and sciences; D. B. R. Johnson, dean of pharmacy; Lewis Salter, dean of fine arts; Ellsworth Collings, dean of education; and new deans John G. Hervey of Law and George Lynn Cross of the Graduate College. The meeting's participants debated sending a group letter of "no confidence" to the OU Board of Regents. Although the majority voted to send the letter, Cross advised them against it. "If we fail, the position of the deans with the president becomes untenable," Cross recalled saying. "If we succeed and the Regents pick a new man, he will always wonder if he can trust his deans." The group voted to scuttle the group letter but some deans wrote to the Board of Regents independently.

President Brandt *(top center)* enjoys an OU–Missouri football game with his wife, Sallye, and guest Oklahoma Governor Leon C. Phillips *(right of Brandt)*. *(OU Photo Services 14025)*

President Brandt was popular with students for his quick wit and lively spirit, as seen in these two images of him clowning on a rocking horse during a student formal *(Brandt 29)* and surrounded by students at the president's home. *(Brandt 37)*

Another conflict erupted, this time involving academic tenure. Dean Meacham sought permission to ask the OU Board of Regents to dismiss two popular but antagonistic young English professors, Martin S. Shockley and Charles G. Walcutt. Brandt instructed Meacham to send the issue to the committee on tenure and grievances. When news of the internal fight was leaked to newspapers, misplaced criticism rained down from students and faculty who believed the president was railroading the two young faculty members. It was one more strike against Joe Brandt. As Cross summarized: "In no sense of the word could Brandt be considered a popular president. At the time he left the University, he did not have the majority approval of any segment of the University family."

Brandt's struggles for a democratic faculty, his work to establish University College, his efforts to help OU survive the war, even his misunderstood wishes to honor President Bizzell, had taken a toll both personally and professionally. Brandt's family was under tremendous pressure. To complicate matters, Brandt learned in late 1943 that Oklahoma Governor Robert S. Kerr planned to cut state appropriations to higher education by 15 percent for a state budget gain of $7 million. The decision represented the final line in the sand that Brandt had drawn the day he accepted the OU presidency.

A NEW CHAPTER

Brandt's distress was short-lived. He was offered a position as director and general editor of the University of Chicago Press, then the largest university press in the nation. Brandt announced he would resign as OU's president effective January 1, 1944. "One does not choose the time when opportunity knocks," Brandt said in a public statement, adding that the offer from Chicago represented the opportunity of a lifetime. The occasion also served as a platform for Brandt to criticize Governor Kerr's recent cuts to education, which even the *Oklahoma City Times* had called "economy applied in the wrong places."

"I would be doing myself and my family a grave injustice," Brandt said if he were to reject the Chicago offer, "for the will-of-wisp future which the financing of Oklahoma's higher education holds. No president of this university can ever be comfortable as long as he knows that worthy faculty members are eking out an existence. . . . If Oklahomans would only gain the vision of the real service their University could render, they would feel no pride in a $7 million balance in the state treasury."

George Cross led a presidential search committee composed of faculty members. Cross was surprised a month later when several Regents asked that he accept an appointment as interim president. He was publicly congratulated at a reception attended by the Brandts shortly before they moved to Chicago.

Brandt's last act as president of the University of Oklahoma was to forward the name of four individuals he believed were deserving of OU's highest academic acclaim. He had already resigned in November 1943 when the OU Board of Regents named Jens Rud Nielsen, professor of theoretical physics; Edward Everett Dale, professor of history and director of the Phillips Collection; Charles E. Decker, professor of paleontology; and Oscar B Jacobson, director of the School of Art, as OU's first research professors.

The Brandts' time in Chicago was short-lived, lasting but two years. Joe Brandt was hired as president of Henry Holt Publishing Company in New York City in 1945. In 1949, he returned to academia and established the graduate department in journalism at the University of California, Los Angeles.

The following year, former OU dean of admissions Roy Gittinger leveled a scathing criticism against Brandt's administration in a radio address aired on WNAD and later published in *Sooner Magazine*. Gittinger, a member of OU's administration since 1915 and author of *The University of Oklahoma: A History of Fifty Years, 1892–1942*, had witnessed every major campus event since his days as a student under OU's first president, David Ross Boyd. If there was an "old guard" at OU, Gittinger embodied it.

"The difficulty was that President Brandt had had no educational experience," Gittinger began. "As a newspaper man he had a flair for publicity, and he seemed to think that the important thing was to say or do something to keep the University and its president in the public eye."

Gittinger went on to criticize Brandt's establishment of the Faculty Senate, his efforts to bring young faculty members who had not yet served their "apprenticeship" into academic administration, and the creation of University College. His perceptions may have been colored by decades of struggle to keep OU steady during countless interventions by Oklahoma governors and legislators.

"Those who had to do with the management of the University of Oklahoma for many years prior to 1941 had sought to maintain and emphasize stability," Gittinger said. "It seemed better for the University to be known for its conservatism than for its willingness to experiment. Unfortunately," he wrote, "reforms of this sort are apt to cause discontent." He added, "When President Brandt found to his disgust early in his third year that there was as much discontent with University Administration as ever and this discontent chiefly among his special friends and advisers, he decided that he did not want to be a university president."

Gittinger concluded: "A cynic once said of Joe Brandt that he could never be a successful gardener. If he planted a seed today, driven by his restlessness and inquiring mind, he would have to dig up the seed tomorrow to see if it had begun to sprout."

Brandt responded to Gittinger's attack in a 1950 *Sooner Magazine* article titled, "A Former President Speaks." He expressed admiration for Gittinger, but did not hesitate to refute the retired administrator's charges or to defend his presidential legacy. "I know that as president my aims were only for the betterment of the University," Brandt wrote. "My administration was a stormy one because uprooting and spading is always a turbulent task and that is what the Regents wanted and what I felt the school needed." The Board of Regents had wanted change, Brandt said, and he made no apologies about the speed with which it had come. "Had I planned to spend the rest of my life as president of the University, I would have sharply altered the tempo of reforms. On the other hand, had I done so, the danger would have been that most reforms would have been compromised into non-existence," he wrote. "My motives were those of a loyal and devoted graduate to the University of Oklahoma who was impatient that the University take its rightful place with sister universities as a leader in education."

OU was in the hands of a new reformer beginning in August 1944, when the Board of Regents asked Cross to remain in office. Cross would serve twenty-five years, the longest term to date for any OU president, and become one of the most beloved and admired figures in university history.

The Brandts retired to Laguna Hills, California, and in 1965, Joe Brandt received OU's highest honor, the Distinguished Service Citation. It would be almost twenty years later that the Brandts received a "long-overdue" visit from George Lynn Cross and his wife, Cleo. The occasion gave Cross the opportunity to express how much he owed to his predecessor. "When I succeeded him as president, I was reminded constantly of the many changes he had made that made my job easier," said Cross, who dedicated his 1981 book, *Professors, Presidents, and Politicians,* to Brandt. "As the years passed my respect for him changed to admiration." Later Cross said: "He paved the way for my nearly twenty-five years of reasonably successful tenure in office by doing the things that had to be done, but which I could not have done and survived in office." Yet, Cross noted in 1983, "there is nothing on the University of Oklahoma campus that bears his name, nothing to mark his presence there. This is a grave injustice."

Joe Brandt would not live to see that injustice corrected. He died on November 1, 1984, at the age of eighty-five. A year later, OU dedicated the area surrounding the campus Duck Pond as Brandt Park. A marker thanked Brandt for "his courageous stand for academic freedom, the development of the democratic process in university administration, and the reorganization of undergraduate programs of study," adding, "The attractions of open spaces here dedicated figured largely in the life of this scholar, educator, and publisher, who always believed: 'The printed page is the University of Every Man.'"

GEORGE LYNN CROSS
1943–1968

 WHEN JOSEPH BRANDT OFFICIALLY resigned on January 1, 1944, the OU Board of Regents met with members of the Faculty Senate search committee to receive their recommendation for an interim president. Outside the room, dozens of faculty and staff members, along with the Brandts, attended a reception in anticipation of learning the Regents' decision.

Most people expected that they would either be congratulating OU College of Business dean Arthur B. Adams, Arts and Sciences dean Edgar D. Meacham, or OU College of Law dean John Hervey, who was the odds-on favorite. While they waited, a professor approached George Lynn Cross's wife, Cleo.

"I even heard George's name mentioned," Glenn C. Couch joked, and Cleo Cross laughed. She had no way of knowing that, the month before, OU Regents Joe W. McBride and Lloyd Noble had informed her husband that he was their top choice as OU's interim president.

George Cross was torn by the revelation. Although honored to lead OU until a permanent president was named, he had already put his academic work on hold to direct both the Botany and Microbiology Department and the Graduate College. He worried that an interim presidency would delay his research indefinitely.

In response, the Regents dangled the possibility of law dean John Hervey becoming president. The idea appalled Cross, who knew that Hervey did not share his commitment to faculty participation in university policies or the OU research professorships, which had been created by former President Brandt to retain OU's most outstanding faculty. Four candidates had already been named for the research professorships, but they had not yet received the Board of Regents' official stamp of approval. If Hervey became president,

the program might dissolve.

Cross knew that political tides could still turn, so he kept McBride and Noble's vote of confidence to himself, not even telling his beloved wife and partner, Cleo, until the moment that the search committee and the Board of Regents emerged from their meeting on January 1, 1944.

"As everyone began to stream in [to the reception], Dean Meacham came up to me and said, 'The news is wonderful,'" Cleo Cross recalled. "I was so surprised, and I thought, 'Could it be . . . ?' Then the reporters and photographers rushed in and asked me to stand with my husband. I turned to George and asked, 'Did they name you?' He said, 'Yes, I'll tell you more about it later.'"

The smiling Crosses were photographed with outgoing President and Mrs. Brandt, and reporters prodded George Cross for his reaction. "This has happened so suddenly, I don't know what to say," the thirty-nine-year-old professor demurred. But George Lynn Cross

Newly named Interim President George Lynn Cross (*right*) and his wife, Cleo (*second from left*), are congratulated by outgoing President Joseph A. Brandt and his wife, Sallye, at a reception held immediately after the Board of Regents surprised Cross by asking him to fill the vacant position. (*Courtesy* Sooner Magazine)

knew what to do. He went straight to work as president of the University of Oklahoma, a temporary job that he would hold for twenty-five years.

A PRESIDENT IN THE MAKING

Born into a poor farming family in Woonsocket, South Dakota, on May 12, 1905, George Lynn Cross understood the value of education. He was surprised and delighted to receive a football scholarship to South Dakota State College.

Cross made ends meet by washing dishes in the coed cafeteria, a perfect vantage point for spotting new girls on campus. One morning, his eyes were drawn to "a real dazzler, a stunning girl," named Cleo Sikkink, who happened to be in his zoology class. He wooed and won the vivacious science major and, in 1926, married her over the objections of her parents, who were unimpressed by Cross's prospects. He immediately set about proving them wrong. Cross received his bachelor of science degree that year and earned a master's of science in 1928. The Crosses soon moved to the University of Chicago, where George received a Ph.D. in 1929. He was invited to join the faculty at the University of South Dakota and became a full professor and head of its botany department within five years.

Cross's blossoming academic career was interrupted by the blight of the Dust Bowl and the Great Depression. The record drought resulted in significant cuts to state income, and the South Dakota State Legislature slashed appropriations for higher education. Cross took a 35 percent cut in salary.

Luckily, a vacation at a University of Wyoming campsite brought Cross together with Paul B. Sears, then chairman of the OU Department of Botany and Bacteriology. Sears offered Cross a position as an OU structural botanist, though the move would mean Cross accepting a lower faculty position as assistant professor. Cross took his chances in the fall semester of 1935; he became a full professor only four years later and eventually succeeded Sears as department chair.

Another vacation trip changed his career path in 1942. While working on plans for the OU Research Institute in 1940, Cross became friends with Graduate College dean Homer Dodge. He had also collaborated with Dodge and others to create the OU Faculty Senate. Dodge, an avid outdoorsman, invited Cross to camp with a group at the Four Corners of Arizona, New Mexico, Utah, and Colorado. At the end of the two-week trip, Dodge inquired why he hadn't seen Cross smoking his trademark pipe. Cross replied that he knew Dodge had respiratory issues, so he had forgone the habit.

Dodge was taken aback and deeply impressed by Cross's thoughtfulness. When he left OU in fall 1942 for a job with the National Research Council's Office of Scientific Personnel in Washington, D.C., he recommended Cross as acting dean for both the Research Institute and the Graduate College.

While acting dean, Cross worked closely with then-president Joseph Brandt to develop the OU research professorships. The OU Faculty Senate approved the professorship plan over the objection of several deans, particularly law dean John Hervey. The research professorships became the last in a litany of complaints by OU's disgruntled deans and directors, who wanted Brandt to resign or be fired by the Board of Regents. Cross was present for a meeting in which the majority of deans proposed that they send a letter of "no confidence" to the board, but Cross dissuaded the group from taking action.

Regardless, Brandt soon resigned. With Brandt's impending departure, some Regents believed that the research professorships were simply a last-ditch effort to "feather the nests" of the president's OU faculty friends. Brandt asked Cross to defend the professorships to the Regents, which he did in November 1943. The Regents took Cross's word that the new positions would help recruit and retain excellent teachers, but they chose to wait for an interim president before finalizing the issue.

The Regents also asked Cross to join a faculty committee that would help choose the interim president. It was the first time that OU faculty members had been involved in the selection of a president, and committee members Samuel Watson Reeves, Ralph Records, John Bender, and George Wadsack chose Cross as their chairman, never guessing that he would unexpectedly become interim president a month later.

INTO THE FRAY

Only three weeks after being appointed interim president, Cross faced the reality of university politics when the troublesome duo of Martin S. Shockley and Charles G. Walcutt paid him a visit. The associate professors had barely escaped with their jobs in 1943 when arts and sciences dean Meacham had called for their firing on the basis of inciting rebellion within the English Department.

Brandt protested that the two had not received due process through OU's Faculty Committee on Tenure and Grievances. A hearing caught the attention of local newspapers, and students came to the heated defense of the popular professors. The matter soon became an academic hot potato for Brandt and all of OU; as a result, charges were dropped against Shockley and Walcutt, and they retained their professorships.

Hostilities continued unabated in the English Department however. Dean Meacham was determined to get rid of Shockley. It was at this point that Shockley and Walcutt came calling on Cross.

"I remember being favorably impressed by their appearance and mien," Cross wrote in his 1981 book, *Professors, Presidents, and Politicians*. With his classic, dry humor, he added, "In retrospect, it occurs to me that my opinion of them may have been influenced by the fact that they were highly complimentary about my first few weeks as acting president."

The professors offered to serve as volunteer speech-

George and Cleo Cross were a devoted, loving, and formidable duo. They married over the objections of her parents, who thought that the farm boy who would one day lead OU for a quarter-century had no career potential. *(OU 2137)*

writers for any public appearances Cross might make with alumni groups and civic clubs. In fact, they had already prepared a speech they thought he might use, and they told him they would be happy to modify it as needed to save Cross the time and effort. The two also made it clear that the quality of Cross's public speaking could have a direct impact on his future. "If an understanding of my superior performance could be made known to the public, the Regents might finally be induced to name me as President Brandt's successor," Cross wrote.

"I expressed appreciation for all of this and asked why they were willing to put forth so much effort on my behalf," he said. "Shockley quickly explained that, by working together as a team, the three of us could do great things for the University of Oklahoma. We could begin improving it immediately, he said, if I would support their efforts to bring about certain much-needed changes in the Department of English."

A bemused Cross thanked the two and sent them on their way. Not long after, the situation in the English

Department worsened, and Dean Meacham went to the Board of Regents with a plan to dismiss Shockley. Meacham truthfully stated that the English Department budget had been greatly reduced due to decreased enrollment; as a result, Shockley's position would be eliminated. The Board of Regents purposely kept Cross out of the decision. They believed he had the potential to become OU's next permanent president and wished to shelter him from a divisive controversy that predated his tenure.

Cross chose to become involved in the issue and revealed his leadership style by inviting Shockley to his office. There he gently but frankly told the associate professor that there was no future for him at OU. Shockley appreciated Cross's candor and agreed to move on rather than undertake another drawn-out fight for his position. He asked that his dismissal be kept confidential while he searched for another job. Cross agreed and avoided the negative publicity that had plagued President Brandt during the first battle to oust Shockley and Walcutt.

Upon Shockley's dismissal, Cross solidified OU's academic standards by convincing the OU Board of Regents to offer the professor a year's salary. In one fell swoop, Cross helped solve the quandary of two rebellious professors while still maintaining principles outlined by the American Association of University Presidents (AAUP). No action would be necessary against Shockley's collaborator, Charles G. Walcutt, as he soon decided to resign from OU.

The Crosses happily left conflict behind and settled into the routines of a college president and first lady. Reasoning that the Board of Regents might not choose a new president until well after the war ended, they decided to move out of

their house on east Norman's Emelyn Street to occupy Boyd House. With them came children Mary-Lynn, age twelve, and Bill, age seven. Boyd House would soon have a swing set in the backyard and trains in its attic.

Other campus housing issues were not so easily solved. There were fewer than 3,800 students on OU's campus, roughly half the number that had been at OU only five years earlier, and more than 50 percent of the current students were members of the military. Some 900 soldiers were housed in the Woodrow Wilson Center south of the stadium, and others occupied empty fraternity and sorority houses, lived on the naval bases north and south of campus, or rented rooms from Norman homeowners.

OU had only one residence hall, the brick, three-story Jefferson House, which still sits on the corner of Lindsey Street and Jenkins Avenue. Constructed with federal funds, Jefferson House had been an attempt by President Brandt to alleviate OU's overcrowding. Cross knew that OU had not yet experienced true overcrowding; that would arrive with the tsunami of soldiers and sailors who would enroll at OU when the war ended. He also knew that the quickest way to expand OU's residential space came with a political price—closing the naval bases and allowing the university to absorb the navy's land and facilities. He would need to maneuver carefully.

He also moved carefully when he chose to restructure OU's administration. He believed that the number of people reporting to the president and Board of Regents should be streamlined, and he asked that the university's financial assistant report directly to him rather than the board. Cross considered this move essential to his success and reached out

President and Mrs. Cross with their children, Mary-Lynn and Bill, and Slippers, the family pet. *(Courtesy Sooner Magazine)*

to trusted adviser Roscoe Cate, a 1926 OU alumnus who had served as editor of *Sooner Magazine*. He charged Cate with bringing order to the university budget, which was at the mercy of powerful deans who jockeyed for position during annual budget allocations.

The same powerful deans had made former president Brandt's job extremely difficult, and they had complained loudly when Brandt formed University College, a program that allowed freshman and sophomore students to take liberal arts core courses before deciding upon a major. Cross understood how divisive the issue was, and asked the Faculty Senate for its recommendations on the future of University College. When the general faculty asked that the program be restricted to freshmen only, he listened to their concerns and forwarded the recommendation to the OU Board of Regents.

Cross's calm, rational handling of such potentially contentious issues and his ability to plan for the university's future made him the favorite of Regents McBride and Noble during his eight months as interim president. Board members interviewed several prominent candidates during that time, but on August 26, 1944, the board announced that Cross was the board's first and only choice to become OU's permanent president on September 1, 1944. His selection was praised across the campus and state.

"To be named president of our state university is a great honor of which I am very appreciative," Cross said in a public statement. "I am aware also of the opportunities and responsibilities involved in accepting the appointment. I shall do everything possible to justify the confidence of the Board of Regents."

A UNIVERSITY RETURNS FROM WAR

Cross's immediate priority was to prepare OU for postwar adjustment. Adequate student housing topped the list, along with programs of study, guidance, and counseling for returning soldiers. Cross also pledged to fight for faculty salary equity and expressed concern that OU would lose its most outstanding teachers to other institutions if OU's financial security did not improve.

Parts of that security would come in the form of endowed positions and private giving, two areas in which OU had little experience in 1944. Cross built upon the work of previous presidents Bizzell and Brandt and met with Norman attorney T. R. Benedum, president of the OU Alumni Association, and H. L. Muldrow, president of the OU Dads' Association, to draw up formal plans for the University of Oklahoma Foundation in December 1944.

The Foundation's assets consisted of $160 presented by its first trustees, Oklahoma City accountant Tom F. Carey, *Norman Transcript* publisher Fred E. Tarman, and Norman

businessman V. C. Bratton. For a time, the OU Foundation made its home in the bottom drawer of Cross's desk.

Money was also at the heart of Cross's first controversy as president in spring 1945. Cross gained control of the OU budget by first ending the practice of making lump-sum allocations to college deans upon request. Cross established a budget council composed of faculty members from various disciplines; their job was to recommend allocations for each college, approve a budget for each department, and allocate funds directly to the departments without the approval of the college's dean.

This move put Cross on a collision course with John Hervey, who had been considered a top contender for interim president. Hervey came to Cross's office to demand that his own salary be increased from $6,000 to as much as $9,000 and that the salaries of four professors of his choice be increased. Cross agreed to raise two of the four professors' salaries, but refused to give the dean his $3,000 raise, pointing out that enrollment in the law school had dropped from thirty to fourteen students in just a year. He also reminded Hervey that few OU professors had salaries in excess of $4,000.

Hervey threatened to resign. He was confident that the OU Board of Regents would side with him over Cross on the matter, but the board surprised Hervey once again by approving Cross's budget. Furious, the law dean released a thirteen-page statement denouncing Cross, OU, and Roscoe Cate, whose title had been elevated to financial vice president. He also submitted his resignation, which the board accepted. The Regents appointed Maurice Merrill—ironically, one of the two law professors who had received a raise—as interim dean. A search would bring new law dean Page Keeton to OU from the University of Texas.

About this same time, Cross presented the OU Board of Regents with a bound, seventy-eight-page report titled *Plans for the Future of the University of Oklahoma*. The Regents had asked Cross to forecast his vision for OU, and Cross predicted a rapidly growing, vital campus that would be possible only if the university's chronic housing shortages were resolved.

No major building campaign had been undertaken at OU since the late 1920s, and the only additions to campus were Adams Hall and Richards Hall, which had been added to the campus from 1930 to 1944. South of Brooks Street, the top edge of OU's South Oval, the campus consisted of Richards Hall, Hester-Robertson Hall, the armory, the east and west stands of Oklahoma Memorial Stadium, and the recently completed Jefferson House residence hall. Across Lindsey Street, Wilson Center, a wood and stone structure built by the military, housed nine hundred army and navy trainees.

Military men still made up the bulk of OU students even

Veterans swamped OU after World War II, creating a housing crisis that was solved in part with the purchase of five hundred prefabs. *(Courtesy Sooner Magazine)*

into the spring of 1945, when the university graduated only 274 students. Cross knew that the war's end and the massive demobilization that followed would attract thousands of men eager to return to civilian life and earn their college degrees. Congress had already passed the G.I. Bill, which provided tuitiion and the cost of books, plus $50 per month for unmarried veterans and $75 a month for married veterans pursuing their education.

OU's Norman campus facilities were sufficient to handle a maximum enrollment of five thousand students, yet as many as ten thousand students were expected to enroll after the war. Cross predicted that the university would require at least seventeen additional buildings; OU's best hope was that the navy would close its two bases and deed the buildings and property to OU.

Cross's enrollment predictions came true in spring 1946, when some 1,000 married and 1,600 single veterans enrolled at OU and brought the number of students to 5,234. Still, shortages in housing and instructional space forced OU to turn away thousands of applications. Due to these demands, Cross approved a lease for thirty house trailers from a construction company. The trailers would be installed north of Jefferson House. Also, nearly one hundred apartments in four buildings were constructed on the Niemann polo field through a $275,000 bond. The U.S. Navy agreed to loan barracks on North Base to sixty-four veteran families, and one-room efficiency apartments were rented sight unseen in Norman's housing sector.

In 1946, the navy announced that it would close its air station at North Base and reduce personnel at the Naval Air Technical Training Center on South Base. The announcements were received with howls of protest from Norman citizens, who had become accustomed to the steady stream of military income. Claims that as many as 1,600 area jobs would be lost were used to persuade the navy to stay. When Cross went public with his support for the closings, he received furious cards, letters, and phone calls from citizens who threatened to do whatever they could to end his presidency.

With the support of the OU Board of Regents, Cross stood firm. The navy, which under public pressure had wavered slightly in its decision, declared that it was unwilling to stay if the university was in opposition and closed the North Base in March 1946. On May 26, 1946, the navy signed a formal permit to allow OU to use the entire North Base facility, a move that would eventually gain OU properties valued at $7 million, including 1,380 acres of land, $4.1 million in buildings, and equipment valued at $494,000.

Before May 26, 1946, OU's land, buildings and equipment had been valued at $8.7 million; within just one day, its holdings had nearly doubled. That same month the Naval Air Technical Training Center closed. The enormous installation included 2,200 acres and 200 buildings that had previously accommodated 20,000 personnel and was valued at $25 million.

OU requested the use of South Base and its properties, offering to sponsor a veteran's college for men. The navy agreed that OU could use the base for the time being, and the university quickly claimed the immense, five-winged Bachelor Officers' Quarters for use as a residence hall.

Although the veterans' college did not come to fruition, OU was thrilled to occupy the North Base and South Base properties, which allowed the university to advertise for as many as 6,000 new students. The university's welcome attracted 10,126 students that fall, and 6,000 of them were veterans. Suddenly, five times as many veterans were attending OU.

"Veterans swamped the University of Oklahoma veterans liaison office Wednesday as they signed up to enter second semester classes under the G.I. Bill of Rights," the Associated Press reported in January 1946.

Due to this exponential increase in enrollment, OU

housing was once again beyond capacity. Male students joined fraternities just to take advantage of their room and board plans, and OU purchased Albert Pike Hall, a private men's dormitory built in 1921 on the corner of Boyd Street and University Boulevard. OU renamed the building Whitehand Hall in honor of the late OU drama professor Captain Robert Emmett Whitehand, who died during World War II. Still, living conditions at OU remained unbearably tight.

Clee Fitzgerald, an OU student and war veteran, led a group of fellow veterans to Cross's office and threatened to set up a tent city on the North Oval if more and better housing was not soon made available. Luckily, an answer came with a phone call from an unnamed OU alumnus in Dallas. The man offered to sell OU five hundred prefabricated housing units constructed of wood fiber. President Cross immediately agreed, though he had no authorization or financing for the units' $1.25 million price tag. Bonds were used to secure the funding, and three hundred one-bedroom and two hundred two-bedroom houses were on their way to OU.

Soon, an enormous stretch of white prefabs, dubbed "Sooner City," popped up across the land now occupied by OU's residence hall towers. Its houses were rented as fast as they were built. This "temporary" housing development served as home for budget-conscious married couples until 1962, when the units were phased out. The final Sooner City house was removed to make way for Couch Center in 1966.

Cross welcomed the onslaught of new veterans, stating that he hoped to "attract aggressive leaders with revolutionary ideas" about the nation's future. Under the shadow of the atomic bombs that had ended World War II, he believed OU would play an important role in the world's future. "With our very existence hanging in abeyance, we are now being given one last chance to learn to get along with the people of the world," Cross wrote, adding that the Atomic Age would "force us to discard our racial and religious discriminations and make us arrive at an understanding of each other." He would soon learn that he had been far too optimistic.

A TEST OF CHARACTER

Cross was forced to put his beliefs to the test when OU was thrust into a drawn-out war for racial integration. The initial volley had been fired in September 1945, when future U.S. Supreme Court Justice Thurgood Marshall visited the state convention of the National Association for the Advancement of Colored People, or NAACP, in McAlester. At the close of the meeting, Marshall announced to reporters that he intended to test Oklahoma's segregation laws, which had been established at statehood, as part of an effort to overturn *Plessy v. Ferguson*, the 1896 Supreme Court decision that set the doctrine of "separate but equal" education in the United States.

"The southern states, including Oklahoma, had done all to promote the principle of separation and little to honor the principle of equality," Harry F. Tepker, Jr., OU's Floyd and Irma Calvert Chair in Law and Liberty, wrote in a 1992 *Sooner Magazine* article titled "The Sipuel Case."

Marshall chose Ada Lois Sipuel Fisher as a plaintiff for his case. Fisher was the twenty-one-year-old daughter of a Chickasha minister and a recent graduate of Langston University, Oklahoma's only black university. Fisher wished to attend law school, but no program was available to her as a black student.

On January 14, 1946, Fisher came to Cross's office with Roscoe Dunjee, editor of Oklahoma City's *Black Dispatch* newspaper, and W. A. J. Bullock, regional director of the NAACP. Cross recorded his first impression of Fisher in *Professors, Presidents, and Politicians* as "chic, charming, and well-poised. . . . I remember thinking that the [NAACP] had made an excellent choice of a student for the test case," he wrote. "She carried herself through the ordeal that was about to unfold with fearless determination, extraordinary patience, and a serene dignity rare in one so young."

Fisher also recalled the meeting in detail. "We had a very friendly reception by Dr. Cross," she said, adding that she had handed a certified copy of her Langston transcript to admissions and records dean Roy Gittinger, who confirmed that she was academically qualified to attend OU's law school. Regretfully, Cross informed the group that he

Cross became an unexpected ally in the fight for desegregation when Ada Lois Sipuel Fisher applied to the OU law school, making her petition possible by documenting that she was barred from attending solely on the basis of her race. *(Fisher 1)*

was prohibited from accepting Fisher's application.

"An amused and cynical smile spread over Dunjee's face," Cross wrote. "He interrupted and said, 'Dr. Cross, we are completely familiar with the laws having to do with the mixing of races.'" Informed that Cross would refuse Fisher's admission based upon the fact that Langston was not an accredited university, Dunjee implored, "We want an admission from you that Ada Lois is refused permission to enroll solely because she is of African descent."

Dunjee was making an important and canny distinction. People who wanted OU to remain segregated had, in fact, advised Cross that he should refuse Fisher based upon Langston's accreditation. If Cross played along, Fisher and the NAACP would have no basis for a lawsuit. Instead George Lynn Cross freely admitted that OU often accepted white applicants from non-accredited state institutions. A satisfied Dunjee asked President Cross for a written statement to that effect, and Cross complied, knowing full well that he had just given Fisher and the NAACP the ammunition they required.

In July 1946, the Fisher case went before the Cleveland County District Court before moving on to the Oklahoma Supreme Court in April 1947. Both times, Oklahoma's educational segregation law was upheld. Marshall, who would one day become the Supreme Court's first African American associate justice, appealed the decision to the high court.

While he and all of Oklahoma waited for the Supreme Court to hear the case, President Cross still had a bustling university to run. OU hit an enrollment high of 12,350 students in fall 1947, and a handful of facilities were built to help keep pace with student demand. A wing of practice rooms was added to Holmberg Hall, an addition was made to Felgar Hall, and even the OU Press gained a new home. Still, many classes were relying upon extra space available on North Base, with the School of Drama, Extension Division, and School of Architectural Engineering all holding classes in former navy facilities.

Along with OU's rapid growth came the arrival of big-time college football. OU Coach Dewey "Snorter" Luster had resigned in 1945, and the OU Board of Regents purposely seized the opportunity to change Oklahoma's *Grapes of Wrath* image by building a nationally recognized football program. They hired former navy coach Jim Tatum, who brought with him a young assistant coach named Charles "Bud" Wilkinson. When Tatum left OU in 1947 to become athletic director and head coach at the University of Maryland, the OU coaching job went to Wilkinson. Wilkinson led OU to a 7-2-1 record and earned a share of the Big 7 Conference title at the end of his first season.

Sooner fans rejoiced, but on January 8, 1948, all eyes were on the news coming from Washington, D.C., where the Supreme Court was hearing the case *Sipuel v. Board of Regents of University of Oklahoma*. Fisher, who once described herself as "a girl from a little country town," attended the hearing and found herself overwhelmed by the experience and grand surroundings. "This beautiful courtroom—and there I am, sitting on the front row and all of the hearing taking place because of me and my citizenship," she wrote. Fisher and her legal team were optimistic that the court would prevail on their behalf, especially after hearing an Oklahoma lawyer complain that she had not given the state "sufficient notice" that a law school was needed for African-Americans.

"Well, how long ago did she bring this suit?" one of the justices asked.

The defense lawyer answered, "Two years."

"Didn't that give you a hint?"

The Supreme Court announced its decision four days later, in what the United Press International called "almost unprecedented speed," on January 12, 1948. The court ruled that Oklahoma could not deny access to legal education solely on the basis of race, and OU was required to admit Fisher on the same timeline as white students. Spring semester classes were scheduled to begin on January 29, 1948, and the court intended that Fisher would be admitted to the law school before that date. Cross said publicly that the ruling effectively declared Oklahoma's educational segregation "unconstitutional" and commented that it "no doubt opens the way for Negro students to be admitted to other OU schools." But the battle was far from over.

Fisher came to Norman to enroll on January 19, 1948. That same day, the Oklahoma State Regents for Higher Education announced the creation of the Langston University Law School. The college boasted a dean, attorney Jerome Hemry, a faculty of two professors, and one student—Ada Lois Sipuel Fisher. Classes would be held in three rooms in the State Capitol building and the Oklahoma State Library. The move was, as Tepker wrote, "a ridiculous sham that fooled no one," and Fisher declined to enroll. The Supreme Court made its intentions clear: she was to receive the same quality of education available to white students.

Many of OU's white students reacted to the State Regents' legal maneuver by rallying in protest on the North Oval during a bitterly cold day. Among those protesting were Howard Friedman, Wanda Lou Howard, and Jack Bales. "You and I have an obligation to protect the Negro students and any other minority group," Friedman said to the assembly on January 28, 1948. "Second-class citizenship cannot exist. This is an extension of the Hitler myth. We did away with it."

Friedman encouraged the group to send petitions to the State Regents. Then he held up a copy of the Fourteenth Amendment to the U.S. Constitution, which contains clauses on due process and equal protection. Friedman tore the copy into pieces and dropped them into a can held by Howard, where they were soaked with lighter fluid and set ablaze by Bale. The ashes were placed in an envelope addressed to President Harry S. Truman and delivered to the Campus Corner post office while students followed behind, singing "The Battle Hymn of the Republic."

At the same moment, the OU Board of Regents was meeting to consider the application of six additional African American students, who, in a show of support and defiance, had each applied to a different OU graduate school.

Not all OU students supported racial integration. On January 30, 1948, a counter-protest brought four hundred students to Evans Hall, where shouts of "Heil Hitler" and "We Don't Want Negroes" were heard. These students circulated their own petition to ban integration and garnered nearly three hundred signatures.

The Regents knew that, regardless of public opinion, the end of OU segregation was dependent upon the Supreme Court's ruling and the relentless determination of the African American community. OU could never afford to duplicate its seventy graduate programs in separate facilities, as the Oklahoma State Regents had mandated.

George McLaurin, a retired Langston University professor who wanted to pursue a doctorate in education, was among African American students applying to OU. When the university denied his application McLaurin filed suit in Cleveland County District Court and, subsequently, in Oklahoma City's federal district court.

Fisher was back in the courts as well, having returned to the Supreme Court to challenge the State Regents' new gambit. The high court sent her back to petition the Cleveland County District Court, and Fisher found herself starting all over again. Cleveland County judge Justin Hinshaw ruled that the Langston and OU law schools were "substantially equal" and denied Fisher's petition. She appealed to the Oklahoma City federal court.

On the other hand, McLaurin's case received a receptive judge who ruled that if McLaurin was not admitted to OU, the university would be required to discontinue graduate education courses for all white students. While the ruling did not end segregation, it did clarify that the state's educational institutions were required to admit African American students if a comparable program was not available at Langston.

The Oklahoma State Legislature responded by passing a new law requiring absolute segregation within colleges, including separate classrooms and teachers for African American students. OU would be required by Oklahoma attorney general Mac Q. Williamson to develop new segregation procedures.

When McLaurin successfully enrolled on October 13,

Retired Langston University professor George McLaurin became the first black student to attend OU, though he was forced to sit outside the classroom to comply with state segregation laws. *(Fisher 4)*

1948, he became the first black student ever to attend OU. His victory was muffled. McLaurin would take twelve credit hours, but in a classroom unlike any other on OU's campus: he was placed in a small room adjoining the classroom where all of his courses were taught, where he watched and listened through a double-door opening. President Cross and his administrators often met late at night to devise a way around the ridiculous arrangement, but their hands were tied by the State Regents. The strictures of segregation would force them to wait for a solution.

Fisher was also waiting. Finally, the State of Oklahoma, wearied of court defeats, announced that it would close the Langston University School of Law on June 30, 1949. Fisher went to OU on June 17, 1949, to enroll, but was turned away due to the fact that Langston's law school was open for two more weeks.

"Word of the denial came to my office that afternoon," Cross wrote. "I decided it would be absurd not to permit the young woman to get under way immediately with her legal education." Cross had planned to travel to Colorado that day for a fishing trip. Knowing that his presence on campus would require a media response that could possibly expand the controversy, he decided to go ahead with his plans to leave town. He called Academic Vice President Carl Mason

Franklin from the road and ordered him to admit Fisher.

Franklin realized that integrating OU would create a furor, and he privately worried about the possibility of physical violence. "Where will you be tomorrow in case I need to reach you?" he asked Cross, who informed him that he would be twenty-seven miles from the nearest phone. "I could almost see him smile slightly as he added, 'You and Roscoe [Cate] are on your own. I will see you in about ten days when I return.'"

The next day, on June 18, 1949, Ada Lois Sipuel Fisher was at last admitted to the OU School of Law. When news of Fisher's admission was made public, protest calls by the hundreds and hate mail poured into Evans Hall. Reporters from as far away as New York and Europe phoned to interview an absent President Cross. But no violence or other incidents occurred on OU's campus.

Cross returned to OU from Colorado relaxed and tanned. With a wry smile, he asked Franklin how the week had gone. "George, you know very well that we had a devil of a time," Franklin replied. "Now, I think I'll take a few days off and will be at least a hundred miles from the nearest phone." The president smiled, took a puff of his pipe, and strolled into his office.

Fisher had paved the way for herself and twenty-two other African American graduate students who had enrolled at OU in the three and one-half years since instigating her lawsuit. Still, each would study in segregated classrooms. Fisher sat at the back of her law classroom under a wooden standard that read "Reserved for Colored." Her fellow OU law students mocked segregation by moving the sign around the classroom, into the basement, or even onto the roof; on one occasion, they placed it behind the podium where Law Professor Earl Sneed was teaching. He failed to notice the sign, although he did recall later that the students had been especially "attentive and responsive" that day. Sneed finally saw the sign when he was packing up to leave. He simply shrugged and exited while his students roared with laughter.

When Cross learned of the event the next day, he ordered the sign removed. But spaces remained segregated, including OU's student cafeteria in Oklahoma Memorial Union. Fisher and other African American students were required to eat at tables surrounded by chain stanchions; some white students would brazenly step over the chains and join them for lunch. To enforce the state law, OU posted a guard to keep the white students out, and cafeteria workers brought steam tables directly to the black students to avoid any race mixing in the cafeteria line.

Howard Friedman, who led the student rally supporting Fisher's integration, said that OU students showed solidarity with Fisher in small ways that were remarkable for that time and place. Noting people's "inherent sense of decency"

he wrote, "In many ways, I think the student body at the University came of age in this process and stood up to be counted on what was the most important moral issue of the time."

Regretfully, segregation practices continued until 1950, when the Supreme Court ruled on McLaurin's 1948 appeal. The court stated that segregation within a school—including the separate areas where McLaurin, Fisher, and other graduate students had been forced to sit for two years—represented unequal treatment and must cease. Additionally, Fisher's case played a key role in *Brown v. Board of Education*, the landmark Supreme Court case that desegregated all American public schools.

OU's peaceful integration was attributed to many, but none so much as President Cross, whose acceptance of desegregation was clear from the moment he refused to lie while denying Fisher admission on the basis of her race. His very demeanor had set an example for the OU community. "In addressing even the gravest concerns," *Sooner Magazine* editor Carol Burr wrote, "Cross mixed intelligence, objectivity, and common sense with just enough wry comment to put matters into perspective."

In 1956, Cross's work to peacefully desegregate OU was recognized with the first Human Relations Award given by the Southwest Regional Advisory Board of the Anti-Defamation League. His bravery would also be immortalized in a 1988 play, *Halls of Ivory*, by Tulsan Jim Vance.

THE RED MENACE: TAKE ONE

Fresh from the integration fight, Cross was soon battling for academic freedom during a statewide Red Scare. In February 1949, the Oklahoma State House of Representatives announced that it would investigate rumors of Communists among college faculties, especially at OU.

The situation erupted after campus activist, WNAD Radio news editor, and poet Maurice Ogden submitted a guest editorial to the *Oklahoma Daily* titled, "Why Ogden Believes in Socialism." Ogden, who had served as chair of OU's American Veterans Committee, was under low-level FBI surveillance for his Communist leanings, but no action had been taken by either OU or the FBI.

Three days after Ogden's editorial, state representatives passed House Bill 48. The bill required all teachers and students at state institutions to sign a non-Communist oath. Those who violated the law would be penalized ten dollars per day and sentenced to ten days in prison. OU students and faculty objected strongly to being singled out, and Cross stood with them. He suggested that a fairer law would ban the Communist Party in all of Oklahoma.

Even some legislators thought that HB 48 was ridiculous, but Oklahoma state representative William L. Card, who had attended OU from 1946 to 1948, supported the bill. He stood on the floor of the House and said, "I know there are several Communists down there at Norman. At least, they were there when the war was first over. Their way is being paid by the Communist Party. They're instructors for the Communist Party."

Card believed that enforcing the oath would give the state a tool to prosecute Communists, who would commit perjury by falsely signing the oath to avoid discovery. It would also deter other Communists from coming to Oklahoma. State representative Robert Cunningham wanted to punish those who would not sign the oath with a ten thousand dollar fine and ten years in prison, but his idea was defeated by only three votes.

HB 48 was revamped to omit language that inadvertently barred out-of-state students from attending OU when a legislator pointed out that OU would lose such valuable football talent as Texas linebacker Myrle Greathouse. International students were also omitted from scrutiny, as they had already undergone immigration review. This time, the bill passed with a vote of 102 to 7.

Cross heard about the bill's passage on the radio, and reporters soon contacted him for a statement. He tucked himself away to think. "The situation posed a serious dilemma for me," Cross wrote in *Professors, Presidents, and Politicians.* "I was, of course, opposed to the bill . . . on the other hand, if my opposition was not carefully worded, there could be serious consequences for me and possibly for the University of Oklahoma." He crafted a statement, announcing his only objection to the bill was that it applied solely to higher education students and professors, and not everyone in Oklahoma. Cross pointed out that OU worked "in close cooperation" with the FBI in regard to possible Communist activities on campus. "I sincerely believe that communistic activity is at a minimum," he wrote.

Cross's statement was mostly overlooked the next day, when the morning papers arrived and the OU community went into a frenzy of protest against HB 48. Nine student organizations immediately opposed the bill with a petition that garnered two thousand student and faculty signatures. The petition stated that HB 48 was insulting to college students, totalitarian, and "unnecessary to protect the public interest."

The bill reached the Oklahoma State Senate and was rejected, but the Senate proposed its own anti-Communist bill requiring that all faculty and employees of state higher education institutions sign an oath of allegiance. Students were spared such a requirement. The House was troubled by OU's reaction to its bill, "sure that the opposition proved the existence of Communism on campus," Cross wrote. Representative D. C. Cantrell of Stigler penned a resolution suggesting that the House should investigate Communism

at OU and across Oklahoma higher education; the resolution passed 83 to 19.

Cantrell, who would head the House investigative committee, was asked if he had proof of Communist activity among OU's faculty. "No, but by their attitude . . . they show there are Communists down there," he said. "I do know that a hundred of them went down before the Administration Building and burned the Constitution of the United States here a while back." Cantrell was likely referring to students who had burned a copy of the Fourteenth Amendment in protest when Ada Lois Sipuel Fisher was barred from the OU College of Law.

The *Daily Oklahoman* quoted Representative Cunningham as adding, "Dr. Cross ought to be investigated. He's against this non-Communist bill. I don't know why, but I think we ought to know." Cross publicly welcomed the investigation. "Obviously," he told reporters, "if there is anything going on which we do not know about, we would like to be informed of it."

On February 17, 1949, committee chairman Cantrell summoned Cross to his office. Cross said he regarded the state representative as "a dangerous adversary whom I was prepared to dislike very much but who I must treat with the utmost tact and restraint. . . . This investigation, I reflected, would likely turn out to be grim business." Ever cautious, Cross was shocked that Cantrell was warm and welcoming, and the two men shared stories about their mutual background in farming. "He had had the impression that I was from the East," Cross wrote. "He expressed great friendship for the University of Oklahoma and emphasized two or three times that his sole concern in conducting the investigation was to ensure that the institution would not be damaged from within through the activities of even a few Communists."

Cantrell asked President Cross to select fifty to sixty OU employees who would appear before the committee in small groups starting on February 23, 1949. Representatives would be asked questions about their backgrounds, politics, and organizational memberships, and the hearing would be open to the press. Quick-witted and calm, Cross saw his opening and took it. "I agreed readily," he recalled, "and with inward enthusiasm, because I thought that I saw a way to neutralize the investigation and emerge from it without damage to the university, the faculty, or myself."

Cross promptly chose ten of OU's most respected faculty and staff members, knowing that alumni would react poorly when they heard that their favorite teachers and administrators were being investigated for Communist activity. He selected Laurence Snyder, dean of the Graduate College; Glenn C. Couch, dean of University College; Carl Mason Franklin, executive vice president; J. E. Fellows, dean of admissions and records; W. Page Keeton, dean of the

College of Law; Jim E. Reese, chairman of the Department of Economics; Alfred B. Sears, chairman of the Department of History; Oliver E. Benson, chairman of the Department of Government; Charles F. Daly, professor of economics; and Wyatt Marrs, chairman of the Department of Sociology. Cross did not tell the OU representatives that he had personally selected them. "I did not want to take any chance that this information would get to the newspapers, because it would be realized immediately that a group had been picked who would place the university in the best possible light," he wrote. "I was willing for everyone to believe that these highly respected individuals had been selected for questioning by Cantrell and his committee because they were suspected of Communist activity."

Representative Cantrell, a Democrat, opened the closed-door hearing by questioning Graduate College dean Snyder, as reported in the *Daily Oklahoman* by reporter Ray Parr.

Cantrell: "Where were you borned at?"

Snyder: "Kingston, New York."

Cantrell: "What political party are you a member of?"

Snyder: "Democrat."

Cantrell: "What secret lodges or organizations do you belong to?"

Snyder: "None whatever. I belong to the Rotary Club, but it's not secret."

Cantrell went on to ask if Snyder knew anything about Karl Marx or had studied his works. Snyder said that, as a biologist, he had no occasion to study Marx, and denied having knowledge of any secret meetings attended by OU students or faculty members. After Snyder was dismissed, a committee member chided Cantrell for not bluntly asking Snyder if he was a Communist. "Aw," Cantrell replied, "he said he was a Democrat, didn't he?"

Cantrell questioned each of the remaining OU representatives, careful to ask if they knew of any Communist activity on campus. All denied any knowledge. At the end of the day, Parr summed up the hearing by writing, "a nest of Democrats, Presbyterians, and a sprinkling of native-born Texans" had been uncovered at OU, but no Communists.

Behind the scenes, Cantrell was pleased with the committee's work. But State Senator James C. Nance of Purcell was "incensed," Cross wrote. "He realized immediately that some of the best known, mostly highly respected members of the faculty had been subjected to . . . an unnecessary indignity that would reflect unfavorably on the legislature as a whole. He decided to do something about the matter the next day."

Cross arrived the following day with a new crop of hand-picked OU faculty and staff. This time, to ward off suspicion, he had included a sprinkling of people who had been criticized for participating in Oklahoma's civil rights movement. But the investigating committee was already behind closed doors with Senator Nance and Senator Joe Smalley of Norman. After waiting for more than an hour, Cross was ushered inside. "In somewhat abashed fashion Cantrell told me, without explanation, that the committee had decided not to continue the investigation on a person-to-person basis," Cross wrote. Instead the legislature would rely upon university presidents to submit a report concerning Communist activity on their campuses.

Cross later learned that Nance and Smalley had raged at the committee for their irresponsible questioning of distinguished professors and for potentially damaging the teachers' good names and reputations. "You are casting a slur and reflection on the great mother institution of learning in Oklahoma," Nance said. "We've had enough bad publicity about radical political activity in this state. Now, when we're trying to give the nation a better picture of Oklahoma, we raise a Communist hullabaloo."

"I was excused and drove back to Norman with an immodest feeling of elation and triumph," Cross admitted. "A hunch on how to handle a difficult situation had paid off."

Cantrell soon resigned as chairman of the committee. When the group's activity was made public on May 12, 1949, it reported no findings concerning Communism at OU or in all of Oklahoma higher education.

Cross would have another occasion to appear before a state investigating committee that year, to explain the "waste" of state funds at OU, "in particular the purchase of a charcoal brazier and a set of earrings from an ancient Egyptian tomb, which one senator had interpreted as 'earrings and brassieres,'" *Sooner Magazine* reported. Senators also asked about the $1,200 cost of Cross's official presidential portrait, which had been ordered by the OU Board of Regents. "The unflappable Cross replied that presidential portraits normally are done only once, and if the Regents didn't change presidents too often, the cost could be amortized over a period of time."

Cross, ever relieved to turn his full attention back to running OU, had recently passed up a lucrative opportunity to leave the university. Former OU Regent Lloyd Noble had invested his energies in his family's new charitable foundation and asked Cross to serve as director of the Noble Foundation, promising that the president would maintain his annual salary for life. Cross was sorely tempted; he and Cleo had added another son, Braden, to their family, and his five years as OU's president had been filled with constant stress and the upheaval of postwar adjustment. Yet Cross bypassed financial security and chose OU.

The president's challenges continued. A tornado hit North Base in April 1949. Some forty-eight people were injured, and thirty buildings were heavily damaged, including the University School, a K–12 laboratory school operated by the OU College of Education since 1917. The North Base's total loss exceeded $1 million.

Notwithstanding these losses, OU received news that University School alumnus, 1911 OU graduate, and pioneering geophysicist Everette L. DeGolyer planned to establish a library devoted to the history of science at OU. Influenced and inspired by OU professors Charles N. Gould and Vernon Parrington, DeGolyer collected rare science volumes.

DeGolyer confided an idea to friend and OU Press director Savoie Lottinville: he would donate his collection of scientific books to OU if the university would teach the history of science as an academic discipline. "You provide the faculty, and I'll provide the books," he said. DeGolyer's initial gift of six hundred priceless books included a 1632 work by Galileo featuring notes written in the scientist's own hand. The DeGolyer Collection in the History of Science and Technology would form the nucleus of OU's History of Science Collections.

OU was also celebrating the construction of a new women's quadrangle, which would accommodate 848 women and help increase the university's female population, which

1911 alumnus and geophysicist Everette L. DeGolyer donated his collection of rare science materials to OU, forming the basis of the History of Science Collections. *(OU 2334)*

President Cross led an expansion of the student body matched by a construction boom in facilities, including the 1948 "Meacham Wing" of Oklahoma Memorial Union. *(OU Centennial 25)*

had been restricted from growing by lack of available housing. In addition, OU gained a new home for the university's Research Institute on the southwest corner of the South Oval, across from Bizzell Memorial Library. The building is known today as Nielsen Hall. Jens Rud Nielsen returned to OU as director of the Research Institute in September 1949. A member of OU's faculty since 1924, he took time off only to travel for the prestigious Guggenheim and Rask-Oersted fellowships and to work for the U.S. war effort.

The vestiges of World War II still colored much of OU's daily life in the late 1940s, as historian David Levy noted in a *Sooner Magazine* article titled "The Girls They Left Behind." According to Levy, Cross found himself in the unenviable position of playing go-between for male and female students. OU only had 2,400 female students to some 10,000 male students, yet women voiced concern that returning soldiers were "indifferent" to them. They wanted to know why. Cross contacted OU's counselor of men, William J. Mellor, to ask his opinion on the issue. Mellor replied with a detailed letter.

Mellor, himself a veteran, wrote that soldiers returning to college sometimes lacked confidence after having been out of social life for so long. He added that the rigors of war had matured OU's male students far beyond their chronological ages. "Many of the veterans on the campus have been caused to face the sterner realities of life, including death, and look upon the actions of some of the girls on the campus as being infantile," Mellor confided. "Many of the boys are interested in quietly talking with a girl, taking an afternoon stroll, playing cards, etc. They are not interested in the noise, confusion, and action which seem to be rampant at so many of the parties arranged by the girls. Time and time again

Even in the turbulent postwar years, OU's 1947 cheerleaders demonstrated their school spirit. *(OU 1273)*

veterans have told me this." The demand of studies and the financial reality of living on the G.I. Bill also played a role in the men's hesitance to approach coeds, Mellor wrote.

The war, which pulled millions of mothers and wives into the workplace for the first time, changed female expectations as well. Former G.I.s were taken aback by young, assertive women. "Most of the boys with whom I have talked feel that the girls 'chase' them," Mellor wrote. "They want the girl to remain on a pedestal and not stoop to many of the things they, themselves, feel are their privilege and birthright."

Awkward social adjustments aside, OU students eventually embraced their new world. Coke dates at the Sooner Drug were a popular outing in the late 1940s, as were coffee breaks in the student union, where President Cross met daily with students. First Lady Cleo Cross also maintained an open-door policy at Boyd House and often welcomed students with fresh-baked cookies. On special occasions, dates lined up for campus dances, including when big band leader Harry James headlined a huge event at South Base's Building 92.

A large number of faculty members were recruited to chaperone the dance. The crowd's behavior appeared flawless, and a relieved OU president decided to go home early. He threaded his way through the crowd, holding his hat up high to avoid it being crushed. A student stopped Cross and asked what he was doing; when Cross admitted that he was leaving, the young man offered him an alcoholic drink. A startled Cross declined, which offended the student. Cross confessed to being OU's president and said that it would be improper for him to drink with a student. On top of impropriety, alcohol was still illegal in Oklahoma.

The student laughed. "I'll have you know that *I'm* president of the University of Oklahoma, and it's all right for you to have a drink." Cross thanked the student and left.

The next morning, the doorbell rang at Boyd House. Cross opened the door to find Max Genet on his doorstep. "I found out quickly who was the president of the University of Oklahoma, and I'm here to apologize," he said. Cross brushed Genet's concerns away, but Genet insisted upon taking personal responsibility. "I didn't want you to think I was just a drunk student who didn't care what he said to the president of the university," he said. The occasion reminded Cross that although so much in the world had changed, at their core, the wartime generation of OU students were good-hearted, serious, responsible, and conscientious.

FIRE STRIKES AT THE HEART OF OU

A few months later, the lighthearted mood at OU would turn tragic. At approximately 2:45 A.M. on December 3, 1949, the five-winged Base Officer Quarters, or BOQ, on OU's South Base caught fire. Nearly 350 men lived in the building, a wooden dormitory constructed by the U.S. Navy during wartime and acquired by OU just two years earlier. Two BOQ residents used fire hoses to quench the blaze, but it quickly spiraled out of control. Within minutes, three of the five wings were engulfed in flames that lit the night sky for miles. The dormitory's residents ran for their lives into the forty-degree night clad only in pajamas; a few were lucky enough to grab a handful of possessions. Others jumped from second-story windows and broke bones upon landing.

Tales of bravery abounded. Many credited their escape

to Maurice Ahearn, a twenty-six-year-old engineering junior from Killingsworth, Connecticut, who rushed down his hallway shouting and beating on doors. At least fifteen men said that Ahearn had awakened and saved them. The BOQ was engulfed in flames, and within an hour, only chimneys and parts of stairways were visible. At least twenty students would require hospitalization; two had been critically burned.

When the smoke cleared, three students were dead. One was Maurice Ahearn, who had waited too late to save himself. Another was twenty-year-old Sammy LaRue of Clinton, Oklahoma, a fine arts major who had been trapped in his room by flames. These two were quickly identified, but a third body was burned beyond recognition.

Cross was in Enid on business. He rushed back to OU, where University College dean Glenn C. Couch had already set up a desk in the lobby of Evans Hall. Every BOQ resident was asked to report, including those who had gone home for the weekend. Survivors received Red Cross funding, clothing, and a housing assignment. OU's women residents in Hester and Robertson Houses quickly vacated their rooms, doubling up in the new Women's Quadrangle, to make space for the fire survivors.

Frantic parents descended upon OU from across the state. Many spent the long, excruciating day at Boyd House, waiting for their son's name to be checked off the list of potential victims. Reunited families gratefully left Boyd House one by one, until late afternoon, when only a single set of parents remained. Sadly and ironically, Mr. and Mrs. T. P. Starks of Oklahoma City were personal friends of President

and Mrs. Cross. The Crosses waited with them until a call came from Dean Couch at 4 P.M., confirming that the only boy not yet accounted for was their son, twenty-year-old Price D. Starks.

Cross accepted the wrenching duty of telling his friends. "I think it may have been the most difficult responsibility that I faced during my nearly twenty-five years as president," he wrote. "After sitting with us for a few quietly tearful moments, they too went on their way homeward."

In the *Sooner Magazine* article "A Week of Great Sadness: The BOQ Fire of 1949," David Levy details that, within days of the fire, Cross and Couch had sent individually typed letters to each of the 350 involved families. Cross expressed his grief and regret, and also related that local officials had investigated the fire. No specific cause for the $700,000 blaze was ever determined, though a stray cigarette or match in a wastebasket was suspected.

Many parents replied, thanking Cross and OU for their generosity and for taking care of their sons. "Our son Glenn was not hurt physically," wrote G. L. Buck of Gulfport, Mississippi. "We have asked him since he came home, if the fire preyed on his mind. He said it hadn't at all. We believe the most outstanding impressions he retains of the whole disaster are the generous acts of the folks who came to the boys' assistance. He was greatly impressed by everybody wanting to do something for them."

Now OU was again in dire need of student housing. In 1950, the Oklahoma State Legislature passed a $36 million bond issue for higher education. OU's portion would help pay for Cross Center residence hall, which would open two

The tragic Base Officer Quarters fire of 1949 took the lives of three male OU students and injured twenty others. *(OU 1793)*

years later and house 832 male students. Each of the four units were named for alumni killed while serving in the military; the central lounge and dining hall were named for the three students who died in the BOQ fire.

The bond primarily covered new classroom facilities, including Collings Hall, the graduate education building named for Dean Ellsworth Collings. Foreign languages were housed in the newly constructed Kaufman Hall, named for longtime language professor Kenneth Kaufman. Burton Hall would be constructed on Elm Avenue and named for the longtime School of Home Economics director Helen Brown Burton. The building's organic architecture was unique on OU's campus. Classrooms were also added in Oklahoma Memorial Stadium, along with stadium seating to accommodate fifty-five thousand fans and a press box.

Other classroom additions were planned by the time Cross Center opened in 1953, including the modern-style geology building, Gould Hall, named for pioneering geologist Charles N. Gould; Gittinger Hall, a social sciences building named for OU alumnus and administrator Roy Gittinger; an aeronautical engineering building at Max Westheimer Field; and the biological station at Lake Texoma. A new Oklahoma Memorial Union auditorium was dedicated to arts and sciences dean Edgar D. Meacham; and the long-awaited statue of President William Bennett Bizzell was installed in front of the library.

Not to be outdone, the Oklahoma City campus was experiencing its own renaissance. Dr. Mark R. Everett,

a twenty-three-year OU veteran, had become dean of the College of Medicine and superintendent of University Hospital in 1947. His toughest task was to pull OU out of muddy political waters.

OU had been operating without American Medical Association accreditation since 1935, when chiropractors were admitted to practice at University Hospital due to political interference from Governor "Alfalfa Bill" Murray. Murray also used his political influence to select candidates for OU's medical school.

"It had been a highly political art to secure admittance to medical school," Everett said. "I put an end to it. The first year I was dean about eighty legislators contacted me to try and get students accepted. I made it clear that was the very best way for a student to be refused. The next year, no one contacted me."

Everett, known to be blunt and energetic, was an effective administrator who emphasized graduate medical education and expanded research. Among the changes he initiated were a preceptorship program, which made Oklahoma only the second state in the nation to send medical students into local communities for clinical work.

Through Everett's hard work, the OU medical school regained its AMA accreditation on July 20, 1948, with an A rating. Everett believed much of the credit was due to President Cross. "The president, the Regents, and the alumni all stood behind me," he said, "and that was the start of the improvements."

OU continued to grow rapidly through the 1940s and 1950s. Students became accustomed to standing in long lines to enroll for classes. *(OU 1725)*

New housing for married students spread both west and east, as seen in the new Parkview Apartments near OU's Duck Pond. *(OU 1195)*

Another emerging area of OU excellence was athletics. Sooner football coach Bud Wilkinson led his team to a flawless season in 1949, and the team was ranked second in the nation. Then, in 1950, the Sooners won their first national championship.

The impact was immediate, as the University of Oklahoma went from being a mostly unknown college somewhere in the middle of the country to a growing athletic powerhouse with scores of devoted fans. Winning brought other rewards. In the summer of 1951, *Sooner Magazine* reported that OU had received record numbers of alumni donations and memberships. "Never before had the Alumni Development Fund received such solid support from alumni and friends of the University," the author wrote. "It would seem the time was ripe for optimism."

THE RED MENACE: TAKE TWO

OU's optimistic mood faded with the advent of another Red Scare. Members of the Communist Party had been arrested during an Oklahoma City demonstration against the Korean War and the use of atomic bombs. Among those arrested was Giovanni Rossi Lomanitz, a 1940 OU alumnus and brilliant physicist who would later be blacklisted for refusing to testify against J. Robert Oppenheimer, the "father of the atomic bomb."

The American Legion responded to the demonstration by calling for a non-Communist or loyalty oath to be signed by all state employees, including college faculty members. The legislature signed a resolution to that effect in fall 1950. Most OU employees had little issue with signing the loyalty oath, which stated that employees would support and defend the Constitution against all enemies foreign and domestic. Signees also swore that they were not part of any group seeking to overthrow the U.S. government.

But revisions to the legislation, called House Bill 8, changed the oath significantly. Now public employees were asked to swear that they would "take up arms in defense of the United States" and promise that they had not been affiliated with any Communist-leaning groups for the previous five years. Employees who refused to sign the oath within thirty days were subject to firing.

"The implications of these new provisions were enormous and shocking," Cross wrote in *Professors, Presidents, and Politicians.* He added that Oklahoma's attorney general maintained a list of "subversive" groups. The list, Cross said, "represented the opinions of one man, and . . . was subject to frequent change. What about an employee of the university who had innocently joined one of these organizations during the past five years and, having found that it was subversive in nature, promptly dropped his or her membership?"

OU's legal counsel, Maurice Merrill, told Cross that the new law was unconstitutional. Cross visited Oklahoma governor Johnston Murray, who agreed to explore the issue and asked the House and Senate to recall the bill for further study. The House agreed, but the Senate refused. Cross learned that much of the bill's new language had been suggested by the American Legion, and that many legislators had passed the bill without realizing how drastically it had changed.

"It seemed likely that both the House and Senate would have agreed to remove the objectionable portions, but the political climate prevented this," Cross wrote. "Since the beginning of the civil rights movement in Oklahoma, the conservative elements in the state had suspected that Communism was gaining a foothold at the state's leading educational institution."

Senator Keith Cartwright chaired the committee from which the bill originated and conceded that the bill might be unconstitutional. "Let the courts decide it and not a bunch of super intellects at OU," he said. "I think Dr Cross overstepped the bounds when he came up here to oppose the bill. . . . Red-blooded Americans won't object to it."

Minor concessions were made. The state attorney general ruled that the oath would not apply to noncitizens or conscientious objectors, but the major issues remained unchanged. Governor Murray was outnumbered by those protesting changes to the bill, and it passed with the new restrictive wording.

OU's campus was in shock. Dr. Howard Larsh, president of the university's AAUP chapter, led campus opposition, which soon included forty-eight OU employees who refused to sign the oath or scratched out the offensive provisions before signing. Eight of those forty-eight resigned from OU, including Elwyn Hughes, a visiting professor from Canada, who was advised by his embassy that by signing he would forfeit his citizenship.

OU's student paper, the *Oklahoma Daily,* stood in solidarity with those objecting to the oath. On its front page, the paper quoted former University of Chicago chancellor Robert M. Hutchins on the nation's drive to chase down Communists. "The heart of Americanism is independent thought," Hutchins said. "Persons will suffer for acts that they did not commit, or for acts that were legal when committed, or for no acts at all. Far worse is the end result, which will be that critics, even of the mildest sort, will be frightened into silence."

The Oklahoma Supreme Court would uphold the loyalty oath, though it was eventually struck down by the U.S. Supreme Court in 1952. In the majority opinion, Justice Hugo Black wrote, "The Oklahoma statute is but one manifestation of a national network of laws aimed at coercing and controlling the minds of men. Test oaths are notorious tools of tyranny."

The decision was too late for some, including OU assistant zoology professor Richard Blanc. Blanc had freely signed the oath, but President Cross learned that the professor had been under surveillance by the Oklahoma Division of Criminal Investigation for at least six months. Investigators claimed that Blanc had committed perjury by signing the oath, as he belonged to organizations on the attorney general's list. Blanc was also accused of making false statements about OU to the AAUP. Blanc claimed that, during an on-campus meeting with state criminal investigators, OU officials had set him up to be recorded without his knowledge. This claim would prove to be false.

The OU Board of Regents met with Governor Murray and criminal investigation chief Howard Wilson at the state capitol. Afterward, the Regents instructed Cross to ask for Blanc's resignation, but Blanc refused to resign.

Cross recommended that OU follow AAUP procedures, which included a chance for Blanc to appear in his own defense with counsel, the taking of a full stenographic record of any hearing, and issuance of either one year's notice or a docking of one year's salary in lieu of notice unless moral turpitude could be proven. OU had adopted AAUP procedures in 1947; if the university refused to abide by them now, it could face AAUP blacklisting. Blacklisting would put the academic world, including prospective faculty members, on alert that OU did not embrace the concepts of academic freedom or tenure.

Blanc appeared before the Regents during a nine-hour hearing at which he was represented by OU AAUP president and attorney Joseph C. Pray and Paul David, professor of zoology. He denied membership in two left-leaning organizations but admitted he had been a member of a third named

The 1953 memorial service for thirty-seven Navy ROTC midshipmen who died in a plane crash. *(OU 2479)*

the Medical Bureau to Aid Spanish Democracy, which had gone out of existence at least ten years earlier. As a result, he should have been in cooperation with the state loyalty oath's five-year requirement. Blanc also insisted he'd made an honest mistake when insisting that OU had arranged for him to be taped. Cross, at least, believed him.

Regardless, the OU Board of Regents declined to renew Blanc's contract. The Regents were within their rights, but difficulty arose when the board members also declined to offer Blanc either a year's salary or a year's notice, in direct violation of AAUP principles.

The AAUP would consider Blanc's case for three years. In April 1956, OU was censured for its failure to provide Blanc with a hearing in front of his peers rather than the Regents, and for declining to offer either a year's salary or one year's notice. The AAUP also expressed concern about the validity of charges against Blanc and implied that state officials had applied improper pressure on Blanc.

OU's Faculty Senate responded by drawing up detailed procedures for tenure and revocation of tenure under AAUP principles in March 1957. The next month, OU was removed from AAUP censure.

"In reflecting on it all, I had only one regret," Cross wrote. "In my opinion, Blanc had not been treated fairly in that he had not been compensated in lieu of proper notice of dismissal. He had done little to justify the treatment he received. He was not a Communist, as most understood the designation." "He was critical of much that went on in his own country," Cross conceded in his 1981 book, "but for the most part his criticism probably was justified. His views would have attracted little attention today."

IN TRAGEDY AND TRIUMPH

Tragedy grasped the OU community on a scale that had never before been experienced on July 17, 1953, when twenty-three Navy ROTC midshipmen were killed during a devastating air crash in Milton, Florida. The students were among 1,600 Navy ROTC midshipmen being transported from summer aviation training at Corpus Christi, Texas, to amphibious training at Norfolk, Virginia. The airlift of twenty planes had refueled at Milton's Whiting Field; when the second plane took off, its port engine failed and the plane struck a clump of trees before plummeting to earth one mile north of the runway.

Only three boys on the plane survived. Thirty-seven died in the crash, which remains the greatest loss of U.S. Navy midshipmen in a single event. As a result, OU lost almost every man who would have graduated from its Navy ROTC program in 1955. "The news hit the campus and state like a thunderbolt," the Associated Press reported. "Shocked classmates and instructors wept openly." Condolences

OU's glory days in athletics arrived with Sooners football coach Bud Wilkinson (*third from left*), seen here with his coaching staff in 1948. *(OUPS 29755)*

OU students rally before the famed 1957 OU–Notre Dame showdown that ended OU's 47-game winning streak. *(OU 5)*

arrived from across the nation, and Cross called the crash "the greatest tragedy in the history of the University of Oklahoma . . . the loss is personal." Governor Murray called for a special memorial day, and hundreds attended a service on OU's North Oval to honor the dead students.

"All over the state sorrowing families and friends prepared to meet the tragic cargo that was to arrive in railroad baggage cars," a September 1953 *Sooner Magazine* article reported. "A solemn series of funerals marked the young men's return home . . . they were to have been tomorrow's leaders."

That same fall, death struck OU again when a can of gasoline ignited during a painting project at the Phi Gamma Delta fraternity house. Junior Jerry Amundsen of Oklahoma City was critically burned and died.

OU moved beyond its losses, and the university continued to grow throughout the 1950s. In 1955, the university enrolled nine thousand students. Cross stated publicly that OU lacked the necessary resources to provide a quality education for more than eight thousand students. If the legislature was unable or unwilling to fully fund the university's needs, Cross suggested that OU should begin selective admissions. During one legislative meeting, Cross made a detailed presentation and pleaded for more funds. At the presentation's conclusion, he was asked, "But why do you need so much money?"

Cross answered wearily and famously, "I would like to build a university of which the football team could be proud." His point was well taken. Bud Wilkinson had led OU to win seven Big Seven Conference Titles and three national championships in 1951, 1955, and 1956, and the Sooners were the only team to place for seven years consecutively in the Associated Press's Top 10 poll. OU led the nation in scoring for three years. And Billy Vessels became OU's first Heisman Trophy winner in 1952. "They have scored in 95 consecutive games, a national record, and have given the country 18 All-Americans," Joan Flynn Dreyspool wrote in *Sports Illustrated*.

Wilkinson was also voted Coach of the Year by both the National Football Coaches Association and the Associated Press. OU's head coach, who made "Play Like a Champion," the Sooners' mantra, said, "Frankly, I'm not interested in records. The thing I'm proudest of is the type of boy represented at Oklahoma in football . . . in every possible ramification, we're going to try to shoot for the moon."

And shoot for the moon they did. The OU Sooners remained undefeated from the second game of 1953 until the eighth game of 1957, a forty-seven-game winning streak ended by a 0–7 loss to unranked Notre Dame. It was OU's first shutout in 123 games, stretching all the way back to 1945.

In 1956, Prentice Gautt, one of the team's members, became OU's first black football player. The university had been fully desegregated only one year earlier, and would not welcome its first black faculty member until 1959 with the arrival of Melvin B. Tolson, Jr. Several black players had tried out for the team and been accepted, but financial strains had ended their college careers. Gautt came to OU as an honor student, president of his senior class, and a football standout from Oklahoma City's all-black Douglass High School.

Honors student and future Big 8 commissioner Prentice Gautt became OU's first black football player in 1956. *(OU 1082)*

Gautt received multiple scholarship offers, but he was only interested in playing for the Sooners. He arrived on campus exhilarated, frightened, and grateful for the welcome he received from OU's coaching staff. Gautt, who would go on to become an NFL player and Big 8 commissioner, recalled Coach Wilkinson telling him, "You can be part of my program. Regardless of what other people think or feel or do, I want you to be a part of my program."

"My fears turned out to be, for the most part, only in my head," Gautt wrote. "My four years at Oklahoma were marked by acceptance from professors, coaches and teammates. . . . I was able, after Coach Wilkinson's conversations with me, to allow myself to overcome most of the mental blocks of prejudice." When Gautt did face prejudice, his teammates stood by his side. On one occasion, Gautt was refused service in a restaurant. The entire team quickly stood and walked out. Winning was not the only reason Oklahoma had to be proud of the Sooners.

Cross kept working to make Oklahomans equally proud of the university. In 1955, the university libraries established a second special collection with a $10,000 gift from Mr. and Mrs. Harry W. Bass, Sr., of Dallas, Texas. The Bass family would continue to support the collection, which eventually included more than two thousand rare books and reference materials.

OU's DeGolyer Collection in the History of Science and Technology had grown to five thousand volumes and had its own curator, H. Duane Roller, who was recruited to OU soon after receiving a Ph.D. in the history of science

from Harvard University. Roller remained curator of the collection until his retirement in 1990 and helped establish the DeGolyer Collection in a new addition built in Bizzell Memorial Library.

Across campus, OU was expanding in new ways. OU's dean of extension, Thurman J. White, had been striving to meet the needs of adult learners since returning to OU in 1949. Extension classes were well suited to the needs of returning military men, and White realized that continuing education was a ripe area for universities. But OU lacked adequate facilities. "For adults to be properly educated and trained, they needed a unique physical facility, one that recognized them as different from eighteen- to twenty-two-year-olds, and faculty committed to the kind of program that adult students required," White wrote.

White researched the best methods of adult education before convincing the W. K. Kellogg Foundation to fund "a community in miniature," an architectural design that would foster the development and sharing of ideas. The $1.84 million grant was the largest in the history of Oklahoma higher education in 1958 and provided both construction costs for the Oklahoma Center for Continuing Education and $245,000 for operation costs and program development.

Among programs generated by the grant were OU's Bachelor of Liberal Studies degree, which offers adult learners the chance to earn a broad-based liberal arts education at their own pace, and Advanced Programs, which today offers courses to tens of thousands of military and civilian personnel in more than fifty locations around the world.

OU dean of extension Thurman J. White *(left)*, Oklahoma governor J. Howard Edmondson, and President Cross examine a model of the future Oklahoma Center for Continuing Education (OCCE). *(Courtesy* Sooner Magazine)

Still, traditional students remained the primary focus of OU life, and the students of the 1950s were enjoying a time of relative innocence in which news of the Korean War and the Army-McCarthy hearings paled next to campus politics. Students were stunned to learn that the union had increased the price of coffee by a penny, and organized a "Tea for Tuesday" campaign to boycott coffee. Other campaigns were aimed at exempting graduating seniors from final exams and the right for students to have cars on campus.

It was a staunchly conservative era when classroom fashions included skirts for girls and button-down shirts and slacks for boys. The students of the 1950s considered college a time to prepare for the world of work in business, industry, and government, and focused on such "bread and butter" majors as engineering, business administration, and education. Most male students expected to participate in the military on some level, and OU's ROTC programs were in demand. In fact, OU's 1952 yearbook was devoted to the "Military Departments of the University."

OU fraternities and sororities flourished in this environment. Sue Barton Huffman, a 1951 OU graduate, recalled that she and her sorority sisters would end weekly chapter meetings with a trip to the County Line, a "grubby little bar south of Norman where they had country and western music on the jukebox, a bowling game, and a pool table. The locals (probably farmers, but we glamorized them into cowboys) bought us beer."

Perhaps the wildest time on record from OU's 1950s era came on May 22, 1952, when more than 2,500 male students stormed the Women's Quadrangle in a light-hearted panty raid that quickly turned into a riot. The event started when some 500 men gathered in front of the quad; the crowd swelled to 1,000 within an hour and surged inside to grab lingerie from unlocked rooms. From there the men went to the Gamma Phi Beta sorority house, where they found locked doors. Not to be deterred, some men climbed onto the roof and forced their way into the second floor.

The mob moved on to several other sorority houses, sometimes being met with buckets of cold water. Police were called in and began to fire tear gas. The men scattered, but regrouped at Sanger House in the Women's Quad, where the fire department deployed crowd-dispersing water hoses. The first spray was a direct hit on President Cross, who had just arrived on the scene.

Most of the 1950s was an idyllic period for OU students. "By any comparison, it was a good time to be in college," said Ralph Thompson, a 1956 business and 1961 law alumnus. Thompson would become a state representative before serving as federal judge for the Western District of Oklahoma. "The University was considered Oklahoma's flagship university," he said, "and students, faculty, and administration took pride in its traditions, image, and ideals."

THE TIMES THEY ARE (SLOWLY) A-CHANGIN'

OU's pride in athletics took a slight hit in 1960, when the Sooners were placed on a one-year NCAA probation for "improper financial assistance" to student athletes and the team was declared ineligible for post-season bowls and TV coverage. Wilkinson led the Sooners through 1963. He retired after sixteen years as OU's head coach and handed the reins to his assistant, Gomer Jones, leaving behind a legacy of three national titles, 145 wins, 29 losses and 4 tied games.

Baseball and wrestling also won national titles for OU in the 1950s, and J. D. Martin vaulted to stardom in U.S. outdoor track. He would go on to win the Pan Am decathlon in 1963.

On the academic side of university life, President Cross was doing his best to maintain OU's standing as Oklahoma's academic flagship, but it required a steady stream of public funds that was gradually drying up. In 1961, the president announced a $20 million fund-raising campaign; a portion of the funds would be used to establish forty endowed chairs. "Since there is no hope at the moment for funds from public sources, we decided to turn to private ones," Cross said frankly.

Some relief for OU's overcrowded, underfunded programs came in 1962, when the Oklahoma State Regents for Higher Education passed stricter fall admissions standards for students who ranked in the lower quarter of their high school graduating class. These students were welcomed to apply again in the spring, when OU's enrollment declined.

Cross, however, "never accepted a shortage of resources as a justification for failure," wrote Carol Burr. In fact, during the early 1960s OU established several of its most successful programs to recognize and foster academic excellence, including the University Scholars program in 1963 and the Honors Program in 1964. President Cross's assistant, David Burr, initiated the President's Leadership Class, which selects Oklahoma's most outstanding students for scholarships and leadership opportunities. OU also became only the second university in the country to offer a ballet program in 1963, taught by famed Oklahoma "Indian Ballerina" Yvonne Chouteau and her husband, Miguel Terekhov. Both had been members of the internationally famed Ballet Russes dance company.

Cross had now spent two decades as OU's president, and was believed to be among the longest-serving presidents in U.S. higher education. He and Cleo were grandparents. The university marked Cross's twentieth anniversary with a special issue of *Sooner Magazine* highlighting the many milestones of his tenure. The magazine summed up, "These were busy years, proud years, in many ways painful years, filled with the hopes, successes, and tragedies of the people who lived them."

George Lynn Cross's steady hand and wry wit led the university through some of its darkest days. *(OU 90A)*

The busy years were not over. On the Oklahoma City campus, Dr. Mark Everett had retired and been replaced by Dr. James L. Dennis, who became dean of the College of Medicine and director of OU's medical center. Dennis led the charge to launch a new concept in health care for Oklahoma and formed the OU Health Sciences Center.

The concept was a consensus between OU's medical faculty, who wished to focus on patient care and research, and the Oklahoma State Legislature, which wanted OU to produce family doctors. Dennis convinced the legislature that Oklahoma could have it all through a center offering the finest medical training and techniques. He also convinced his medical peers of the need to focus on family doctors, which resulted in the new OU Department of Family Medicine.

Dennis envisioned OU and private medical resources clustered in a 135-acre, $200 million Oklahoma Health Center with the OU Medical Center at its core. By 1969, building plans were in place and new colleges in dentistry, health-related professions, and public health had been created. The first building on campus would be University Hospital Tower, named in Dr. Mark Everett's honor.

On the Norman campus, several new buildings were dedicated in 1965, including Rupel J. Jones Theatre, named for the OU School of Drama's founding director; and Carson Engineering Center, named for early engineering dean William H. Carson. A new building for botany and microbiology was also built on the South Oval and named in Cross's honor, along with a massive lecture hall named for OU's first Research Professor, Edward Everett Dale.

Under construction was a cluster of twelve-story residence halls located where Sooner City once sprawled—Adams, Walker, and Couch towers, along with Couch Center cafeteria. Walker was initially planned as part of

Fine arts programs expanded significantly under George Cross's leadership, including the 1965 construction of the Rupel J. Jones Theatre. *(OU 675)*

The famed husband-and-wife team of Miguel Terekhov and Yvonne Chouteau, artists-in-residence who established the School of Dance in 1961. *(OU Dance 23)*

OU's Norman campus as it appeared in the mid-1960s. South of Lindsey Street *(up and to right of center)* is the new Adams Tower residence hall, surrounded by the remnants of the "Sooner City" prefabs. *(OU 53)*

Couch, and had been given the name Couch Center North. But the OU Board of Regents changed the name in 1970 to honor prominent Oklahoma City banker and philanthropist Edward A. Walker. Following soon after was the construction of Kraettli and Yorkshire Apartments. Finally OU had adequate housing for its student population, which had grown from one thousand students in 1944 to over fourteen thousand students in the mid-1960s.

Throughout the first half of the 1960s, OU's student population seemed much like their earlier counterparts. The social turmoil that had begun to envelop campuses across parts of the nation had bypassed Norman, where cultural daring consisted of beatniks, coffeehouses, the Kingston Trio, and river-bottom parties.

OU did have its own chapter of the Students for a Democratic Society, or SDS, but the group featured only fifteen members by 1965. The SDS faculty adviser, William Bittle, once quipped, "This campus is a hotbed of NO protest." In fact, one of the state's largest demonstrations came when 2,500 OU and OSU students held a sit-in at the State Capitol in support of higher faculty salaries.

The absence of angry protest at OU through 1968 can be attributed in part to President Cross, who worked diligently to keep lines of communication open with student groups. He invited each major campus organization to send a representative to a weekly Saturday morning meeting, where he learned of student concerns and tried to explain what could and couldn't be done to solve them. He firmly believed that much of the campus unrest at other universities could be handled through better communication.

One hot topic at OU centered on the fact that all students, including juniors and seniors, were required to live on campus while the bonds for OU's new residence halls were paid off. Older students were required to abide by the same rules as freshmen and sophomores, which included curfews and no members of the opposite sex visiting in rooms. Cross "promised a new kind of more adult housing [with visiting hours] because I agreed that it was silly to treat juniors and seniors like high school students," he said. Cross suggested that a forthcoming student demonstration be held in late afternoon, and members of the media came to cover the event. Cross went to observe.

"About dinnertime, the kids began to drift away. I knew most of the reporters, and I thought they all had left, too. One boy asked, 'Suppose it is 11:30 P.M. and my girl is in my room, and I have a bottle of bourbon. Would that be all right?'"

Cross thought for a moment, then answered, "That is surely a happy thought." He got the expected laugh and evaded answering the question. He wasn't so happy to see himself quoted in the newspaper the following day, when it became apparent that not all reporters had left the demonstration.

OU was making unflattering headlines in other ways. New OU football coach Gomer Jones had led the Sooners to the Gator Bowl his first year, but the team's performance quickly deteriorated. The 1965 season, termed a disaster, consisted of three wins and seven losses, including OU's first loss to OSU since 1945. The OU Touchdown Club threatened to withdraw its financial support if Jones did not resign. He transitioned to the role of athletic director, which he filled until his death in 1971. In 1966, OU hired Jim McKenzie from the University of Arkansas. With him, McKenzie brought coaching assistants Chuck Fairbanks and Barry Switzer.

McKenzie began to turn the team around, posting a six-win, four-loss season and beating the University of Texas.

The George Lynn Cross Botany and Microbiology Hall, dedicated in 1965, was among thirty-seven buildings added to the university's campuses during Cross's tenure. *(OU 1889)*

Then, during a spring practice, he suffered a heart attack and died on April 28, 1967.

President Cross asked the board to appoint Chuck Fairbanks in McKenzie's stead, but the board wanted to continue looking at other options. Cross appointed Fairbanks by executive order subject to Regents' approval. The board agreed, but restricted Fairbanks to a nine-month contract. He won the board over by earning a nine-win, one-loss record and winning the Big 8 title. Fairbanks also groomed Steve Owens, the new Sooner running back who would win the Heisman Trophy in 1969.

Other sports experienced drastic change during the 1960s as well. OU's gymnastics team became a varsity sport for the first time in forty-eight years, though it would later wane and be resurrected in 1965. Basketball went through a rapid succession of coaches, including Doyle Patrick, Bob Stevens, and John MacLeod. Tennis coach Jerry Keen joined OU and won eight consecutive Big 8 championships, while wrestling coach Port Robertson handed his program to Tommy Evans, who led the Sooners to two national championships. And in baseball, Coach Jack Baer retired after twenty-three years, to be replaced by Enos Semore, who would become a legend.

Cross mulled the idea of his own retirement. He told the Board of Regents that he planned to resign the OU presidency on June 30, 1968, which would give the Regents plenty of time to find a deserving candidate. Cross and the board crafted a plan for a smooth succession: a search committee would be formed, headed by longtime history professor Gilbert Fite, and the committee would take suggestions for presidential candidates from OU faculty, students, staff, and alumni. The lead candidate would be named president-designate by the board and work closely with Cross during his final year of service before assuming the presidency.

OU students were undergoing a transition of their own. In January 1966, a Campus Corner boardinghouse was raided for marijuana, and eleven OU students were arrested and charged with possession. Newspapers carried the story statewide, and conservative Oklahomans began to look uneasily at OU.

Then, that December, a student group planned "Religious Education Week" for the following March. Oklahoma State University would host a similar event, so the groups collaborated to share the expense of two keynote speakers: James A. Pike, a former Episcopal bishop from San Francisco, and Thomas J. J. Altizer, a theologian from Emory University. Cross described the speakers as "somewhat radical theologians." For his part, Altizer was well known for his theory, "God is dead."

"Within hours a near avalanche of protesting messages—letters and telegrams—reached the presidents' offices at both schools," Cross wrote. "The ones I received carried identical messages: this godless man should not be permitted to speak at OU." Members of the legislature chimed in, and OSU's new president, Robert B. Kamm, announced that his campus would cancel the lecture. Kamm went even further, forbidding OSU faculty members from participating in unapproved demonstrations. Nine OSU sociology professors resigned in protest.

Cross, nearing the end of his presidency, had less to lose than Kamm. "After giving relatively little thought to possible consequences, I told the press that Altizer would appear on the campus," he wrote. When asked why he was giving the lecture his support, Cross conceded that OU's policies on academic freedom and tenure probably did not cover the appearance of a controversial outside speaker.

"At stake only, I said, was the question whether students had the right to hear speakers of their choosing—the right to listen and explore ideas occasionally unpalatable to the public at large," he wrote. "I contended that the students did indeed have that right and that to deny it to them would be prejudicial to the basic purposes of the university."

Altizer and Pike's lecture in OU's Union ballroom was attended by 1,200 people, yet otherwise uneventful. Cross continued to receive letters of both criticism and support, and the Oklahoma State Senate snubbed him indirectly by passing a resolution praising OSU's president for canceling the lecture.

But President Cross continued to lead OU with his convictions. OU human relations professor Dr. George Henderson was only the third African American faculty member on the Norman campus in 1967, and quickly became distinct when he and his wife were the first black family to purchase a home in Norman city limits. The sale led to death threats and blacklisting against the Norman realtor who had sold the house, and the Hendersons were the subjects of threatening phone calls and racial slurs. Garbage and a wooden cross were thrown on their lawn, and raw eggs at their cars.

Cross ensured that the Hendersons were encircled by the OU community. Cleo Cross hosted a tea party at Boyd House for the Hendersons' young daughters, and the Hendersons received a long list of social invitations from faculty and staff eager to offer their friendship and support. "It became clear to us that we would either eat our way into social acceptance or we would be the best-fed wannabes in the history of Norman," Henderson wrote in his book, *Race and the University: A Memoir.*

As 1967 wore on, OU's presidential search committee reviewed the curricula vitae of two hundred candidates. At last, Cross was pleased to hear that the committee had recommended forty-eight-year-old J. Herbert Hollomon, a metallurgist who was serving as acting undersecretary of the U.S. Department of Commerce. On May 27, 1967, Hollomon was named president-designate of OU, and he and his wife, Margaret, moved to Norman that summer. Hollomon would become familiar with the university and form his plans for OU's future, while Cross continued overseeing the university's day-to-day operations.

"Dr. Hollomon has much to offer the university and the state," OU Foundation director and *Sooner Magazine* executive editor R. Boyd Gunning said by way of introducing alumni to Hollomon. "By nature, he is an exciting, quick, impatient man of ideas who expects results."

At his initial press conference, Hollomon stated his support for academic freedom and said that a university's duty was "to train, to educate, to do research . . . to challenge the accepted views of society and to aid society. . . . A university is a special place where the accepted wisdom does not have to be accepted."

Hollomon would get a lesson in accepted wisdom in October 1967, when several student groups, including the SDS and OU Committee to End the War in Vietnam, brought militant black socialist and Marxist Paul Boutelle to speak to an audience of five hundred. Critics alleged that Boutelle had previously called the United States flag "a rag" and the nation's president "a liar." He was also thought to be a Communist.

The Oklahoma American Legion immediately asked Governor Dewey Bartlett to investigate OU, and newspapers, which had been supportive throughout the Pike and Altizer controversy, began to criticize Cross.

"That such a man should be permitted to speak on the university campus was incomprehensible to most Oklahomans, or so it seemed from the flood of protest that reached my office in letters, telegrams, and telephone calls," Cross wrote. "I announced to the news media that, while I thought the selection of Boutelle was unfortunate, I would not interfere with his appearance."

Several student groups withdrew their sponsorship of the event, but Boutelle's lecture was not canceled. In response, state Representative Texanna L. Hatchett of Oklahoma City pledged to investigate OU, particularly regarding the presence of radical student groups and its scheduling of outside speakers. A legislative committee was formed, and State Representative David Boren, a friend of Cross, got himself appointed to the committee and worked with Cross behind the scenes to smooth ruffled feathers. Cross met with the legislators on OU's campus.

"I sensed that certain of them, especially Representative Hatchett, were not in a mood to discuss freedom of speech or freedom of students to listen." Cross said. The president agreed that Boutelle's OU appearance had been mishandled. But the legislators likely didn't expect what came next. The lecture "should have been sponsored, I said, by the university rather than by a small radical student group and the lessons to be learned shared by as many students as possible," Cross continued. "I suggested that, because of the mishandling, the student body as a whole had lost an opportunity for a valuable educational experience."

The meeting ended cordially, but Cross soon learned that the committee was not satisfied and demanded the firing of SDS sponsor Jack Middleton, who directed intergroup relations for OU's Southwest Center for Human Relations Studies. Considerable pressure was applied to Middleton's boss, Thurman J. White, now dean of continuing education. Cross took the issue straight to Governor Bartlett.

"I explained carefully my ideas concerning academic freedom, freedom of speech, freedom of students to listen, and the need for students to experience the disagreeable products of society as a part of their general educational experience," Cross wrote. "I found the governor completely receptive." Bartlett agreed that he would not pressure OU to fire Middleton, though the university eventually did reassign him. The controversy was Cross's last as OU president.

THE LONG GOOD-BYE

The president's final year in office was what one author called a long "love-in befitting the '60s" that celebrated all Cross had achieved during his quarter century of leadership. President and Mrs. Cross were the guests of honor at innumerable dinners and meetings, and Homecoming 1967 was dedicated to the Cross presidency. At the Homecoming

President Cross spoke to students on campus in 1967, a year before his retirement after twenty-five years leading the university. *(Courtesy Sooner Magazine)*

parade, each float represented some phase of Cross's life at OU, and the Homecoming game halftime show, "Era of Excellence," was dedicated to President Cross. The show closed with the Pride of Oklahoma marching band forming Cross's profile, complete with his famous pipe at a jaunty tilt.

The OU Board of Regents did their part to remember Cross by naming OU's research professorships in his honor. The move represented the closing of a circle, as Cross was the person whose support made the research professorships possible in 1944, when the controversial faculty appointments were proposed by outgoing president Joseph Brandt.

Cross had much more to his credit than the research professorships, of course. OU's student body had quadrupled during his tenure to nearly seventeen thousand students, and graduate enrollment had increased from less than one hundred to more than thirty-six hundred students. In fact, Cross had awarded more than half the degrees in OU's entire history, including 80 percent of all doctoral degrees.

The university budget had increased from $2.8 million to $20 million since 1944, and faculty salaries had risen from an average of $2,450 to $11,000. OU's faculty also had greater research resources, including a library with more than one million volumes.

OU's very campus had been transformed during the Cross era. Some thirty-seven buildings were constructed or enlarged, and hundreds of acres had been added to OU through the acquisition of the naval bases. Student housing increased from 250 rooms to more than 7,200 single-student rooms and 778 family units.

As R. Boyd Gunning wrote, however, the greatest legacy of George Lynn Cross's presidency was far more intangible than buildings or books or even students. "The character of a university is determined by its president more than by any other factor, and in this respect the University of Oklahoma has been fortunate," Gunning wrote. "A man of integrity, prudence, high principles and standards, patience, wit, and intellect, George Lynn Cross has imparted these qualities to his institution and given it a purpose and a sense of direction which have kept it moving forward in its pursuit of excellence."

Gunning credited Cross for creating a climate of reason, tolerance, respect for academic freedom, intellect, and humanity. "The Cross years have come to an end, but the Cross influence will continue," he wrote. "It's an invaluable legacy of which Oklahomans should be proud and protective."

George Lynn Cross stepped down as president on June 30, 1968. He served as chairman of a local bank and continued teaching OU botany courses while writing seven books on the history of the university from his campus office. He and Cleo remained deeply involved in OU life for three more decades and were frequently seen about campus.

Dr. and Mrs. Cross, seen here
meeting with student recipients of
the Cleo Cross International Student
Scholarships, remained active
and at the heart of the university
community long after retirement.
(OU 2329)

Among those visiting Cross in the mid-1990s was recently appointed OU president David L. Boren, who had
come to know Cross while an OU law student and as an
applicant for the Rhodes Scholarship. Although Boren had
been both Oklahoma's governor and a longtime U.S. senator, he relied upon the Crosses' experience and wisdom in
his new role as president.

"In an age when all too many people tend to use important institutions for their personal gain, George Cross,
along with his wife, Cleo, lovingly and faithfully invested
his entire life in building a great university for the people
of our state," said Boren, who acknowledges Cross as his
presidential role model. "His example will always challenge
us to be faithful to the best that is in us."

Dr. Cross and Ada Lois Sipuel Fisher,
who became a civil rights leader
and OU Regent, were bound in
friendship by the shared experience
of helping to desegregate a
university. *(OU 2235)*

Cross's example now stands on OU's North Oval for all to see. A statue of the former president was dedicated in 1996 and features Cross seated in a chair, facing campus. The base of the statue carries an inscription of Cross's own words: "The success of university graduates should and ultimately will be measured not by the effectiveness with which they compete with others but by the quality of service that they render and the integrity of their relations with their associates." In an especially appropriate touch, the opposite side of the statue's base features an engraving of Cross's wife and life partner with the dedication, "Cleo Cross: First Lady, Mentor, Friend."

Cross was present for the dedication, but alone. Cleo Cross had become too ill to venture into public and died at the age of ninety in 1997. The Crosses had been married for seventy-one years. "When Cross lost the love of his life, the spark went out for this remarkably resilient man," Carol Burr wrote in *Sooner Magazine*. Cross died at age ninety-three on New Year's Eve 1998. Flags across OU's three campuses were lowered to half-staff, and a memorial service was held in his honor with friends, family, and colleagues surrounding his statue.

"With each passing year, the greatness of George Lynn Cross, the man and the educator, becomes more clear," President Boren said of his own mentor and friend. "He stands among the small handful of giants in Oklahoma history."

OU president David L. Boren introduces Dr. Cross at the 1996 dedication of a statue in his honor, placed in front of Evans Hall.
(Courtesy Robert Taylor, OU Public Affairs)

JOHN HERBERT HOLLOMON
1968–1970

 AFTER A QUARTER-CENTURY of nearly idyllic leadership from George Lynn Cross, the transition to any new OU president was destined to have its challenges. But the convergence of a deadly war, a counterculture movement, and a brilliant, brusque personality meant that the J. Herbert Hollomon presidency would be brief, volcanic, and unforgettable.

Hollomon was nominated as OU's president after an exhaustive search in 1967. By all appearances, he was an impressive and fortunate find for OU. A graduate of the Massachusetts Institute of Technology (MIT) and an army veteran, he had been general manager of General Electric Company's engineering laboratory before joining the Kennedy administration as first assistant secretary for science and technology at the U.S. Department of Commerce. Hollomon was instrumental in legislative proposals for the Highway Transportation Safety Act, one of the earliest laws addressing consumer safety, and established the Environmental Sciences Services Administration, which was the precursor to the National Oceanic and Atmospheric Administration.

During the Lyndon Baines Johnson presidency, Hollomon served as undersecretary of commerce and was offered the post of secretary of commerce. According to William McKeen, a former OU professor of journalism and author of the OU doctoral dissertation "Field Day: Student Dissent at the University of Oklahoma, May 5–12, 1970," Hollomon was flattered, but he declined the offer because he did not support Johnson's handling of the Vietnam War.

Still, Johnson offered to further Hollomon's career; when Hollomon stated that he would like to become president of a university, Johnson spread the word. Soon Hollomon's name had reached the OU search

committee, and on May 27, 1967, he was named OU president-designate, an unusual move that allowed Hollomon to study the university and introduce himself to constituents while President Cross finished his final year.

Hollomon moved into temporary offices on the first floor of Buchanan Hall and met regularly with the Board of Regents. During one meeting, he announced his intention to establish a series of committees that would study OU from every possible angle. Findings would form the basis of a "blueprint" for OU's progress during the next two decades. Twenty-three panels with 572 volunteer members formed committees and subcommittees featuring members from OU's faculty, staff, students, alumni, and the Norman community.

"One clearly deep and essential question is being asked," Hollomon said of the study. "Is the university only a sort of supermarket? Is it a place where students come to select a series of courses that, put together,

J. Herbert Hollomon meets the press at the 1967 announcement of his selection as OU's President-Designate. With him are *(from left)*, his wife, Margaret Hollomon, presidential search committee chairman and OU research professor of history Gilbert Fite, and current president George Lynn Cross. *(OU 1161)*

become an education? Or is it living in more of a connected process?"

Hollomon's blueprint, *The Future of the University*, was written by his assistant, Gordon Christenson, and was released in time for Hollomon's inauguration. OU community members waited for the report's findings with a mixture of anticipation and foreboding, realizing that significant change was on the horizon. The report was farsighted and reached across the entire scope of university life. Many of the changes suggested in *The Future of the University* took effect almost immediately; others would not be implemented until long after J. Herbert Hollomon departed OU.

Among the plan's physical recommendations was adding a multipurpose arena and new student health center (the Lloyd Noble Center and Goddard Health Center, both completed in the 1970s under President Sharp), a multistory parking lot, a physical education and recreation facility, and a music building/concert hall (the Oklahoma Memorial Union Parking Garage, Huston Huffman Fitness Center, Catlett Music Center, and Paul Sharp Concert Hall, all completed in the 1980s under President Banowsky).

Undoubtedly the most significant academic change stemming from the report was the addition of the Office of the Provost, the second-highest ranking officer behind OU's president. The provost's job was to integrate all academic functions on the Norman and Oklahoma City campuses. Other academic recommendations of the plan included encouraging women to seek nontraditional degree programs, establishing a career information and placement services office, expanding OU's cooperation with private enterprise through grants and contracts, offering concurrent enrollment for high school students, and creating more rigorous OU admission standards.

One of the marquee achievements of the campus-wide

plan was creation of a representative, three-branch system of student government that would control the disbursement of student fees. The first members of the University of Oklahoma Student Association played a crucial role as conflict unfurled at OU and produced a generation of Oklahoma leaders, including U.S. representatives Mike Synar and Dave McCurdy, state representative Cleta Deatherage Mitchell, Governor David Walters, and Lieutenant Governors Jack Mildren and Robert S. Kerr III.

Hollomon pledged to use *The Future of the University* to transform OU once he officially became president on

Hollomon officially became OU's eighth president on September 1, 1968. *(OU 101)*

September 1, 1968. His inauguration was an impressive, grand event, made all the more memorable because it was the first of its kind in forty-eight years. Neither President Brandt nor President Cross had held inaugurations, due to the fiscal austerity of World War II. A temporary platform was erected on OU's South Oval with a giant OU seal and Bizzell Memorial Library as backdrops. While four thousand spectators looked on, a line of seven hundred faculty members and dignitaries filed into the celebration, where Hollomon recited an intellectual, heady address on the challenges faced by OU and all of higher education, and the challenges he faced.

"Coming to this university last year . . . it crossed my mind that I might be expected to be all things to all people," he said. "A sorcerer who uses magic to change things instantly; a charlatan, mouthing everyone's righteous causes; a Steppenwolf who sits outside society's circle with a grin on his face, waiting to lead a revolution. But after all, my humanity is the same as every man's. And we all are expected to face these same questions.

"Is it possible for us to accept the fact that conflict does and will continue to exist within our universities and in society?" Hollomon asked the assembly, before making an almost prescient statement: "Under these conditions perhaps a sharing of values will come about only through a ritualistic battle, not a real one, within new forms where the confrontation can be made explicit, open, and nonviolent, and the resolution understood, accepted, and accepted peacefully."

Within two years, Hollomon found himself caught in a conflict between state officials and students, struggling to manage a ritualistic battle in which his presidency and students' very lives were on the line.

A NEW REALITY

From his first day, Hollomon demonstrated that he was a president for a new age. While Hollomon's distinguished guests celebrated his inauguration in the ballroom of Oklahoma Memorial Union, downstairs in the union cafeteria students danced to psychedelic rock band Strawberry Alarm Clock and to the Kingsmen, whose signature song was "Louie, Louie."

The new president also demonstrated his focus on students by creating an administrative level called University Community, a vice-presidential post filled by former assistant to the president David Burr. Burr's role encompassed all nonacademic aspects of student life and served as a touchstone between students and the OU administration.

Hollomon's other administrative changes nearly doubled the number of OU vice presidents to nine, a drastic change from the streamlining that President Cross had

Brilliant, charismatic, and dynamic, Hollomon angered conservatives and won over students with his casual, open style and willingness to relate to the growing counterculture movement. *(OU 103)*

fought for early in his own administration. Hollomon kept Cross's vice presidents, including Pete Kyle McCarter, who would later become OU's first provost. He added Burr; Thurman J. White, vice president of university fund-raising; Edward L. Katzenbach, Jr., vice president of research and public service; and John O. Dean, vice president of university relations.

Never self-doubting, Hollomon plunged into making changes recommended by the *Future of the University* report and immediately created hard feelings with such established faculty members as law dean Page Keeton and vice president for Medical Center affairs Dr. James L. Dennis. Keeton hoped to run a nearly autonomous operation, as did Dennis, who planned to greatly enlarge the Health Sciences Center. Both ideas were in direct conflict with Hollomon's plans.

The president also clashed early on with Governor Bartlett. Hollomon asked the State Legislature for a $7 million increase in OU's budget only a month after becoming president and disputed the formula that the State Regents used to calculate faculty salaries. Further, Hollomon publicly announced that Oklahoma was sadly lacking in education funds compared to its neighboring states. His claim offended Bartlett, who prided himself on being a champion of higher education.

Back on campus, Hollomon also offended some faculty and students with his hiring of William T. Jones, OU's new director of campus security. According to findings in *The Future of the University*, OU's security was woefully inadequate to handle the emerging national issues of campus unrest, and Hollomon charged Jones, a twenty-four-year law enforcement veteran, with developing a professional police department for OU. One of Jones's initial acts was arming OU's security forces for the first time.

Many OU students found the addition of weapons threatening, and a coalition of faculty members protested the change with a letter to the OU Faculty Senate. "Little evidence exists for the need of weapons in university precincts," the letter stated. "There is certainly nothing in the past record of the University of Oklahoma to prompt the assumptions that campus violence is likely."

Jones would transform a security force into one of the nation's first accredited university police forces and stood firm on the issue of arming officers. He did concede to university life by uniquely outfitting his officers. Rather than wearing a standard police uniform, OU Police Department officers wore wool blazers and slacks, a small distinction that played an important role in the years to come.

OU was hardly a center of radical activity like the University of Wisconsin, where the underground group the Weathermen claimed responsibility for a bombing that killed three people. But arrests for marijuana possession occurred with regularity in residence halls and boardinghouses, and parents were disquieted by television broadcasts showing OU students with long hair and beards. Greek life on campus was slowly faltering, and OU had its own popular underground newspaper, the *Jones Family Grandchildren*, as well as a chapter of the Students for a Democratic Society. The activist organization led the charge against involvement in Vietnam at other campuses across the nation, but OU's SDS members were primarily focused on local issues, including the university's compulsory housing policy.

OU required all students below the age of twenty-four to live in student housing to help pay for the construction cost of Adams Tower and the two Couch towers. Students pasted SDS-distributed posters proclaiming, "We Want Out!" on their dorm windows, and at least one hundred students held a sit-in in the lobby of Couch Center North, now known as Walker Tower. Burr and dean of men Stanley Hicks visited the sit-in and promised students a meeting with OU's Board of Regents. Before that could happen, President Hollomon found a solution that would both pay OU's debt and allow upper-class students to leave university housing: Hollomon

used his federal ties to attract the U.S. Postal Training Center to Norman. Trainees would be housed in OU's Couch Tower for decades to come, and the SDS was neatly cut out of any political bargaining in student housing.

Still, OU students were aware of the political and cultural upheaval of their time, and student leaders brought to campus such speakers as Columbia University's SDS "Weatherman" Mark Rudd and black activist and comedian Dick Gregory, whose controversial speech to an audience of more than three thousand angered the American Legion so much that one member publicly called it "treason."

Gregory's speech was moored in the fact that many of OU's four hundred black students felt isolated in a sea of seventeen thousand students. They found the university climate repressive and their classmates apathetic about the unique challenges they faced. The OU Afro-American Student Union was a new expression of a growing awareness of cultural identity. Its members, stymied by a lack of progress in OU race relations, wrote and presented a "Black Declaration of Independence" with fourteen requests, including race-specific offices for student affairs and admissions, minority representation on OU's athletic coaching staffs, athletic competition with black schools, and a Black Studies program. Hollomon openly denied the majority of the requests, but vowed to enter into a dialogue with black students to address racism in university life.

Native American students were also frustrated, as illustrated in their reaction to longtime OU mascot "Little Red," a role filled by a Native American student who stomp-danced at OU football games in traditional attire. The mascot was termed "a war whooping idiot who misrepresents American Indians." Hollomon sent the issue for review by the newly created University Human Relations Committee, chaired by noted philosophy professor and Presbyterian minister J. Clayton Feaver. By the following spring, Little Red was banned. It was not a popular move with many Oklahomans, including traditionalists and some members of Native American communities who saw Little Red's presence as a point of pride.

Then, in the fall of 1969, Hollomon angered conservatives and Governor Bartlett further by allowing OU students to participate in the "National Moratorium," during which campuses across the country canceled classes to protest the Vietnam War. OU's afternoon classes were dismissed and students were encouraged to attend a dialogue featuring retired general Clyde Watts and U.S. senator Fred R. Harris of Oklahoma.

Hollomon worked to keep dialogue open with all students and tried to relate to them on their own level. His efforts paid off with many student leaders, including Joe Foote, OU '71, a member of the President's Leadership Class who today is dean and Edward L. Gaylord Chair in OU's Gaylord

The Pride of Oklahoma Marching Band performing at Band Day in 1969. *(OU 2404)*

College of Journalism and Mass Communication. Foote, then a nineteen-year-old student from Durant, Oklahoma, remembers being deeply impressed by Hollomon. He found OU's president to be urbane, articulate, and highly intelligent. "He was the very picture of what an academic should be. He carried himself differently and spoke differently," Foote said, recalling that Hollomon spoke in clipped tones contrasting with his own Oklahoma drawl. "He was an exciting thinker; I was very taken with him."

Many students also admired Hollomon for his casual, open style and his obvious connection to young people. But that same style attracted unwanted attention. Former OU Board of Regents chairman G. T. Blankenship served as Oklahoma attorney general during Hollomon's tenure. According to William McKeen, Blankenship was invited to a backyard barbecue where Hollomon was a fellow guest; there the attorney general saw OU's president sitting shirtless on the grass, "rapping with about ten or twelve dissident leaders." The sight struck Blankenship as grossly inappropriate, and he left the party.

At the same time, former president Cross heard his share of complaints about Hollomon. Cross told McKeen that he received a visit from concerned faculty at the end of Hollomon's first semester as president. "Some parents were disturbed because he'd have student groups over to the president's house and lie on the floor, barefooted, with a can of beer on his chest," Cross told McKeen. "Which, of course, has nothing to do with his abilities."

Unfortunately, Hollomon was also gaining a poor reputation with alumni and supporters who thought he was brusque and egotistical. At one event the OU president ignored donors and spent the evening visiting with a bartender. Hollomon's case was not helped by the fact that he and his wife Margaret had separated and would divorce in early 1970. Margaret Hollomon had been ill for several years and was unable to fulfill the role of OU first lady.

Faculty members who visited Cross went so far as to ask how OU could get rid of Hollomon. "It startled me a little bit and I said, 'I haven't had any experience getting rid of university presidents, but if half of what you told me is true, I'm not in favor of getting rid of him,'" Cross quipped. "'He's done more for my image in a semester than I could have done in 25 years.'"

Almost three decades later, Cross admitted to new OU president David L. Boren that he had seen trouble coming during the year that Hollomon had served as president-designate. But Cross felt strongly that it was the OU Board of Regents' right and responsibility to choose a president, and that he should not influence the process. "I took too much of a hands-off position on my successor," Cross told Boren. "I felt it was inappropriate for me to make any suggestion at all to the Regents, sometimes even to answer their questions."

No one doubted that J. Herbert Hollomon was a brilliant man with a vision for higher education, and one hugely popular with student leaders. But in less than two years he had managed to alienate virtually every key OU constituency except the student body, including Governor Bartlett. Bartlett made no secret of the fact that he believed

Hollomon was pandering to the growing counterculture movement and, in the process, damaging OU.

It was a recipe for disaster that only lacked one key ingredient: a divisive conflict. The first week of May 1970 would provide that missing piece. It would also reveal that Hollomon was both the wrong choice for OU and the best-possible president for a critical moment in OU history.

A NATIONAL TRAGEDY STRIKES HOME

Early May 1970 was already a time unlike any other in U.S. higher education. President Richard M. Nixon had announced on April 30 that the United States was invading Cambodia to expand its war efforts in Vietnam and that more than 150,000 new troops would be drafted for the campaign. Across the nation, college campuses erupted in protest.

Ohio's Kent State University was no different, though its protest quickly spiraled out of control with students rioting and setting fire to the university's ROTC facility. Ohio governor James Rhodes called nine hundred National Guardsmen into campus, and on May 4, a heated confrontation between protestors and the National Guard turned deadly when guardsmen fired into a crowd, killing four students and wounding nine others.

As the impact of the tragedy swept across the United States, unrest flared to dangerous levels at universities, and more than four hundred campuses closed due to protests. OU students responded with a candlelight march and memorial for the dead, and a student group, the People's Liberation Front, manned a table in Oklahoma Memorial Union to advertise a peaceful protest at OU's armory on the afternoon of Tuesday, May 5, 1970. That same day, McKeen writes, two students were seen walking through the union carrying a Republic of Vietnam flag. Asked by authorities to put the flag away, they complied.

On Tuesday afternoon students began to gather outside OU's armory, waiting for Army ROTC cadets who traditionally drilled in full uniform and with weapons on a field adjacent to Brooks Street. ROTC Commander Leroy Land considered canceling the event, but changed his mind because his students needed to rehearse for an ROTC awards ceremony scheduled for the following week. However, he conceded that his students should leave their weapons behind.

When the ROTC cadets exited the armory they faced approximately five hundred student protestors enjoying a carnival atmosphere, with members dancing, tossing Frisbees, and chanting antiwar slogans. Many in the crowd had come to simply observe, and some girls were seen wearing bikinis. The cadets marched to the parade ground on Brooks

Fallout from the 1970 Kent State tragedy reached OU with a series of protests and a potentially explosive face-off between students, state leaders, and law enforcement. President Hollomon stepped into the breach to ensure students' safety while protecting their right to free speech. *(1971 Sooner Yearbook)*

Street, trailed by protestors, supporters, and newspaper and television reporters, who recorded protest speeches delivered against the backdrop of a growing spectacle. While ROTC students marched in drill formation, some protestors danced through their ranks to heckle and spray them with water guns. "We are fighting the absurd with the absurd," one protest organizer explained to a student reporter for the *Oklahoma Daily*. ROTC supporters stood across the street and were chanting their own slogans.

Absurd or not, university officials, law enforcement, and Oklahoma's governor took the protest seriously. OU vice president Burr and legal counsel David Swank were on site and in constant contact with President Hollomon via two-way radio. OU Police Department officers also were present, and Chief Jones had asked Governor Bartlett to supplement his small staff by placing Oklahoma Highway Patrol on standby. But Jones did not realize that Bartlett had gone a step further and notified the National Guard to be on alert.

Yet no move had been made against the protestors, even when motorcyclists began weaving their way among the ROTC cadets. McKeen says the crowd's mood shifted abruptly when OU graduate student Keith Green brandished the Republic of Vietnam flag. Many mistook the flag for the Vietcong banner and ROTC supporters began to react with virulent shouts. The possibility of physical conflict flared between the protestors and ROTC supporters.

In a decision that would be examined and reexamined, OU administrators and OUPD officials decided that the flag had to go. OUPD officers grabbed the flag from Green and his companion; the two groups struggled until Green was forced to the ground and arrested for flying the flag of an enemy nation.

"That," McKeen wrote, "was when a rally turned into a riot."

Green and his friend were moved to a police car and the crowd of five hundred protestors swarmed the vehicle and blocked officers from driving away. Jones used a bullhorn to repeatedly ask the crowd to disperse, but students refused. Some tried to free Green from the car while others beat on the hood and roof, released air from the car's tires, and attempted to set the car's gas tank on fire. Two students were arrested. OU Student Association president Bill Moffitt—who had been elected as UOSA's first black president only the day before—did his best to quell the conflict, but to little effect.

President Hollomon and special assistant Gordon Christenson drove to Brooks Street while maintaining a distance, where they could watch without causing more chaos. What they saw was unnerving. Chief Jones finally resorted to calling in the Oklahoma Highway Patrol. The OHP members arrived an hour after the conflict began and combined forces with OUPD and the Norman Police Department. More than one hundred officers marched onto the scene, using billy clubs to push students away from the besieged OUPD car. A few students fought back and received minor injuries. The majority, however, quickly scattered, allowing Jones to transfer Green and his companion to a police van. Police then used their clubs and bodies to clear an exit path for the van and damaged patrol car.

Nearly twenty years later, Jones told McKeen he believed the riot could have been considerably worse and expressed regret for the moment that set it all in motion. "We could have avoided most of that incident had we let that flag alone and let that crowd dissolve in the manner that it was scheduled to," he said. "That was a mistake."

Jones and the OU administration would soon encounter much larger student protests. But they would not act rashly in a volatile situation again, despite tremendous pressure brought to bear by Oklahoma's governor.

A CAMPUS IN SHOCK

That night, Gordon Christenson stood on a stage at the Wilson Activity Center and faced an assembly of 350 student leaders with newly elected UOSA president Bill Moffitt. He was prepared to accept the students' criticisms, to quell their fears, and to answer questions about Green's arrest. Christenson's job was to urge calm and peace on campus and to deliver a message from President Hollomon.

"There is disagreement in our country about the war and about the law," Hollomon's statement read. "Today, this disagreement was expressed in disruptions and arrests. What is needed now is calm and understanding. Members of the university community, no matter how they feel, must not excite others to react violently. . . . I therefore call upon the students to express their various views peacefully."

After Christenson exited, the UOSA passed a resolution that would allow the OU student body to vote for a strike two days later "to express their dissatisfaction with the widening horror of the war in Southeast Asia and horror over the death of four students at Kent State University." Moffitt was officially sworn in as UOSA president and departed for a protest rally on the South Oval, where two thousand angry students were waiting.

"Avoid violence," Moffitt urged the crowd. "We must keep cool. We can't change the world with dead students." Moffitt called for a second rally outside OU's administration building the next morning and returned to the UOSA office, where he enlisted several volunteers to serve as "peace marshals" Wednesday morning. He hoped fellow students could mitigate crowd temperatures and avoid any more conflict.

Meanwhile, OU President Hollomon was hosting a long-planned faculty awards dinner at his home on Pickard Avenue. Hollomon would remember the night not only as an incongruous end to a violent day, but as the first evening he spent with his future wife, OU associate professor of theater Nancy Gade. Hollomon had noticed Gade at campus events and arranged to be seated next to her at the faculty dinner. Guests were to follow dinner with a special viewing of a student play that Gade had produced.

Gade recalled that the dinner was interrupted several times by phone calls and messages updating the president. McKeen said: "He briefly described what had happened, that people were actively trying to keep the peace, and that it was hectic, trying to manage the campus when it appeared likely to explode."

Gade sat with the president during the play's performance and noted that Hollomon excused himself for a lengthy phone call. When the play ended, Hollomon and Gade walked out to discover an OUPD officer waiting with a car. The officer had been instructed to keep Hollomon moving, and they soon learned that a bomb threat had been made on the president's home. Once the bomb threat was cleared, Hollomon and Gade returned to Pickard, where they found more than a dozen OU faculty, staff, and students offering to help diffuse the next day's event however they could.

Hollomon left Gade with his guests, and he and Christenson went to a student planning session for the next day's rally. There UOSA president Moffitt asked Hollomon to speak at the rally and told the president about the plan to enlist student marshals. OU administrators and students were united in their desire to avoid violence, which they agreed might provoke a show of force from Governor Bartlett. They even feared that Bartlett might declare martial law at OU.

Hollomon returned to his home to find Gade still with students and OU employees. Chief administrators, including Burr and Jones, worked until the early hours of the morning as students shared concerns about what might

Although the counterculture movement had reached OU by 1971, the fashions of the 1960s were still popular, as seen in this photo of Walker Tower sixth-floor residents. *(OU 1815)*

happen the next day. Gade noted that the students were angry yet devoted to protecting OU from dangers within and without. "Their passion to take care of the university was really astounding," she said.

The next morning, copies of the *Oklahoma Daily* were circulated while some three thousand students gathered for the 9 A.M. protest rally on the North Oval. The issue featured a column by editor Karen Vineyard calling Tuesday's riot "the sickest day in the history of this campus." Hollomon hoped to keep May 6, 1970, from being described in the same fashion.

OU lowered the North Oval flag to half-staff to honor the Kent State victims and provided a flatbed truck as a platform for the two-hour rally, which started with a moment of silence. Some rally speakers promoted the impending student strike, while others preached nonviolence to the crowd. Among the speakers was President Hollomon, who was greeted with catcalls and heckling. "I believe you people have a right to an opinion and other people have a right to their opinion," he told the crowd. "And I'll die before that is taken away from you. . . . The most important thing we can do is give the right to you to disagree . . . to express yourself in a way that people can hear."

"Hollomon understood how the earth beneath our feet was shaking," said Joe Foote, whose job as a KTOK Radio reporter gave the student a unique perspective on the week of May 4. "The guy really got it, and he was on our side."

Hollomon backed up his words by opening his office to any student who wanted to talk. Hollomon spent most of two days addressing student concerns while his staff fielded phone calls from reporters, worried parents, and politicians.

The state's leading politician, Governor Bartlett, held a press conference in Oklahoma City that day. He informed the public that the Highway Patrol remained on standby and that he had called a National Guard "training alert." A control center had been set up for Bartlett to direct any use of force.

Back on OU's Norman campus, Hollomon continued to meet with students while small bands of students roved from office to office, holding temporary occupations. OUPD encouraged the students to leave; their efforts were unsuccessful and Hollomon soon received a phone call from Governor Bartlett's office demanding a solution. The president's only course of action was to expel the occupiers, so Hollomon chose to let sleeping dogs lie. One group in OU's Evans Hall purchasing office grew to seventy-five students who were happily talking and listening to music, while staff members tried in vain to work around them. At the end of the business day, the occupiers cleaned up after themselves before voluntarily leaving.

In the UOSA offices across campus, President Bill Moffitt met with his own endless stream of visitors. Then a phone call came inviting him to meet with Governor Bartlett at the executive mansion that evening. Moffitt, accompanied by fellow UOSA members Mike Kelly and Jim Todd, listened as the governor informed the students that he had the National Guard on standby, and said he "would not tolerate any disruption of the university," Moffitt told McKeen. When one of the students asked frankly who was in charge of OU, Bartlett said, "I run the university."

"We left the meeting with the clear impression that if there was peaceful picketing, it was going to cause something to happen," Moffitt said. The students returned to OU and awoke President Hollomon to discuss their plans for a strike vote the next day. They left with the confidence to move ahead with the strike vote.

While the daylong strike voting occurred on May 7, 1970, Hollomon and Moffitt worked to encourage nonviolence. "At a moment's notice," Moffitt informed a large group of student organizers, "troops are ready to pour onto this campus. If they do, somebody's going to get hurt and you know it won't be them."

The strike vote failed by a little more than two hundred votes. Through his network of students, Burr learned that focus was shifting to the May 12 "Field Day," an ROTC awards ceremony. In addition, student protestors picketed ten classroom buildings on Friday. Peace marshals, representing both students and faculty and wearing makeshift armbands with peace signs, took positions around the North and South Ovals to discourage conflict. During this period, McKeen states, Hollomon received several offers from Governor Bartlett to provide additional law enforcement. But Hollomon declined; OU would take care of its own.

The peace was kept in many ways. During the Friday demonstrations, Colonel Leroy Land noticed picketers shivering in the cold outside the OU armory. Land ordered an urn of coffee to be positioned within reach, and his spontaneous show of kindness effectively ended the demonstration. "Two young girls threw down their signs and said, 'If this is the way they're going to treat us, we're not going to picket anymore,'" Land told McKeen. Still, campus peace marshals kept a close watch leading up to the May 12 Field Day, even during two Jimi Hendrix concerts at the OU field house.

OU's administration and student leaders were busy preparing for the Field Day demonstration, scheduled at Oklahoma Memorial Stadium and coordinated by student Mike Wright. Wright led an evening planning session with more than four hundred students. When they learned that Chief Jones was nearby, he was invited in to answer questions. "Who makes the decision to call the Highway Patrol?" one student asked. "That is my decision," Jones replied. "If the campus police can't control the situation, I will summon the Highway Patrol."

Jones spelled out ground rules to ensure public safety:

Demonstrators would be required to stay in the south end zone and not interfere with ROTC students marching on the field. A demilitarized zone between the two groups would be patrolled by student and faculty marshals, including Mike Wright and Jody Bateman, a student normally considered one of OU's most committed radicals.

OU was as ready as it could be for Field Day.

A CRUCIBLE MOMENT

An hour before the May 12 Field Day demonstration was to begin, Chief Jones met with several hundred students on the South Oval and went over the rules once again, telling the crowd that there was "a thin line between lawful and unlawful assembly, and it can be crossed very quickly." OU legal counsel David Swank also reminded the students of the rights and responsibilities of assembly.

"They listened and there was an intercourse there, and a dialogue," according to Jones, relaying that students and administrators "understood each other fairly well when we left that forum." When the protestors moved to the stadium, however, they promptly went to the middle of the football field and sat, blocking the ROTC cadets from taking formation on the field. The gesture, in direct violation of the agreement the protestors had made, compelled Burr and the peace marshals to circle the nearly four hundred students, entreating them to move, while Jones requested cooperation via a bullhorn.

Watching from high above was President Hollomon, who stood in the press box near an open telephone line connecting directly to Governor Bartlett. Bartlett had sent Attorney General G. T. Blankenship and Public Safety Commissioner Bob Lester to the demonstration. In the west stands of the stadium were three thousand spectators. Many were family and friends of ROTC students; others simply wanted to witness what was about to unfold.

After an hour and half of cajoling, all but four demonstrators moved to the south end zone. The peace marshals and Burr pled with the four before they chose to peacefully submit to arrest in protest of the killings at Kent State and the escalation of the Vietnam War.

While student marshals like Mike Wright and Jody Bateman patrolled the south goal line and six OUPD officers in wool blazers manned the sidelines, OU football coach Chuck Fairbanks and two of his players arrived to volunteer. Their task would be to ensure that upset and vocal ROTC supporters stayed in their seats.

Unbeknownst to the students, spectators, and media, just beyond the stadium walls were 150 Oklahoma Highway Patrol members awaiting orders to quell any violence. The OHP officers were in position on the Sooners' practice field on the orders of Governor Bartlett, who had also staged contingencies from the Norman Police Department and National Guard a few miles away. All were prepared to move if the governor called.

OU administrators grew more nervous when the hundreds of protestors spilled outside the end zone and encroached upon the designated parade ground. Administrators discussed their options; rather than quit, Land chose to accommodate the dissidents by tightening the formation of his cadets. Field Day commenced with a military band and honorary guest Lieutenant General William Peers circling the cadets in a Jeep. The ceremony was greeted with catcalls, boos, and obscenities from the demonstrators.

In the midst of all this, President Hollomon received a phone call from Governor Bartlett announcing his intention to send in the National Guard. When Hollomon objected, Bartlett asked what OU's president could do to stop him. "I'll broadcast what they do to these kids," Hollomon said. "Every mother and father in Oklahoma will be on your back." The governor, undeterred, pledged that he would send in the guard if the demonstration deteriorated.

On the field, protestors maintained a steady stream of loud chants and obscenities while ROTC students received awards. Chief Jones watched carefully, while repeatedly reassuring Public Safety Commissioner Lester that it was not necessary to bring in the Oklahoma Highway Patrol officers. Jones could see that the university was achieving its goal of nonviolent protest through the efforts of student and faculty marshals, the Sooners team members and staff, and OUPD's officers. His belief was strengthened when two protestors helped carry an overheated ROTC cadet off of the field.

Field Day lasted for one excruciatingly long hour. At its closing, the demonstration had not descended into chaos and no students had been physically hurt. A total of four students were arrested for disrupting a lawful assembly and released that same evening. President Hollomon, Burr, Jones, and the student leaders all sagged with relief.

Student activist Mike Wright stated that he was well aware just how badly the day could have gone if any one of the factions involved—antiwar demonstrators, police, ROTC members, or supporters—had overreacted. "There would have been an explosion three ways. So it was a very tense and delicate situation, and it came off."

The worst had been avoided. Through the involvement of wildly disparate parts of the university community, OU had honored its students' constitutional right to assembly and allowed them to vent their fear and anger without one incident of violence, an overwhelming police presence, or overt threats. OU had closed ranks against interference from the governor and maintained its autonomy.

That evening Hollomon reflected on May 12 during a

Although he withstood the battle for his presidency, the often passionate and combative Hollomon chose to resign rather than continuing to make OU a center of controversy. *(OU 103)*

panel discussion before members of the media. Always a lightning rod, his remarks angered many. "It was peaceful and nobody got hurt and no bricks were hurled and no windows were broken, and I thought that was beautiful," Hollomon later explained. It was "certainly more pleasant than bloodshed and the horror of Kent State."

THE END BEGINS

Governor Bartlett was incensed by the Field Day demonstration. His sentiments were echoed by Commissioner Lester, whose report to the governor was unearthed by McKeen at the Oklahoma State Archives. "Although I was personally alarmed at the permissiveness toward the demonstrators, . . . I could not in good [conscience] request permission from you to bring state forces into the stadium, because there had been no open violence," Lester wrote. "It was apparent that the university officials were determined to permit the students and others who were there to carry out their intended purpose of disrupting the parade activities."

Both the governor and President Hollomon received bags of letters lambasting OU's handling of Field Day. Bartlett held a press conference criticizing Hollomon, and called for the OU president to meet with him privately on May 15, 1970. After the meeting, the governor publicly pledged his support of Hollomon and OU. But privately Bartlett plotted to end Hollomon's presidency.

Bartlett pressured the OU Board of Regents to fire Hollomon. He appointed supporter Bob Lollar to the board and made veiled comments to media that the Regents would force Hollomon to resign. Just when it looked as though the board would dismiss Hollomon on June 24, 1970, a single key vote swung the other way and his contract was extended for one year. Realizing the dangerous precedent they would set by buckling under outside pressure, the Regents righted their course. Hollomon, ever bold, credited the extension of his contract to the attention of local and national media, media he may have tipped to the controversy. Understandably his maneuver dismayed OU's Regents.

"You profess to love the university above yourself," Walter Neustadt, Jr., wrote to Hollomon. "Your apparent invitations [to national media] . . . were nothing more than an attempt to ridicule and embarrass the university while enhancing your own image. This action alone renders your words meaningless, mere rhetoric without substance."

On his part, Governor Bartlett responded negatively to the board's decision to keep Hollomon. He boldly stated during a press conference that Oklahomans had "lost patience with a divisive and less than professional performance by the university administration."

Yet other prominent voices supported Hollomon. "I don't know why everyone is so mad at Herb now," former President Cross told David Burr. "What he did that day [Field Day] was the greatest thing he ever did."

Despite winning the battle for his presidency and the support of so many, Hollomon shocked the university and all of Oklahoma by offering his resignation "with hesitation and anguish" at the very next Board of Regents meeting, on July 23, 1970.

Hollomon used the occasion to denounce Governor Bartlett and to warn the OU community of "the real tyranny we now face." "When my continued presence becomes the excuse for denying citizens and members of this community those fundamental values on which our way of life depends," Hollomon read from a public statement, "then I can no longer stand in silence. I cannot and will not be so used. . . . It is a noble enterprise that we embarked

upon together. And it must not fail. It will not die if the innovations we have attempted here can be separated from my personality, my style, or my beliefs. . . . *The Future of the University* must not be shelved."

Hollomon stipulated that his resignation would be effective on September 1, 1970. Before leaving the meeting, he asked the Regents to name Provost Pete Kyle McCarter as interim president.

Joe Foote, recording the meeting for KTOK and seated next to the president, was flattened by the announcement. "It was one of the most dramatic things in my life," he said forty-three years later. Foote and many other OU students were dismayed that Hollomon's stand for student protest in the wake of Kent State had resulted in his downfall. "It was a time that no human being could have governed at an optimal level," Foote said. "He did everything in the world to diffuse the situation; it's a shame that history has written him as the cause of it."

Despite his faults, Foote maintained, Hollomon may have been the best possible leader for OU during a crucial moment. "You could argue that he was the right person at the right time. What I saw with my own eyes as a student and a reporter was an intelligent, articulate, sophisticated man who sincerely wanted to lead the university in the right direction."

Hollomon reviewed his decision to leave OU in a 1980 interview. "I don't believe I could have efficiently and effectively led the university in the face of the governor and some of the newspapers bickering and harping on details which were of no significance to the future of the university," he said. "I left because I didn't think I could be useful any longer."

Years later, then–U.S. senator Dewey Bartlett looked back on the events of May 1970 and told Chief Jones that the university had handled a potentially explosive situation correctly. According to McKeen, the former Governor Bartlett admitted that he had been in the wrong.

"I've never regretted any part of it, either going to Oklahoma or leaving Oklahoma," Hollomon recollected a decade after leaving OU. "I came out of Oklahoma with the most cherished of possessions; I have a wife I would never have met." Herbert and Nancy Gade Hollomon married in December 1970 and moved to Cambridge, Massachusetts, where he served MIT as a consultant to the president and provost before taking the title of Japan Steel Industry Professor of Engineering.

Hollomon served as the founding director for MIT's Center for Policy Alternatives, which developed national technology strategies for the United States and other nations and helped to establish graduate programs in technology and policy management. He suffered a massive stroke in 1979, but recovered and joined the faculty of Boston College in 1983. Hollomon authored six books on technology and science.

"When people ask me what was the most interesting thing I've done in my life," Hollomon offered late in his career, "I say, 'To be president of the University of Oklahoma.'"

Gade and Hollomon would remain married until his death in May 1985. In commemoration, MIT named a memorial symposium in Hollomon's honor that explores the role of science and technology in solving critical issues of our times. Above any achievement, however, Hollomon is remembered as a passionate, driven man who stood for the things he believed in at any cost.

"Hollomon tore through life, leaving in his wake myriad expanded minds, changed lives, and reformed institutions," colleague and friend Donald Frey wrote upon Hollomon's death. "Combative, controversial, often ahead of his time, and always pushing those around him to do more and do better, he was a colorful and complex man. He touched all those around him in an intense and personal way."

PETE KYLE McCARTER
1970–1971

WHEN LOOKING BACK ON his year as OU's interim president, Pete Kyle McCarter once summed up, "We kept the doors open." Others viewed his appointment more generously. *Sooner Magazine* editor Connie Ruggles wrote when introducing the interim president to OU alumni and supporters: "An almost audible sigh went up in some quarters when Dr. Pete Kyle McCarter walked out of the provost's office and into the president's office."

Handpicked as OU interim president by President J. Herbert Hollomon upon his abrupt resignation in July 1970, McCarter had served as OU's first provost under Hollomon. Previous to his appointment as provost, he had served as vice president of the university under President Cross. McCarter initially came to OU as a professor of English in 1953 and played a key role in the development of OU's College of Liberal Studies.

The soft-spoken Mississippi native was a natural antidote to the anxiety and anger left in the wake of Hollomon's divisive departure. Known for a folksy manner and self-deprecating wit, McCarter pointed out the downside of his role, however: "I have been seeking a great deal of advice from a great many people on what an acting president, who is a lame duck by definition, can do to keep the university from going lame also," he said in an early address to faculty, "especially when no one can tell him how much time he has to do anything in."

TEARING AT
THE UNIVERSITY'S FABRIC

Greeted by a faculty divided between those still loyal to Hollomon and those resentful of the profound changes the former president had tried to implement, McCarter stated his support for Hollomon's plans and encouraged faculty members to "keep up our good labor." He also called for unity among the OU community. "This is the University of Oklahoma," McCarter said. "It is my earnest conviction that this institution occupies a place in the regard of the citizenry of this state that no other institution occupies." But he also cautioned faculty that many citizens felt OU was "in disarray" and encouraged them to put aside infighting and "petty carping." "We

have been tearing at our own fabric," McCarter told the faculty. "We have been wounding ourselves, and we have lesions to attend to. Fortunately, they are the kind of lesions, I think, that can be quickly healed. I ask you to do a very simple thing. Let's get back together."

Ever forthright, he voiced his concern that OU might stagnate during this interim period. McCarter instituted a plan that included goals to reestablish good public relations for OU, to recruit more minority faculty and staff members, and to build cooperation with the OU Medical Center campus. True to his word, McCarter appointed Wilbur Walker as OU's first black senior-level administrator, special assistant for minority affairs.

McCarter was an unexpected ally in OU's ongoing racial struggles, according to Dr. George Henderson, Sylvan N. Goldman and David Ross Boyd Professor Emeritus and the founder of OU's human relations program. Henderson, one of OU's first three black faculty members, admitted that he had made assumptions about McCarter based upon McCarter's background as a white southerner. "McCarter was not someone I counted on to help me push through changes that would open the university to more ethnic minority people," Henderson wrote in *Race and the University.* "After he took office, it became crystal clear to me how wrong I had been about him."

The medical campus posed its own problems. Vice President Dennis had resigned after butting heads with President Hollomon over the medical campus's autonomy, so that campus was without leadership. Dennis had formed his own comprehensive plan for the future, but left OU without a financial blueprint for the medical campus's growth. In his absence the Oklahoma City campus floundered.

Faced with contentious student relations, especially with student dissidents and student leaders who were shocked by what they saw as Hollomon's ouster at the hands of state politicians, McCarter soon inherited a series of student confrontations beginning with a cafeteria sit-in by black and Native American students on November 20, 1970. The sit-in occurred after a group of black female students insisted that they had been insulted by a Cross Center cafeteria worker and the Cross Center housing director. More than 150 angry students filled the cafeteria lobby and blocked its entrance, trapping several frightened cafeteria patrons and staff inside.

Black student leaders enlisted mediation from Dr. Henderson, who was their trusted adviser and friend. He spoke to the protestors and advised them to contact Jack Stout, director of OU Resident Programs. Stout and vice president of the university community David Burr came to the cafeteria and listened to the students as they stated their grievances. According to Henderson, Stout promised to address the students' concerns "with all deliberate speed." The students believed Stout and dispersed. Once again, OU used respect and goodwill rather than force to end a potentially volatile situation.

PEACE IN THE MIDST OF TROUBLE

Unrest, particularly related to the Vietnam War, was rife across the nation that year, but McCarter did his part to maintain the peace with dissident students. "I never failed to meet with them," he said of those participating in demonstrations and sit-ins, "but I refused to have any shouting matches. I like to think some of the diminution of tension was because I tried and so many others helped." McCarter said a key factor in his success was the relationship and camaraderie that OUPD chief Bill Jones and his staff had built with student demonstrators during Hollomon's presidency. "He had the confidence of the student dissidents. They would talk to him," McCarter said of Jones. "He was a very tall man during those troubled times. . . . He knew he wasn't dealing with criminals; he was dealing with students."

Nonetheless vandals made their mark at OU during the weekend of April 10 1971. Ku Klux Klan crosses were painted in orange on the lawn of the traditionally black Alpha Phi Alpha fraternity, Threshold '70 minority tutoring center, and Afro-American Cultural House. Swastikas were also found on the wall of OU's Hillel Foundation.

McCarter ordered additional night patrols of campus and met with seventy black students in a two-hour, closed-door session. He listened to the students' concerns and took their ideas into consideration. But McCarter's diplomacy could not quell all tensions on campus, such as when Afro-American Student Union chairman Erik Barnett interrupted proceedings at the annual Law Day luncheon to demand an end to institutional racism in the College of Law.

The ongoing U.S. involvement in the Vietnam War continued to create division at OU. McCarter worked out a compromise with protestors by approving an OU Student Association vote to cancel classes on March 3, 1971. Students were encouraged to use their free day to attend a national teach-in featuring former New York congressman and antiwar leader Allard K. Lowenstein and Pulitzer Prize–winning *New York Times* reporter David Halberstam.

Not everyone approved of OU's concessions to student protest. Outside Norman, OU supporters and conservative Oklahomans were disaffected by the campus conflicts and shied away from donating to the university. When plans were unveiled for a new multipurpose arena, McCarter remained skeptical of the project's success, until he was

able to convince former OU Regent and Phillips Petroleum Company board chairman John M. Houchin to head the $2 million private fund-raising drive.

McCarter did what he could to ease public fears and made it a point to invite alumni, faculty, and friends to attend OU football games and after-game parties at the president's home on Pickard Avenue. Even OU football games were a target for disruption, however, and bomb threats were common before most home games. "We usually had about fifteen minutes to decide whether to cancel or whether it was a bluff—again," McCarter said. "Each time, we decided to go ahead, but I didn't enjoy any football game."

The games also served as the stage for a battle to bring back Little Red, the longtime Native American mascot who had been banned during Hollomon's presidency. On two occasions, Native American students who had served as Little Red stomp-danced without permission at OU games and stirred arguments both favoring and opposing

The Pete Kyle McCarter Hall of Advanced Studies was named in 1971 to acknowledge McCarter's contributions to the university.
(OUCT 698)

the mascot. McCarter held fast to the ban on Little Red.

Yet another issue arose when the 1971 *Sooner Yearbook* was printed with a thirty-three-page section featuring contentious photos from the May 1970 demonstrations, a photo of a man smoking marijuana, and a heavily screened shot of a nude woman. The book won mention by the Associated Collegiate Press but was vilified by alumni and parents.

Many small crises competed for McCarter's attention, but he never lost focus on OU's central mission of education. "We tried to maintain a sense of humor," he said. "We always were mindful that we had an obligation to the faculty and to the majority of students." McCarter's obligations included the decision to reshuffle Hollomon's administration. He would allow vice president of university fund-raising Thurman J. White to return to his first love of administering continuing education. In his place McCarter appointed Burr as vice president of development, making Burr the first administrator to focus solely on private giving.

McCarter surely felt relief on April 20, 1971, when the OU Board of Regents named Paul F. Sharp as OU's next president and thanked McCarter for his service. "The excellent job that Dr. McCarter and his staff did, coupled with the loyalty of the faculty during this unsettled period, cannot be over-emphasized," board chairman Horace Calvert said. In appreciation, the Regents christened a six-story building at OU's Oklahoma Center for Continuing Education as the Pete Kyle McCarter Hall of Advanced Studies.

McCarter would continue in his role as interim president until Sharp took office in August 1971. He happily served as provost again until January 1973, when he returned to teaching as a Regents Professor in OU's English Department. The following year, McCarter received OU's highest award, the Distinguished Service Citation. A scholarship for graduate English majors was named in McCarter's honor, and he lived in Norman until his death in 1988.

"Pete Kyle McCarter was a gentleman of the old school," reflected friend J.R. Morris, OU provost emeritus and Regents Professor emeritus. "He was the prototype of the scholar-administrator."

PAUL FREDERICK SHARP
1971–1978

IN SPRING 1971, OU was still reeling from the abrupt departure of its charismatic but divisive president J. Herbert Hollomon. Hundreds of candidates for OU's ninth president were reviewed and the list was narrowed down to three finalists. Among them was Paul F. Sharp, president of Drake University in Iowa.

Sharp was an obvious contender. The Missouri native had served as president of Hiram College and as chancellor of the University of North Carolina at Chapel Hill. A history scholar, he had received prestigious academic awards, including the Fulbright Scholarship, Ford Faculty Fellowship, and a Guggenheim Fellowship. He held a doctorate from the University of Minnesota and was the author of *Whoop-Up Country: The Canadian-American West, 1865–1885,* which had won the coveted Spur Award for nonfiction from the Western Writers of America.

Sharp had Oklahoma roots. His mother had taught in Oklahoma Territory and sent her eighteen-year-old son to attend their church school, Phillips University in Enid. There Sharp met fellow debate team member Rose Anderson. "We've been debating ever since," Sharp once said of his marriage, "and I'm still losing."

Paul and Rose Sharp made a winning team, and their combined talents convinced the OU Board of Regents to look no further. The board offered Sharp the presidency, along with three expressed goals: to restore the public's confidence in OU, to gain legislative support for the university, and to launch a major fund-raising campaign. More than capable of completing all three goals, Sharp, nonetheless, had reservations about OU after learning of his predecessor's troubles with then-governor Dewey Bartlett. Before accepting the board's offer, he met with newly elected Oklahoma governor David Hall, who

pledged in a public statement that he would not interfere with the university.

In April 1971 Sharp was introduced as OU's next president during an Evans Hall press conference. "Dr. Sharp returns to Oklahoma with an understanding of the people of this state and with proven ability," Board of Regents chairman Horace K. Calvert said by way of introduction. He called the fifty-three-year-old administrator "a person of great personal warmth and integrity . . . his ability to establish rapport with individuals of diverse ages and backgrounds enhanced our opinion of him. Last but not least, we came to know his wife, Rose, and we were thoroughly delighted with her."

For his part, Sharp expressed great pleasure at being back in Oklahoma and promised to "use energy, imagination, and hard work" in his new role as president and professor of education and history. "I've never worked with people I enjoy more than students," he said. "That's why I'm here."

THE REALITY OF THE TIMES

Enthusiasm notwithstanding, Sharp was realistic about the challenges he faced. Oklahoma's education spending ranked near the bottom nationally, and OU enrollment had declined while inflation and rising energy costs took a toll on operating expenses. The news was even worse on OU's medical campus, which was teetering on the brink of insolvency. The Oklahoma State Legislature established a special committee that revealed the medical campus faced issues ranging from poor administration to neglect in collecting unpaid bills.

The mood was understandably bleak among OU students, faculty, and staff on both campuses. The conflicts surrounding Hollomon's presidency and resignation had not abated, and factions of the OU community still longed for the stability of the George Lynn Cross era. Faculty and staff also lacked a sufficient retirement plan, an injustice that Sharp vowed to fix. Additionally, supporters and alumni were leery of OU's growing reputation as a hotbed of radical activity. An unnamed OU Regent had told Sharp that the university was in "total disarray."

"In all truth, I was shocked by the disgruntled and disenchanted faculty and the restless, almost hostile student leadership," Sharp later stated. "It took a long time for me to gain acceptance."

Sharp had always enjoyed cordial relationships with students during his previous university presidencies and as a professor. He respected students' rights to self-determination but also recognized that student unrest was often aimed inappropriately at higher education. "It has to be an irony that in some places in this country students have

Dr. Paul Sharp and future first lady Rose Sharp at the press conference announcing his selection as OU's ninth president. *(OU EMP 71-116)*

President Sharp visits with students on OU's Norman campus.
(OU EMP 72-139)

First Lady Rose Sharp gives a tour of the president's home to members of the Cwens women's honor society (now Lambda Sigma). *(OU EMP 71-161)*

tried to destroy their best friend," he told reporters.

If student protest had brought about many positive changes nationwide, it had also produced serious side effects. In addition to student deaths at Kent State University and the University of Wisconsin at Madison, the deaths of several university presidents had been linked to protests. Multiple university presidents had also been fired for either being too strict or too lenient with protestors. "Universities are singularly inept to handle this kind of a revolt," Sharp said. "They are places of reason, and you can't reason with a mob."

The mob at OU had focused its protests on the issues of individual freedom, the war in Vietnam, and racial and gender inequities. The OU Student Association was charged with addressing many of these student concerns and was considered a pacesetter in American student government. OU's Student Code, with its origins in President Hollomon's tenure, was deemed "a magnificent document, a triumph for students striving for responsibility," *Sooner Yearbook* contributor Michael Vitt wrote. Yet the UOSA was split by an invalidated election and quickly lost student backing. "It appeared to be headed for an end, smothered in internal dogfights and external apathy," Vitt added.

While student leaders fought, Sharp focused his early efforts on achieving parity for OU's black students. The presidential search committee had secured a promise from Sharp that he would finish the affirmative action initiatives started by Hollomon and interim president Pete Kyle McCarter. He quickly made several key black appointments and encouraged OU Personnel Services to write an affirmative action plan that would increase the number of minority employees.

Sharp's reforms, although appreciated, were considered inadequate by black students frustrated by the glacial pace of change in the decades since Ada Lois Sipuel Fisher had faced the Supreme Court. Black students frequently came to OU from segregated hometowns and expected diversity to be appreciated on a college campus. Instead they often found themselves surrounded by unwelcoming white students and even hostile professors.

"The smoldering fire of racial discord had reached a searing level by the fall semester of 1971," George Henderson wrote in his book, *Race and the University: A Memoir.* Henderson was the third black professor ever hired at OU and became the first black citizen to purchase a house in Norman in 1968. He founded the university's Human Relations Department and he was duly recognized for his excellence in teaching and service.

Henderson's fiery metaphor unfortunately became reality during Sharp's first months at OU, when arsonists attacked four residence halls across campus. More than twenty-five people suffered smoke inhalation, and the damage to OU's residence halls was in excess of $200,000. According to rumors, the fires were intended to trigger a race riot. Both blacks and whites pointed the finger at each other. Fistfights between black and white students became commonplace on campus, including a large fight between members of the black fraternity Alpha Phi Alpha and white fraternity Phi Kappa Sigma. Racial slurs shouted at black students frequently prompted violence; the same slurs and epithets had also been written on the pavement in front of the Alpha Phi Alpha house. Soon the conflicts became even more physical. "Intramural games were broken up with tire chains and fistfights," Sharp recalled.

"The extent of the verbal and physical conflicts on campus was grave," Henderson wrote, "and because of it, black-white relationships were edging closer to the edge of irreparableness." The OU Regents were warned to do something before students were injured. An already volatile situation threatened to erupt when a pellet gun was fired at a black female student walking across campus and a bullet was fired into the Alpha Phi Alpha living room.

Against this backdrop of chaos, Henderson calmly offered a series of recommendations. In an *Oklahoma Daily* column, he implored students to stop telling racial jokes, to include black students in informal gatherings, and to invite them into their homes. Henderson also asked that OU commit to promoting blacks in upper levels of the university administration and advocated the appointment of a black OU Regent.

Sharp responded with the help of vice president for the university community J.R. Morris. The president ordered his administrators to work harder on communication with black students, to include black history courses in the OU curriculum, and to hire more black faculty and staff members. In 1973 alone, OU's Black Ethnic Studies program was established, Gloria Smith became OU's first black dean, at the College of Nursing, and Walter Mason was appointed as the university's first affirmative action officer. Soon thereafter, OU's first biracial residence hall was established with one hundred students, making the university home to the largest racially integrated student housing unit in Oklahoma. Henderson, who extolled Sharp as "a president with a heart for oppressed people," wrote that it would be several more years before integration spread across OU student housing; however, the biracial residence hall was an important first step.

FIGHTING FOR BALANCE

Other minority groups, including Native Americans, gays, and women, also demanded changes at OU. Women celebrated when the OU Board of Regents welcomed its first female member, Nancy Davies of Enid. But the university's three hundred Native American students were dismayed when the UOSA cut funding for the Sequoyah Indian Club, which had been overshadowed by the more political American Indian Student Association. The Norman Gay Alliance for Sexual Freedom was formally recognized by the UOSA in 1972, which qualified the group for a portion of student fees. However, the resulting onslaught of negative feedback from citizens and members of the Oklahoma State Legislature led the OU Board of Regents to form a committee to examine student organization funding and the role of the UOSA. The gay alliance chose to withdraw its request for recognition rather than risk the board curtailing student oversight.

Disquiet among OU's student body continued unabated. President Sharp met twice weekly with students in the cafeteria and encouraged them to express their complaints. But some issues were simply beyond Sharp's reach. "Week after week, militants confronted us with angry and sometimes impossible requests," he said. He credited Morris with using constructive leadership to fulfill reasonable requests and calming those students he could not help. Peaceful demonstrations were a fixture of the times and continued at OU; unfortunately, occasional violence continued as well, including firebombs set off outside Evans Hall and

The president and first lady *(left photo, second from right)* promoted the university whenever possible, from offering personal alumni tours of the Norman campus to posing with members of the university's janitorial staff. *(OU EMP 72-238, 72-284)*

In the early 1970s, demonstrations, fights, and deepening chaos at OU culminated in the 1973 firebombing of the president's home on Pickard Avenue. *(OU EMP 7394)*

a plethora of false bomb threats. Due to safety concerns, large-scale events traditionally held at the president's home on Pickard Avenue were relocated to campus or canceled altogether.

During this same period, two OU graduate assistants stripped naked in front of students in separate incidents as a means to make anti-establishment statements. Though certainly less serious than arson and fistfights, the incidents created yet another flurry of negative publicity aimed squarely at Oklahoma's flagship university.

"It was a tense time," Rose Sharp recalled of her family's first few years at OU. Legislators and alumni called frequently to complain, along with concerned parents. "Students' families wanted the university to straighten them out," the president's wife said. The Sharps focused on engaging students by bringing in challenging speakers, such as those provided by the new Oklahoma Scholar-Leadership Enrichment Program, established by Governor David Boren with its headquarters at OU, and involved students in as many decisions as possible. "Students wanted to be included in everything, and you could do that to a certain extent," she added.

Sharp and his administration were eager for any tools that might help them navigate the constantly choppy waters. Help came in the form of a Cornell University symposium at which university presidents could exchange best practices for weathering unrest. A sample of the group's suggestions spotlighted the grave concerns Sharp and his colleagues faced daily: establish a secret exit in the president's office to avoid behind held captive by demonstrators; establish a designated hiding place in the president's home in case of attack; enact evacuation procedures for the president's children at the first sign of trouble; establish a single spokesperson for the university during crisis; and install separate phones in

the president's home for media and the public, staff, and family, and a direct line to university police.

The Cornell guidelines may have helped the Sharps avoid injury on February 23, 1973, when a firebomb was launched at the front door of the president's house. "We were asleep one night and we heard this noise. It sounded like a transformer blowing," Rose Sharp recalled. President Sharp peered out the front door and, realizing that it was on fire, ran to the OUPD phone. As smoke began to fill the house, the Sharps became separated and exited by different doors. OUPD was at the scene in moments; as they swarmed the property, they could not locate Rose and worried that she was trapped inside. Luckily, the Sharps reunited outside their home unharmed, but the president's house did not fare as well. The home suffered extensive smoke damage and was uninhabitable for six weeks. The Sharps moved into the cottages at the Oklahoma Center for Continuing Education while the house and all their belongings were cleaned. When the couple returned to Pickard Avenue, they were greeted by OU Native American students who asked to conduct a cedar blessing for their home.

The Sharps watched as the students burned cedar boughs collected at a sacred site and waved them in each corner of the house and over the president and first lady while praying—both in English and their tribal language—that the Sharps would never be touched by fire again. "It was a beautiful service," Rose Sharp said. "We were very touched by their emotion and their sincerity."

Unfortunately, OU had more tough times ahead in 1973, when six students were killed in a private airplane crash at the nearby Goldsby airport and five OU students made state headlines after being arrested for illegally entering Tinker Air Force Base to protest the Vietnam War.

With the Paris Peace Accords in January, the Vietnam

War was finally coming to an end in spring 1973. "When news of peace finally came . . . radios blared in dorms, in the apartments of veterans already returned to school, and in the newsroom of Copeland Hall, where [*Oklahoma Daily*] students anxiously prepared to print the story of the year . . . of the decade," *Sooner Yearbook* editors wrote. "There was a feeling of bitter relief, silent sadness, and joy simultaneously."

"SOONER MAGIC" PULLS OU THROUGH TOUGH TIMES

Although relieved of the hardships of war, Oklahomans and all Americans still faced the toughest economic period since the Great Depression. State funding for education plummeted, along with federal monies for research. President Sharp instituted cuts across the board and kept OU administrative expenses below that of all other Oklahoma state schools. But there were casualties from the cuts, including WNAD Radio and the University School, the well-respected College of Education laboratory site that had operated at OU since 1917 and produced several Rhodes Scholars.

Other dour OU news that year included the resignation of Sooner football coach Chuck Fairbanks. Fairbanks invited assistant coach Barry Switzer to join him as offensive line coach for the New England Patriots, but Switzer remained at OU to become the Sooners' head coach. The football program was soon under scrutiny when the NCAA accused assistant coach Bill Michael of conspiring (while Fairbanks was still coach) to falsify the high school transcripts of two incoming freshman players. Michaels resigned, and OU was forced to forfeit nine of the 1972 season's twelve games, as well as the team's Big 8 championship and Sugar Bowl victory over Penn State University. The Sooners were also banned from participating in bowl games until 1975 and from television appearances until 1976.

Football fans were additionally dismayed when the OU Athletic Department announced that it would begin assigning tickets based upon fans' financial support. The plan raised $500,000 a year and financed the $5 million renovation of Oklahoma Memorial Stadium, which included the addition of nine thousand seats in an upper deck, a "prestige area" with chair seating, the Jack Santee lounge, and a new press box. Still, OU football enjoyed tremendous success under Switzer, going undefeated in 1973 and 1974 and winning back-to-back national championships in 1974 and 1975.

The Sooner basketball team had gone through its own trials in 1973, as Head Coach John MacLeod resigned and was replaced by former OU All-American Lester Lane. Before the season began, Lane collapsed and died, at age forty-one, following a pickup game with OU faculty members in the

President Sharp poses with OU's new football coach, Barry Switzer, at a 1973 football recruiting dinner. *(OU EMP 7346)*

Field House. A bright spot in OU athletics was the success of the university's wrestling program, which won the NCAA championship in 1973. The new Murray Case Sells Swim Complex and the $5.3 million Lloyd Noble Center were also dedicated that year. The Noble Foundation made OU's first $1 million gift to name the facility in honor of the late oilman and philanthropist. Settling into the new facility was OU's brand-new women's basketball team, one of several women's sports that would be added under the provisions of the new Title IX federal law requiring equal treatment of women in athletic programs.

The Sooners happily celebrated their first national football title since 1956 when Switzer led the team to a flawless season and won the Big 8 title. Most remarkably, the team won the 1974 national championship without competing at a post-season bowl, due to its unbeaten record and number-one Associated Press Poll ranking. Among the team's standouts were quarterback Steve Davis, defensive linemen Lee Roy and Dewey Selmon, and "Little Joe" Washington, a five-foot-ten running back whose silver shoes were almost as famed as his speed and agility. "When Little Joe carried the ball he created more confusion and utter chaos among defensive lines than a panty raid in an old folks' home," *Sooner Yearbook* quipped.

Panty raids had been the fad of the 1950s. The 1970s featured its own fad—streaking—and Rose Sharp credits the running joke with vaporizing tensions and helping OU to regain its sense of humor. "There were streakers everywhere," she recalled with a grin. "They came by our house, painted and with nothing on. It was funny. You laughed, and you looked for them."

At commencement one year, OU Police Department chief Bill Jones anticipated streakers and set aside a stack of blankets that could be thrown over television cameras. Rose Sharp said Jones's foresight came in handy when "all of a sudden the laughter started and it got louder and louder and you knew what had happened." A streaker, his body painted silver, emerged from behind the commencement stage on a bicycle and rode halfway across the football field before escaping capture.

For a brief time in 1974, OU's attention shifted away from football and fads to focus on the university's internal politics. Former interim president and provost Pete Kyle McCarter returned to teaching, and OU hired Dr. I. Moyer Hunsberger of the State University of New York at Albany as provost. Hunsberger's controversial, restrictive policies on tenure at SUNY had prompted student sit-ins; his reputation preceded him to Oklahoma and created friction with OU faculty who believed that Hunsberger unfairly ascribed to the philosophy of "publish or perish." The *Oklahoma Daily* reported that faculty openly resented the new provost, and it alluded to a nickname of "Attila the Hunsberger." He would resign within the year, citing the unfavorable publicity that had followed him from New York.

OU soon appointed its first female provost, Barbara Uehling. OU women celebrated Uehling's addition as provost, which represented the university's second-highest post and was the most advanced position that a woman had ever held at OU. Uehling would stay at the university for only two years before being named chancellor at the University of Missouri, where she attracted national attention as the first woman to lead a land-grant university.

In Oklahoma City, attention was focused on the remarkable recovery of OU's newly renamed Health Sciences Center. Sharp had committed early on to saving and growing the OU College of Medicine, an effort that paid off substantially year after year. In 1970, the Oklahoma City campus consisted of two hospitals and the College of Medicine building, and only one thousand enrolled students in medicine, allied health, and nursing courses. Sharp oversaw the completion of the $3.5 million Basic Sciences Education building, followed by the 1971 opening of the OU College of Dentistry. The Oklahoma State Legislature approved the OU College of Medicine–Tulsa in 1972 as a clinical branch of the Oklahoma City campus, and practice clinics were proposed in several communities across the state. The following year OU transferred Children's Hospital to the state welfare system and made administrative changes at University Hospital. The $12 million Everett Tower was scheduled for completion at University Hospital in 1974.

Most important, Sharp hired Dr. William G. Thurman as the first provost for the Health Sciences Center. Thurman established a strong administrative and financial system that was considered a model among peer institutions. Through his leadership, the Health Sciences Center made plans for the Biomedical Sciences Building and College of Dentistry building, both $10.5 million projects; the $5.2 million College of Nursing building; and the $6.3 million library building.

A key to the Health Sciences Center's success was ongoing collaboration between OU, state agencies, and private medical facilities that were part of the 1964 consortium known as the Oklahoma Health Center. Associated clinics and research facilities cropped up near the Health Sciences Center, including the Dean A. McGee Eye Institute, which housed OU's Department of Ophthalmology; Presbyterian Hospital; and the Oklahoma Medical Research Foundation. The OU College of Pharmacy was also scheduled to move from the Norman campus to Oklahoma City in 1976. Sharp considered the completion of the Health Sciences Center his most difficult challenge and his most significant accomplishment. "It was the product of a great dream," he said. "We faced a crisis and out of it came a great center."

Much of the Health Sciences Center's success was due to private donors, and Sharp knew that OU's long-term future would depend upon successful fund-raising. "To have a truly quality university, private giving is essential," he said. "It can't be done with state funding alone." Previously, OU focused fund-raising appeals on special projects, such as the $4.2 million raised for the new OU Law Center in 1974. But Sharp envisioned an integrated program of fund-raising that would allow OU to pursue academic excellence as well as special projects. He appointed Vice President of Development David Burr as the first vice president for university affairs, making Burr responsible for private fund-raising as well as alumni, donor, and public relations. Burr's decades of OU experience, his warm but dogged nature, and his absolute devotion to the university made him uniquely qualified to move OU into the top twenty of public institutions raising funds from private sources.

NEW EXPECTATIONS AND OPPORTUNITIES

The University of Oklahoma was in sore need of private monies. State funding for all of higher education was only $14.5 million, which was insufficient to cover even regular operating expenses. Costs had been cut in every possible area, to the point that OU and Oklahoma State University chose to consolidate several graduate programs. Private funding allowed Sharp to identify academic areas that were underperforming yet had the potential for excellence. He directed private funds to business, philosophy, geology, geography, chemistry, and meteorology; as a result, he revitalized each program.

The president also endowed five chairs with private funds, including the Merrick Chair in Western American History and chairs dedicated to energy, banking, oncology, and surgery. In addition, private funds paid for an electron microscopy laboratory and established OU's Oil Well Blowout Prevention School on South Base.

Private giving made other long-range achievements possible, including a $200,000 endowment from the family of Mrs. Walter Neustadt of Ardmore to establish the biennial *Books Abroad* literary prize, which today is known as the Neustadt Prize for International Literature awarded by *World Literature Today*. And a $1 million endowment established the Karcher Distinguished Lecture Series in the sciences to honor the 1916 OU alumnus Dr. J. Clarence Karcher, who developed the reflection seismographic method of oil exploration. Karcher's method was credited with identifying most of the world's petroleum reserves.

OU's rise continued in 1975, the year fresh-faced 1968 law alumnus David Boren swept past the political old guard to become Oklahoma's governor at the young age of thirty-four. Earlier, George and Cleo Cross, who usually stayed out of politics, had attended a capital rally carrying brooms, the symbol of Boren's reform campaign. As governor, Boren openly supported Sharp and often telephoned members of the Board of Regents to urge them to do the same.

Most statewide headlines were dominated not by politics, however, but by another winning Sooner football season. Having ended NCAA probation, the Sooners won

Students outside Brown's College Corner at the intersection of Boyd Street and Asp Avenue offer a glimpse into both the fashions and landscape of 1977. *(OUCT 4482)*

the Big 8 championship and a second national championship after defeating the University of Michigan in the Orange Bowl. Baseball also won its third consecutive Big 8 championship that year, and the Sooner men's basketball team welcomed new head coach Dave Bliss. Bliss helped lead the team, which had not won a conference title since 1949, to the Big 8 championship and to the NCAA championships for the first time in thirty-one years. "It was a wonderful time, and it really did help," Rose Sharp said of OU's 1970s athletic successes. "It helped in the state, it helped with the students. There was a buoyancy."

The football team's winning ways were bolstered by the charismatic personality of Coach Barry Switzer, who lent his charm offensive wherever it was needed. On one occasion, Rose Sharp called on the coach to attend an annual luncheon for the wives of Oklahoma state legislators. "When Barry Switzer walked into a room, everything stopped," Rose related. "There was a presence there." Switzer gave a rousing speech, and then promised the ladies that he would dedicate a play in their honor. He even confided the exact moment for them to watch for the play during the annual OU-Nebraska game.

The Sharps rode the wave of OU popularity into 1976, the year that the Sooners welcomed their first black quarterback, Thomas Lott. "Let me tell you, we had more telephone calls over that than anything else," Rose Sharp said, recalling with steely dismay that more than three hundred people from across the nation called OU to say that a black man was not talented enough to lead the Sooners.

Lott quickly proved them all wrong, leading the team to victory against the University of Wyoming at the Fiesta Bowl in his first year and to the national championship game at the Orange Bowl in 1977. There the Sooners lost to the University of Arkansas. The next year, the Sooners would return to the Orange Bowl and beat the University of Nebraska. However, the national championship went to the University of Alabama for its Sugar Bowl win.

Rose Sharp said that one side benefit of football was getting to know the coaches and players. The Sharps frequently traveled with the team, and Rose enjoyed sitting next to a "chatty" Dewey Selmon, whose outgoing personality belied his huge defensive presence on the football field. The president and first lady also proudly represented OU at grand dinners and dances held before each Orange Bowl, where Rose wore a custom-made ballroom skirt meticulously embellished with a scissortail flycatcher, Sooner Schooner, and the Oklahoma state seal.

Campus spirits remained high throughout 1976, as the entire nation celebrated the U.S. Bicentennial. Patriotic fever swept the country, and OU brought back traditional Homecoming events that had been curtailed during the turbulence of the late 1960s and early 1970s, including a bonfire,

President Sharp and Vice President for the University Community J.R. Morris pose in costume for the "Welcome Back" party, an annual event for faculty and staff that often featured skits and other programs. *(OU EMP 77450)*

pep rally, and parade. A Bicentennial concert capped off the weekend at the Lloyd Noble Center featuring famed comedian and actor Bob Hope and Boston Pops Orchestra conductor Arthur Fiedler.

Not everyone celebrated, however. A column in the *Oklahoma Daily* reminded students that black citizens still did not fully share in America's promise in 1976. Yet a sure sign that many of OU's tensions had melted away came when the UOSA sponsored a series of "White Paper" meetings in which students were invited to air their concerns. Only a handful of students attended, and the problems addressed were limited to such issues as basketball tickets, parking, and classroom pencil sharpeners.

As tensions eased, large social events returned to the president's home, including student luncheons and an annual "Welcome Back" party for faculty and staff that often offered televised football games in one room and music in another. The evenings culminated in a program; one year, Rose Sharp proved she was both a good sport and an accomplished dancer by performing the Charleston for her guests.

OU also invited the public to its celebrations, such as when the inaugural Medieval Fair was held in spring 1977 on OU's South Oval. The Medieval Fair, now Oklahoma's largest weekend event, has been named one of the top one hundred local events in the nation by the Events Media Network.

A TIME TO CELEBRATE, A TIME TO MOVE ON

OU pride had clearly returned to the campus and state, and countless supporters from the across the nation sent congratulatory letters and calls to the president's office. "One was raving about how he liked Paul and the things

OU's inaugural Medieval Fair in April 1977 featured a sword fight in the sunken garden of the South Oval. Today the fair has grown into Oklahoma's largest weekend event. *(OUCT 2173)*

The newly built Biomedical Sciences Building in 1975, seen here against the backdrop of downtown Oklahoma City, reflected Sharp's focus on the OU Health Sciences Center. *(Courtesy Robert M. Bird Library)*

Germany while it was still under Communist control. "We enjoyed meeting people from all over; it was a bonus I never expected."

President Sharp was determined to bring a different type of bonus to OU and made good on his early promise to provide retirement benefits for faculty and staff by enrolling the university in TIAA-CREF, long believed to be the national standard in education retirement. The university paid all of its employees' required 15 percent contribution and earned the loyalty of employees, who were now assured of a decent, reliable retirement benefit.

Not content with all these accomplishments, President Sharp moved OU forward even further in 1977 through private giving. State funding continued to decrease, from 17.1 percent of OU's total budget when he had become president in 1971 to 9.5 percent in 1977. To help bridge the gap, Sharp instituted the President's Council, an association of alumni and friends each donating $1,000 to OU annually. The group would later transition into the OU Associates program. And, in an even more ambitious effort, Sharp launched the $50 million Gift of Quality campaign; within a year, $10 million of the campaign total had been secured.

Enthusiasm for OU continued to rise, bolstered by the university's success in athletics. OU gymnast Bart Conner participated in the 1976 Montreal Olympics and won the American Cup in 1977. That same year, near-capacity crowds supported the OU Sooners basketball team, and women's softball was established under head coach Marita Hynes. The coming months would thrill Sooner football fans as running back Billy Sims rushed for 1,896 yards, a record that would not be broken at OU for nearly thirty years and that later earned Sims the 1978 Heisman Trophy.

The Sharps continued to follow the Sooners football team on the road, and one such trip would forever change Paul and Rose Sharp's lives. While on the bus to the annual

he'd read about OU in the paper," Rose Sharp recalled with a laugh. "He went on and on about how impressed he was with the administration and then added, 'I would have sent you your picture from the paper, but they don't allow scissors here.'"

OU's image had also reached around the globe, thanks to the Oklahoma Center for Continuing Education's Advanced Programs, which provided degree opportunities to more than 1,500 U.S. military members serving at bases overseas. President and Mrs. Sharp made a point of traveling to each of the twenty Advanced Programs sites during his tenure. "It was such a wonderful cross-cultural experience," she said, adding that their adventures included sleeping in the Saudi Arabian desert and traveling to East

The Sharps worked hard to bolster OU's image both at home and abroad, promoting the internationalization of the campus. Here, Rose Sharp poses with members of the OU International Women's Club in 1975. *(OU EMP 75503)*

To promote a spirit of service and community, the Sharps and other OU administrators offered an evening of free babysitting for married students in 1978.
(OU EMP 78226)

OU-OSU game in Stillwater on November 4, 1978, President Sharp complained of a headache. His symptoms worsened and the couple rushed back to Norman with his staff. The president was admitted to Norman Regional Hospital, where the attending physician informed Rose that her husband had suffered a stroke.

"He said Paul would probably never walk again and would certainly never drive again," she recalled. "But they underestimated him and his determination, and the skill of the OU Physical Therapy Department."

"I thought he should resign immediately, that this was a warning," Rose said. With his mental faculties still untouched, Sharp and his team of OU vice presidents agreed, however, that he would not resign for the time being. He began the hard work of recovery as physical therapists taught him to crawl and walk again. Sharp regained his physical functions slowly and painfully. Still, "when our [adult] children came home at Christmas, we had long discussions and finally convinced Paul that twenty-four years as a president was long enough," Rose said. The president announced his formal resignation at the January 1979 Board of Regents meeting. He agreed to remain president until

August, which would give the university time to search for a successor.

"OU has passed its transition period," Sharp said in announcing his retirement to the public. "It has kept up with social issues and is ahead on some. It is time to think of a third career." The Sharps, ready for their next chapter, had no regrets about the years they had spent as OU's president and first lady. "It really was wonderful, because it was one of the few team jobs left," Rose Sharp later said. "It was exciting, it was busy, it was full."

With J.R. Morris stepping in as acting president until a national search could be conducted, Paul Sharp was granted a six-month leave of absence. He and Rose traveled to many places they had visited during their travels with OU Advanced Programs and toured Australia, where they had lived during the year that Paul was a Fulbright Scholar.

Upon their return to Norman, the former president accepted an appointment as Regents Professor of History and Higher Education. He taught at OU for twenty-four years, with his last four years spent teaching in OU's revitalized Honors College. Sharp also remained active in the Norman community and with many of the professional associations he had led, including the Federal American Council of Education, the Board of Association of American Colleges, and the Board of Educational Testing Services. He worked as an educational specialist for the U.S. State Department and served on the North Central Association Commission on Higher Education.

"Paul was a natural-born leader," Rose Sharp said. "He would be on a committee, and by the second meeting he'd be the chairman of it." She pointed out that Sharp's work as an education mentor also helped steer a dozen former OU deans and administrators toward careers as university presidents.

The Sharps stayed involved with OU, attending many games, plays, and arts events. When then–OU president Frank Horton invited the Sharps and their administrative team to a dinner on Pickard Avenue, he asked for details about the conflicts and fears they had faced in the early 1970s. The group talked for more than three hours. "When we were ready to leave, President Horton looked at all of us and asked, 'Why did you stay?'" Rose said. "There was dead silence for a minute and then someone said, 'Well, I guess it was because we were committed to something bigger than ourselves. We not only wanted the university to survive, we wanted it to be stronger because of the crisis.'"

The Sharps had done just that by helping OU outlast the turmoil that had swept its campuses and leading the university toward prosperity. Paul Sharp would finally retire from the OU classroom in 1998 at the age of eighty-one, and his and Rose Sharp's efforts were recognized in many fashions. In 1994, a new concert hall in Catlett Music Center was given

Although President Sharp retired after suffering a stroke, he fully recovered and returned to teach at OU for two more decades. The president emeritus and former first lady remained devoted to the university. *(OU EMP 80124)*

President Sharp's name to honor his long support of the arts. He was inducted into the Oklahoma Higher Education Hall of Fame and received an honorary OU degree. Mrs. Sharp received OU's Distinguished Service Citation, and OU scholarships carry both of their names. President and Mrs. Boren also commissioned an OU rose garden to be designed in Rose's honor.

Perhaps no honor meant quite so much as when the Oklahoma Health Center Foundation recognized Paul Sharp in 2003 as a "Living Treasure" for his dedication to saving the OU Health Sciences Center. The award noted that Sharp was "the consummate teacher, mentor, and role model in higher education. "To say that he was instrumental [in the formation of the Health Sciences Center] is an understatement," said Hershel Lamirand, executive director of the Oklahoma Health Center Foundation. "He was critical."

In accepting the award, Sharp offered a brief speech titled, "What I Have Learned in Eighty-five Years of Life," which Rose Sharp calls a crystallization of her husband's core beliefs. "The most important decision you will make in your lifetime is your choice of a lifetime partner," the speech began, before Sharp entreated the crowd to pursue lives imbued with integrity, education, and humor. He closed by saying, "To complete your life, you must commit yourself to something greater than yourself—to a cause—to an institution, to an idea."

For thirty-eight years, Paul Sharp's cause was the University of Oklahoma. When OU's ninth president died on February 19, 2009, he and Rose had never moved farther than two miles from the university. OU remembers Paul Sharp, like all of its presidents, with a statue placed in a niche of Evans Hall. Paul Sharp's statue also pays tribute to a marriage and partnership that lasted more than sixty years and helped shape the university we know today. Nestled in the statue's hand is a long-stemmed rose.

Under Sharp, OU's medical campus rapidly gained new ground. The Robert M. Bird Library, Biomedical Sciences Building, College of Dentistry, and Everett Tower were all built during his presidency. *(Courtesy Robert M. Bird Library)*

WILLIAM SLATER BANOWSKY
1978–1982

WHEN OU WAS SEEKING its tenth president in spring 1978, members of the Board of Regents made their wish list clear: they wanted someone who would continue Paul Sharp's focus on repairing the university's reputation among Oklahomans. They also wanted someone whose energy and vision would propel OU into the future.

Unexpectedly they found exactly who they were looking for twelve hundred miles away on the Malibu coast at Pepperdine University, a conservative Christian university. Pepperdine had been transformed by the sheer willpower, charisma, and determination of William Slater Banowsky.

The grandson of a prolific Church of Christ pastor and religious music composer, Banowsky had been raised in the faith and began preaching as early as age seventeen. He attended the Church of Christ–affiliated David Lipscombe College in Nashville, Tennessee, on a baseball scholarship and was voted student body president. While still a student, he married homecoming queen and head cheerleader Gay Barnes. Banowsky supported his growing family by preaching on the weekends, a practice he continued as a graduate student at the University of New Mexico. He was soon juggling ministry with doctoral studies in communication at the University of Southern California and a new job as assistant to the president of Pepperdine College, a thirty-three-acre Church of Christ school then located in the heart of inner-city Los Angeles.

Banowsky became a protégé of Pepperdine president M. Norvel Young, who promoted him to dean of student life. Others also recognized Banowsky's talents, and by 1963, he had attracted the attention of Broadway Church of Christ in Lubbock, Texas, then the largest church of its denomination in the United States. He

became head pastor of the church at age twenty-seven and doubled Broadway's membership within five years; he also gained national acclaim during a televised debate on moral issues with Anson Mount, *Playboy*'s religion editor.

Banowsky maintained his ties to Pepperdine and served on the president's board. He knew that Pepperdine's enrollment and fund-raising had been stagnant since the school found itself in the middle of a war zone during the 1965 Watts Riots. Parents and supporters debated both the college's safety and its future, and Pepperdine's private-school expenses could not compete against nearby USC. Pepperdine was by all accounts in crisis.

"We never got over the shock of having been in the middle of things during the riots," Banowsky told *Sports Illustrated* in 1977. As early as 1966, President Young knew that Pepperdine's survival hinged upon building a new campus. He visited with Banowsky in Texas as sites for relocating the campus were considered. When land in Malibu was offered to the school, Young reached out to his protégé and Banowsky returned to Pepperdine as its vice president.

His job was to lead the design, funding, and construction of an entirely new campus. "We were either going to make it or not, and it was a fundraising challenge," Banowsky said frankly. "If we made it, everybody would win, but if we didn't, everybody would lose." He rose to the occasion, securing $36 million to build the campus and developing a master plan that would shape the school's physical form and curriculum. In 1969 he became the college's first chancellor, and Pepperdine moved to its Malibu home in 1970. The following year M. Norvel Young decided to step down from the newly renamed Pepperdine University, and at age thirty-four Banowsky became one of the nation's youngest college presidents.

Over the following decade, Banowsky brought all his considerable gifts to bear upon Pepperdine's growth. His ability to cultivate relationships with donors brought in an astonishing amount of money, including a $300 million estate gift from oil heiress Blanche Seaver. Just as significant, by 1978 enrollment had increased from fifteen hundred to seven thousand students, and Pepperdine's endowment skyrocketed from $6 million to $125 million. Banowsky's fund-raising efforts were helped by strong ties to California Republican political leaders, including then-governor Ronald Reagan and U.S. President Gerald Ford. He also hosted a weekly interview program for the local NBC affiliate that attracted a wide variety of political figures and national newsmakers.

Then, in March 1978, Banowsky received a phone call from recently retired OU Board of Regents chairman Mack Braley inquiring about his potential interest in the OU presidency. Braley had contacted John Hospers, the philosophy chairman from Banowsky's days at USC. Braley, a former campaign manager for Hospers, asked his friend to suggest a conservative presidential candidate for OU.

Banowsky brushed the idea aside. It was not uncommon for him to receive calls from presidential search committees several times a year; also, he didn't know Braley and wasn't sure if he could take him seriously. Then came calls from current OU Regents, and Banowsky began to consider the possibilities. He had grown up only a few hours away from Norman in Fort Worth, Texas, where his parents still lived, and his mother's family had lived in eastern Oklahoma for four generations. Oklahoma was an important part of his roots, and OU football had loomed large in Banowsky's childhood. "Bud Wilkinson was a hero, and I thought that OU was just like magic. It was beyond imagination that I would get to be the president of the University of Oklahoma."

Former president Paul Sharp (*left*) welcomes William S. Banowsky at the August 1978 press conference announcing his selection as the university's tenth president. (*OU EMP 78435*)

A FUTURE AT THE UNIVERSITY OF OKLAHOMA

Banowsky came quietly to Norman for an interview. That evening he took a customary jog and wandered toward the football field where Bud Wilkinson had once ruled. He found the stadium gates locked. "In my sweaty jogging clothes I literally crawled over the fence into Oklahoma Memorial Stadium about dusk," he said, recalling that he stood on the field and wondered what it would be like to become OU's president. The next day Banowsky returned to California to await a decision from the Board of Regents. The wait would stretch out for six months, in large part because the board was split by political allegiances. Oklahoma was then a majority Democrat state, and Banowsky heard that several Regents were hesitant to appoint an outspoken minister and politically active Republican. Their reluctance was furthered by faculty members on the search committee wary of both Banowsky's politics and his public stands on morality. Several months into the process, Banowsky learned that William Thurman, then-provost of OU's Health Sciences Center, was another top candidate. By May, Thurman had the majority of board votes, and Banowsky chose to withdraw his application. Then, in mid-August, Banowksy was surprised to receive a phone call asking if he would accept OU's presidency. Board members had been advised that Thurman was filing for divorce, which could be a liability for a prominent public figure even in 1978. "It was bad to be a Republican, but it was worse to be in the middle of a divorce," Banowsky quipped.

That same day, joint announcements were made in Malibu and Norman, mere hours before Banowsky caught a red-eye flight to Oklahoma City. At 10 A.M. on August 15, he walked into OU's Oklahoma Memorial Union ballroom for a well-attended and highly celebratory press conference. "It was very, very exciting," Banowsky said. "To come to Oklahoma was not a dream come true—it was an absolute, unbelievable blessing out of the blue."

Not everyone was enthusiastic. Faculty Senate chair Bernard McDonald lamented and expressed "shock, sadness, and disappointment" at Banowsky's appointment in a newspaper interview. "Why is he here?" a second, anonymous faculty member bemoaned. "OU has not been a hotbed of liberalism, but it certainly has been a voice of moderation in the state."

From the moment he arrived on campus, Banowsky set about proving to critics that he understood the importance and role of the university, and he gathered the faculty together to address their fears. He recalls saying, "The faculty is the university, and I am here to advance the best interests of the University of Oklahoma faculty." Listening to faculty members' concerns, Banowsky learned that faculty salaries were the lowest in the Big 8 and that faculty shortages had led to overcrowded classes frequently taught by graduate assistants. Of critical concern was OU's Bizzell Memorial Library, which had one of the smallest collections of scholarly books and research materials among comparably sized institutions in the Southwest. The OU Regents also told him that the university should have a greater presence throughout Oklahoma.

Spotting the opportunity to sell himself and the university in the onslaught of invitations that poured in from civic clubs and organizations across the state, Banowsky set off on a whirlwind tour of Oklahoma that would last throughout much of his presidency. "We've got to do all we can to make our case in the state," he told the *Norman Transcript* days after arriving at OU. "I regard the boundaries of the State of Oklahoma as the responsibilities of my office."

A habitual record-keeper, Banowsky to this day has a stack of "Month at a Glance" calendars that he used while serving as OU's president. One month shows him making forty-four speaking appearances in thirty days, and

Banowsky's former administrative assistant, Mary Jane Rutherford, remembers a day in which he spoke to six separate groups in six cities. According to Carol Burr in *Centennial: A Portrait of the University of Oklahoma,* "He spoke to every group in Oklahoma that owned a microphone—and several that did not." No gathering was too small; in one instance, Banowsky traveled to a tiny town near Oklahoma's Panhandle to deliver a commencement address to three graduates. If the people of Oklahoma wanted him, Bill Banowsky would be there. Patterned after his successful programs in Southern California, he also began taping monthly "Bill Banowsky Visits" for Oklahoma City's NBC affiliate. His combined exposure built an irreplaceable goodwill among Oklahomans who were dazzled by Banowsky's personal trifecta: charm, good looks, and the trained oratory of an impassioned revivalist.

"We were riding the crest of a wave," Banowsky said, explaining that curiosity about OU's new president gave him a distinct window of opportunity to gain support for the university. "The fundamental offensive weapon that I had was my public speaking. It was something I could do; it put me in touch with people and it gave the university direct access to groups all over the state."

A handwritten note in OU's Western History Collections shares a taste of Banowsky's impression on the public. The note makes it clear that Banowsky met *Oklahoma Journal* editor and OU 1949 alumnus John Clabes briefly at a civic club event and later recognized him on sight at an OU football game. The president followed up the chance meeting with a letter to Clabes.

"You are the damndest guy I ever met," Clabes replied in October 1978. "I have told many people you are destined to go down as the greatest president ever to sit at Norman. We think you know what you are doing and how to get there from here. I volunteer my services in your crusade to make the University of Oklahoma a great institution."

Clabes was not alone in pledging his service. After decades of stagnant state spending, alumni and friends stood ready and, perhaps more important, financially able to help. Oklahoma's oil economy was experiencing a record-setting boom. Drilling was increasing dramatically; by 1980, the value of Oklahoma oil would be nearly $10 billion, an average of $10,000 for each family of four in the state.

THE PRICE OF EXCELLENCE

Banowsky seized on these opportunities and set audacious goals for OU that included sharply increasing faculty salaries. A slew of deferred academic appointments would also be a priority; among Banowsky's first was the new dean of libraries, Dr. Sul Lee. "When I came to OU, we had a 1930s building with a 1958 addition," Lee said, describing the library as cramped and awkward. He advocated for OU to build a new library and, with Banowsky's blessing, took a $30 million proposal to the Board of Regents. He came away with a $12 million annex proposal for which Banowsky immediately began raising funds.

"The university cannot fulfill its responsibilities, either to instruction or to research, without an excellent library," the president argued during his November 18, 1978, inauguration. "No priority can be higher, no progress more consequential. . . . For a great comprehensive university, there can be no substitute for excellence. No matter how much we conserve or how shrewdly we manage, we cannot sustain excellence unless we pay the price."

Banowsky knew that price would also require dramatic increases in state appropriations, and he spent much of his first year in office improving relations between OU, the State Legislature, and the Oklahoma State Regents for Higher Education. Regents Chancellor E. T. Dunlap soon became an avid supporter who would help OU tap into Oklahoma's plentiful oil proceeds.

As the fall wore on, many were captivated by the news that OU Sooners running back Billy Sims had become only the sixth junior in NCAA history to win the Heisman Trophy. Sims, OU's third athlete to receive the award, was preceded by Billy Vessels in 1952 and Steve Owens in 1969. Other OU headlines were not as celebrated. An ongoing battle between the administration and OU's Gay People's Union (GPU) had

landed on Banowsky's desk a little more than a month after he arrived. The GPU asked to be recognized as an official student organization, thereby making it eligible to receive funding from student activity fees. These fees were paid per academic credit hour, meaning that most funds originated either from federal dollars or from students' parents and guardians. OU's Student Association had passed a resolution approving the GPU as a student organization. The resolution was quickly overturned by the OU Board of Regents, who in turn gave OU's president the sole power to decide which student organizations would be officially recognized. Banowsky weighed his options. If he refused the petition for recognition, many students and faculty would think he was a rigid moralist who would allow his own religious beliefs to rule the university. If he formally recognized the GPU, he would risk alienating Oklahoma's conservative base at a time when OU badly needed its support. He denied the GPU petition and was symbolically censured by the OU Student Association by a vote of twenty-one to sixteen for "violation of the student code process."

"I regret having inherited such a controversial and potentially divisive issue. It is my responsibility to face such issues squarely," Banowsky wrote in a 1978 *Daily Oklahoman* column. The president stressed his commitment to academic freedom and reached out to the gay and lesbian community. "I respect and affirm genuinely, at the deepest possible level, every other person as a human being of value and ultimate dignity."

Newly elected U.S. senator David L. Boren congratulates President Banowsky upon his inauguration. (*Courtesy* Sooner Magazine)

William Slater Banowsky in the official regalia of the presidency, June 1979. (*OU EMP 79351*)

OU students are gathered on the lawn of Walker Tower to meet their president at a cookout during "First Four," a freshman orientation program held before the official start of the fall semester. *(Courtesy Sooner Magazine)*

"Deep down, I agreed with them. They should have been able to use student fees like anyone else," Banowsky clarified in a 2013 interview. "But my antennae told me that this was not the sort of thing we should do in the first two or three months I was at OU. The bottom line was that I just didn't believe the taxpayers of Oklahoma were ready yet." Some three years later, the Oklahoma Supreme Court ruled that OU must recognize the renamed Gay Activists' Alliance as a formal student organization, though the court stopped short of requiring OU to provide either university space or funding. In light of that ruling, OU Regents chose to remove the administration from the organization recognition process and to allow the UOSA more autonomy in deciding which groups received activity funds.

One divisive issue aside, Banowsky risked his popularity again by juggling OU's administration. He appointed more than a dozen key administrators and deans in his first year and demonstrated an innate fairness by promoting several faculty members who had been among his harshest critics. He also eliminated two vice-presidential positions and streamlined OU's structure, allowing most divisions to report either to new provost J.R. Morris, Vice President for University Affairs David Burr, or Vice President for Administrative Affairs Arthur J. Elbert. Elbert was new to OU, but Morris and Burr had a combined fifty-five years of university service. Health Sciences Center provost William Thurman resigned to become president of the Oklahoma

Medical Research Foundation, and executive assistant to the president Joseph Ray also stepped down. Banowsky had brought only one person with him from Pepperdine: personal assistant Phyllis Dorman. But now he reached back for professor Gerald Turner, who would take the title of executive vice president. Turner, who stayed at OU throughout Banowsky's tenure, later became president of the University of Mississippi and then president of Southern Methodist University.

Capitalizing on his fund-raising success and experience at Pepperdine, Banowsky modified OU's existing President's Council, a $1,000-giving-level club. He renamed the group the OU Associates and designated special benefits for support that included an annual black-tie dinner. Banowsky believed the Associates would form a broad platform of unrestricted gifts to address academic needs and seize new opportunities; donors would also increase their support of OU as their personal wealth grew. In February 1979, he gathered OU's development staff around a table and asked them how many donors they believed would sign on as Associates. R. Boyd Gunning, then-director of the OU Foundation, suggested three hundred. "Okay," Banowsky told the development team, "Go get them." Banowsky and his staff spent the weekend calling potential Associates and were overwhelmed by the response. The goal of three hundred Associates was reached within weeks. Before a year had passed, more than eight hundred members would attend the first OU Associates dinner featuring keynote speaker and former secretary of state Henry Kissinger. The OU Associates became the most successful giving program in OU history.

Banowsky also continued fund-raising at the grassroots level by crisscrossing the state. By the time of his first

President Banowsky addresses the OU Associates at their first annual black-tie dinner. *(Courtesy Sooner Magazine)*

anniversary as president, Banowsky and his development team had raised $10.8 million. Much of that money was devoted to construction and capital renovation projects across OU's three campuses.

AN IDEA WHOSE TIME HAD COME

One construction project had its genesis when OU Regent Dan Little suggested the university should centralize and unify all its energy disciplines. The idea "lit a fuse" in Banowsky, and he took the concept to the leaders of OU's energy programs, including the newly formed College of Geosciences. "They were very excited," Banowsky said, recalling that College of Engineering dean Martin Jischke and other faculty members quickly took leadership roles in the project that became known as the OU Energy Center. The center's concept was unlike anything being done at that time in higher education. "It was creative academically, in the bringing together into one central force various disciplines through the unification of curriculum and research," Banowsky said. "The project just seemed to have a life of its own and made sense to everybody. It was an idea whose time had come."

In the early months of 1980, many felt the time had come for another radical idea. Oklahoma's longtime U.S. senator Henry Bellmon announced that he would not run for reelection, and within days a movement began to draft Banowsky as Oklahoma's Republican senatorial candidate. Banowsky had plenty of political experience and connections from his days in California, and his popularity and renowned speaking style would make him a strong contender. Hundreds of people called and approached Banowsky. Without his input, the local GOP chair gave up her position to start a "Draft Banowsky" campaign, going so far as to hold a press conference at the State Capitol.

"I was getting tremendous encouragement to run, even

from Bellmon," he said. State Democrats also began to push Banowsky to reveal his cards. He said publicly that he would need time to think, and OU's Regents encouraged him to take all the time he needed. Banowsky had been OU's president little more than eighteen months, there was much he still wanted to accomplish at OU, and his family was settled in Norman. Finally Banowsky announced in March 1980 that he would not run.

"It was agonizing," Banowsky disclosed in 2013. "When it came right down to it, I felt it was too early to leave the University of Oklahoma. If it had come four or five years later, it would have been perfect. But it was just too painful; I loved the university, and I hated the timing." He smiled wryly. "But once I said 'no,' it hurt, because I had been bitten. I was tempted by the political serpent, and I could see myself as a United States senator."

Diving back into OU life, Banowsky quickly became immersed in plans for the future, including the $13.1 million library addition, which would add 150,000 square feet of space in the four-story structure. The library also joined the prestigious Research Libraries Group, whose members included Yale, Princeton, and Harvard. "It gave me great joy," Banowsky said. "The library became a symbol of our determination."

OU's valiant efforts led to 1980 and 1981 becoming record-breaking years in student enrollment, with twenty-five thousand students making up the largest enrollment on record. The OU Associates program had grown to fifteen hundred members and was contributing $1.5 million to the university's budget. OU's $6.1 million Huston Huffman Physical Fitness Center opened in the midst of student residence halls during the summer of 1980 and was among $101 million in capital projects being undertaken by OU, more than in the previous ten years combined. On the Health Sciences Center campus, academic offerings grew to include graduate programs in dentistry, nursing, and a doctoral program in pharmacy.

A wrecking ball destroys a turret of OU's Women's Building to make way for the expansion of Bizzell Memorial Library. *(1980* Sooner Yearbook*)*

President Banowsky presents President Emeritus George L. Cross with a piece of cake to celebrate OU's ninetieth birthday in December 1980. (*Courtesy* Sooner Magazine)

In fall 1980, OU launched the $103 million Campaign for Academic Excellence, whose eighteen major goals focused on energy research and studies, health professions, the library, endowed chairs and professorships, and the burgeoning OU Energy Center. The campaign kickoff coincided with OU's ninetieth birthday on December 19. The celebration, marked with a giant cake lit by ninety candles and served to hundreds of celebrants that included former presidents George Lynn Cross and Paul Sharp, was highlighted by the groundbreaking for OU's new library wing.

Banowsky set other goals for OU in 1981, including the start of construction for the $29.7 million Energy Center, the $13.4 million Catlett Music Center, and a new pharmacy building at the Health Sciences Center. Comprehensive master plans for construction, renovation, and landscaping on both the Norman and Oklahoma City campuses were a priority, and three thousand trees were added to the two campuses through the David Ross Boyd Tree Planting Program.

Of special importance were faculty salaries, which had already increased 33.5 percent on average in thirty-six months. Overall, Oklahoma higher education was emerging from decades of underfunding. While neighboring states were cutting funds, appropriations to Oklahoma's higher education institutions had increased by more than $71 million in the previous two years. Ever savvy, Banowsky understood the importance of the public-private partnership and wasn't content relying solely on the state for funding. His development team raised $18 million in private contributions.

"This fall, the University of Oklahoma could look back on three Banowsky years and draw the inescapable conclusion that after generations of preparation, the 'time

of the Sooner' in higher education may be at hand," *Sooner Magazine* effused. "If a single accomplishment had to be drawn from the record of the past three years, it would have to be one of attitude."

"We have suffered for so long from a cultural inferiority complex that most of us have come to settle for academic mediocrity, even in our best university," Banowsky agreed. "For all these years we have thought it ludicrous to seek to be as good as Michigan, Texas, Wisconsin, the University of California at Berkeley. But if we believe we can, we can."

The summit of OU's 1981 growth and prosperity was reached in October when 1951 College of Business alumnus and Dallas oilman Bill Saxon and his wife, Wylodean, donated $30 million to the Energy Center campaign. Half of the donated funds would be used for construction costs and the remainder earmarked for creating endowed professorships. Saxon's donation was the largest private gift in Oklahoma history and among the most generous in U.S. higher education. With the Saxon pledge, OU extended its fund-raising goal for the Energy Center to $65 million: $45 million for construction and $20 million to endow academic programs. "The real reason for this gift is to say how proud we are to be Oklahomans. And to say that America gives you the opportunity to achieve and acquire—and to give," Saxon declared at a press conference.

Many more gifts would be needed to make the Energy Center a reality, and OU established the "Energy Center Founders" society for donors who gave $100,000 or more to the effort. Saxon's gift ignited interest and gave Banowsky the incentive to optimize his speaking talents during visits to alumni and potential Energy Center supporters.

Paul Massad, then OU's director of development, was with Banowsky at a Houston dinner for seventy

President Banowsky addresses Norman's civic clubs during a meeting in the ballroom of Oklahoma Memorial Union. (*Courtesy* Sooner Magazine)

President Banowsky, Oklahoma governor George Nigh, and Sooner head coach Barry Switzer pose with the Governor's Trophy, exchanged between the governors of Oklahoma and Texas depending on who wins the annual OU-UT game. Unfortunately, the trophy went to Texas in 1979. (*Courtesy* Sooner Magazine)

potential donors. Each was asked to consider giving $100,000. Banowsky delivered his typically rousing speech and had no more than finished when one woman jumped to her feet and yelled, "Bill, count us in!" Her husband's jaw dropped, but at the end of the evening OU had seven new Energy Center Founders. More than seventy-five people had signed up as Founders by that November, for a combined total of $12.5 million in funding. The State of Oklahoma would provide an additional $15 million toward the project.

Even as university fund-raising went well, OU was tied up with a case against the NCAA that would have long-term financial implications for the university. At that time, the NCAA controlled how often teams could appear on television and doled out coverage in turn. "The NCAA took a governmental approach that 'what's fair for one is fair for all,'" Banowsky said, adding that OU's Board of Regents felt strongly that the practice was illegal. They wanted OU to have the right to negotiate its own television deals, especially as cable television expanded. "OU was a football power, and somebody wanted us on television every Saturday. It was worth millions of dollars a year in TV revenue. We could not only fill our stadium, we could have people everywhere watching our football games. The TV companies were very willing to pay the schools, but the NCAA was in the middle of it all."

In the case, *The University of Oklahoma and the Georgia Athletic Association v. The NCAA,* OU charged that the NCAA's television policy violated the Sherman Antitrust Act and essentially fixed prices. Experts estimated that as much as $280 million in football contracts were at stake for all U.S. college teams. In turn, the NCAA contended that giving up the right to schedule television coverage would "threaten the entire fabric of the NCAA" and endanger competitive balance between small and large schools. OU would win its case on the federal level in 1982, and the NCAA appealed to the Supreme Court.

The U.S. Supreme Court agreed to hear the case against the NCAA. The court would rule in favor of OU and the University of Georgia Athletic Association in 1984, defeating the NCAA for the first time in its history. Justices declared that the NCAA's television plan for football represented a violation of the Sherman Antitrust Act. "The free enterprise approach won," Banowsky commented. In his book, *The 50-Year Seduction: How Television Manipulated College Football, from the Birth of the Modern NCAA to the Creation of the BCS,* author Keith Dunnavant called the decision "the most important event in the history of college athletics."

SHIFTING TIDES

Headlines foreshadowed troubling economic indicators in the year to come, but very few were listening. During an economic outlook conference in Oklahoma City, a Merrill Lynch economist predicted a weak year for business in 1982; the economist softened her forecast by adding, "Oklahoma will refuse again to participate in this recession," a statement met with cheers. More warnings arrived by December 1981, when the federal government told OU that severe cuts to financial aid were to come. At that time half of the money OU received for student aid came from the federal government.

For the moment, OU was still steaming along under the power of the oil economy and private donors. One of Banowsky's primary goals was reached in March 1982 when, for the first time in its history, OU topped the Big 8 in faculty salaries. The ranking was especially noteworthy because only four years earlier OU had ranked last in the Big 8. Faculty members had received an on-average 45 percent salary increase, and OU had experienced a 102 percent increase in state appropriations and $1.8 million in academic improvements. Private fund-raising continued to be strong; more than $15 million had been raised through Energy Center Founders in less than five months, and OU Foundation assets had increased by 154 percent. Some 150 faculty members had been added to classrooms, and $127 million in construction and renovation projects were scheduled for the Norman and Oklahoma City campuses.

The Doris M. Neustadt Wing of OU's Bizzell Memorial Library was dedicated on May 3, 1982, marking the completion of Banowsky's first construction project as president. "It is our one hope that this university remains the last great bastion for the free exchange of ideas," said Walter Neustadt, who, along with siblings Jean, Allen, and Joan, had chosen to honor their mother with a $2 million naming gift. The new wing doubled the library's existing capacity and faculty study areas. Elsewhere on OU's campuses, four athletic construction projects and the Henry D. and Ida Mosier College of Pharmacy Building were also reaching completion.

Another of Banowsky's construction projects did not go as smoothly. The president announced that he planned to bar traffic from OU's North Oval and close all streets within the campus core. The North Oval's drive went almost to the

Faces are installed in the E. T. Dunlap Clock Tower adjoining Bizzell Memorial Library in 1982. One of the faces would crash to the ground during a massive ice storm in 2010. *(OUCT 443)*

very steps of Evans Hall; one morning in June 1982, students and faculty awoke to find the Oval closed and workers tearing up concrete to replace it with turf. The Board of Regents soon approved $500,000 to dramatically redesign the Oval as Banowsky wished, though negative public reaction and a lack of funding eventually deterred most of the plans and limited spending to $75,000 in lighting and landscape design. Banowsky had other projects to oversee, including the September 11 groundbreaking for OU's Energy Center and completing its $62 million fund-raising campaign.

Students learn computer research methods inside the library's newly opened Neustadt Wing in 1982. *(WHC)*

Then, on June 22, 1982, the OU community was stunned by news that President Banowsky was resigning to become the first salaried president of the Los Angeles Chamber of Commerce. He would leave by September 1. "Universities are here for the ages. Our work is never finished," he said at a press conference announcing his decision. "I would have liked to have broken the ground on the new music center. . . . I could give a long list of the things I would have liked to have accomplished."

Even those closest to Banowsky expressed disbelief and bewilderment at his decision, alongside a deep appreciation and abiding gratitude for all that he had accomplished. OU Regent and 1933 alumnus Charles Engleman pondered Banowsky's announcement in his paper, the *Clinton Daily News*. He credited the president with "furnishing the leadership for the most remarkably progressive four years in the history of OU" and called Banowsky "a motivator, a spellbinder, a preacher, a politician, a visionary, an idealist—and a fund-raiser deluxe. . . . We didn't want him to leave, but he's gone, so we can only wish him well . . . and be thankful and grateful." OU provost J.R. Morris would serve as interim president, and Executive Vice President Gerald Turner would be acting provost. A presidential search committee was formed.

OU had barely recovered from the announcement of Banowsky's impending departure when even more ominous news broke. On July 2, 1982, Oklahoma City's Penn Square Bank was the first of nearly 140 state banks to fail amid an oil glut that meant the beginning of the end of Oklahoma's economic boom. Among those most adversely affected were Energy Center Founders Bill and Wylodean Saxon. The stock they had donated to OU as part of their $30 million gift had plummeted in price, and the cash remainder they had pledged was now uncertain. Banowsky and Vice President David Burr forged ahead, saying that the future of the project had been assured by the $15.7 million already donated by Energy Center Founders. The Saxons later gave in excess of $1 million to the Energy Center and hundreds of thousands of dollars to other OU projects. "Come what may, the Saxons have already earned and will always have a very special place in the hearts of their countless friends at the University of Oklahoma," Banowsky said.

In late August, almost two thousand faculty, staff, and students came to Banowsky's farewell reception, where the president said the move had been the hardest decision of his career. "I don't feel very much like making a speech—an indication of my emotional condition right now," he told the crowd.

During a 2013 interview, Banowsky stated publicly for the first time what had led to his resignation. "I made the move to run for the United States Senate," he said frankly. Political connections in California had suggested that he take the Los Angeles Chamber of Commerce job to establish residency before they positioned him as a 1984 Republican Senate candidate. But Banowsky soon realized that he had taken the wrong path. "I only stayed five weeks, I was so miserable. I missed OU and I just knew I had made a mistake. I've had a good life, I'm seventy-seven years old, I've been real lucky, and that is still the stupidest thing I ever did. I decided I wasn't going to run." Banowsky contacted members of the Board of Regents and soon had their blessing to return. "We came back with great relief," he said.

Banowsky returned to a very different OU. The 1982 oil crash had hit Oklahoma hard and fast, and the State Regents advised all colleges and universities to trim nearly $6 million in spending. Banowsky immediately froze hiring, travel, and equipment purchases and asked administrators to plan for a 4 percent across-the-board cut to their budgets.

President Banowsky laughs with newspaper publisher and OU Regent Charles Engleman in 1982. *(Courtesy Sooner Magazine)*

OU athletics kept the university in the national spotlight during Banowsky's presidency. Sooners halfback Billy Sims became only the sixth junior to win the Heisman Trophy in 1978, and Bart Conner won two gold medals in gymnastics during the 1984 Olympic summer games. *(1979* Sooner Yearbook*)*

By spring 1983, OU had a $2 million budget shortfall. Staff and faculty cuts were suggested as a remedy but rejected. Instead OU imposed furloughs and cut benefits, including medical and life insurance plans. The president warned state legislators that funding shortages would undo much of the progress that OU had made in the previous four years. "We'll be cutting into the muscle and tissue of our institution," he said.

Some of that muscle came from OU's Energy Center. Just as the project was ready to enter its first phase of construction, the state temporarily withdrew nearly half of the pledged $15 million in funds. Banowsky and his development team continued an aggressive pursuit of private fund-raising, but their work was made difficult by the financial strain many donors experienced.

In the midst of OU's tough times came a near-tragedy when head men's basketball coach Billy Tubbs was struck by a car while jogging. Tubbs, who had just led the Sooners to its first Big 8 basketball title, suffered a skull fracture and was sidelined for months. His first public appearance was a grand entrance at the basketball awards banquet, where he stood under a banner reading, "Another Miracle for Coach Tubbs."

Like Tubbs, OU persevered, though the state's budget woes continued through 1983. The university broke ground on the new music building in October and opened the College of Pharmacy building a month later. Admission standards became much more rigorous and OU was admitted into the National Merit Scholarship program, setting the groundwork for OU to one day become the public university with the most National Merit Scholars enrolled on its campus. Back in Oklahoma, Banowsky was educating legislators

President Banowsky stands against the backdrop of the incomplete OU Energy Center. *(University Archives RG15, Box 181)*

However, the eternal optimist in him maintained that OU would emerge from the morass, and he declared the university "bloodied but not bowed."

A TIME FOR GOOD-BYES

Amid OU's continuing financial troubles, the university faced another controversy when football superstar recruit Marcus Dupree abruptly abandoned the Sooner football team. The nineteen-year-old recruit who was called "the greatest high school player in history" had failed to return to campus following the annual OU-Texas game in Dallas. Athletic staff members found Dupree in his Mississippi hometown, where he announced that he was leaving OU for the University of Southern Mississippi. OU's Athletic Department underwent a tsunami of scathing national criticism regarding how Dupree had been treated both as an athlete and as a student. In an interview with the *Washington Post*, Banowsky called Dupree a "victim of the high-pressure process of big-time intercollegiate football. We crowned him a hero."

Mississippi also soon gained OU executive vice president Gerald Turner, who left his role as the president's right hand to become chancellor at the University of Mississippi. Banowsky called Turner's elevation "an inevitable moment" and celebrated his achievement.

Banowsky also celebrated the establishment of the \$1 million Henry Bellmon Chair of Public Service, OU's most lucratively endowed chair to date. The Energy Center was steadily rising, and Banowsky had helped to secure \$250,000 in private funds for new Associates Distinguished Lectureships to supplement salary and support teaching and research for OU's most outstanding faculty. Faculty salaries were still stagnant in 1984, but the president was able to announce that furloughs would end.

OU reported that private contributions had increased by \$2 million from the previous year for a total of \$18 million raised, the second-highest amount of annual giving in the history of the university. Banowsky marked his sixth anniversary as president while looking forward to new goals, including the creation of a weather center that would allow collaboration between state, federal, and private organizations and increase weather-related research tenfold. The National Weather Service prepared to move its Oklahoma City operations to OU's north campus, and ten organizations formally joined as the Applied Systems Institute, Inc., which projected \$9.9 million in annual spending. OU's fledgling Energy Center hosted a world energy conference sponsored by the United Nations and the U.S. Department of Energy to focus on the development of shallow oil and gas resources, and the conference brought experts from fifty different countries to campus.

about the inevitably negative impact that decreased state funding would have on Oklahoma's ability to compete for high-tech industries vital to the state's economic future. He and OSU president Lawrence Boger also appealed jointly to the State Legislature for appropriations. OU had already cut fifty sections of student classes and increased class sizes, but still confronted a potential \$8 million in budget cuts. "We are faced with a choice between quality and mediocrity, and that kind of blow will be a decade long," Banowsky said. Some fifty job layoffs and extended leaves without pay were under consideration, and unpaid furloughs would begin over Christmas break and extend through the spring. A survey revealed that more than 30 percent of faculty members were actively seeking new jobs, and nearly 60 percent planned to leave OU if the financial crisis continued.

Banowsky deeply regretted each blow to OU's morale.

More good tidings came in July and August when Bart Conner won two Olympic gold medals in gymnastics and Wayman Tisdale won gold in basketball at the 1984 summer games. The OU community basked in their reflected glory.

In every way OU seemed to be rising from its struggles during the fall of 1984 when headlines reported rumors that U.S. senator Don Nickles was promoting Banowsky as a potential candidate for the post of U.S. secretary of education. Banowsky expressed no interest in the job, but wryly added, "If the president of the United States were to call, I would listen very carefully to whatever he has to say." The call never came, and Banowsky focused his energies on plans to build a $12.1 million family and preventive medicine clinic at the OU Health Sciences Center.

In the end, a very different call came. On December 16, 1984, President Banowsky announced that he was resigning to become president of Gaylord Broadcasting Company, then the nation's largest privately owned broadcasting corporation. "With his skills, he gets opportunities that ordinary mortal men don't get," OU Regent John Imel said of Banowsky's move. "You knew someone was going to come along and take him away."

Gaylord Broadcasting was owned by *Daily Oklahoman* editor Edward L. Gaylord, with whom Banowsky had developed a personal friendship. According to Banowsky, "He came to me with the job offer out of the blue. I wasn't looking to leave again; my family was happy." Remorseful about creating turmoil for OU yet again, Banowsky nonetheless relished challenges and had long expressed a desire to work in free enterprise. "The Gaylord offer was overpowering," he said. Banowsky would depart by September 1, and College of Engineering dean Martin Jischke would serve as interim president.

"You can't put into words what Bill Banowsky has meant to the University of Oklahoma," OU Regent Tom McCurdy said at the time, but the *Daily Oklahoman* tried:

> William Slater Banowsky leaves the University of Oklahoma in far better shape than he found it when he became its 10th president six years ago. If OU wasn't exactly in the doldrums then, it was suffering a severe hangover from the trauma and disruption of the campus protest era of the '60s. Morale had declined, and there was little distinction in the overall academic environment. Banowsky correctly discerned his primary mission: to change and improve OU's image with students, faculty, alumni, the Legislature and potential donors. The record attests he was eminently successful on all counts.

That record would include a legacy of astonishing growth and prosperity that weathered even one of Oklahoma's roughest fiscal storms. Banowsky had led $155 million in new construction, including the debut of world-class music and energy research centers and a library that had doubled in size and now featured the state's largest collection of materials. More than 150 new positions had been added to a faculty that benefited from an on-average 45 percent increase in salary. State appropriations had increased 102 percent in six years. Banowsky also had fully ushered OU into the era of private fund-raising. His work to establish the OU Associates—the giving club that began with weekend phone calls around a conference table and a goal of three hundred members—has helped OU garner nearly $62 million in academic support since the group's establishment. "President Banowsky dared to dream that our alumni and friends might make contributions that would allow the university to reach a level of greatness otherwise unattainable," President Boren said upon the twenty-fifth

President Emeritus Banowsky and former OU first lady Gay Banowsky at the 1999 planting of a tree grove dedicated in his honor on OU's Norman campus. *(Courtesy* Sooner Magazine*)*

anniversary of the renamed OU President's Associates in 2004. "We all owe a debt of gratitude to every donor who helped the university achieve that dream in 1979 and in every year since."

President Banowsky's contributions to OU are remembered fittingly through growth: the Borens established a grove in his name to commemorate the planting of three thousand trees on campus that Banowsky had instituted through the David Ross Boyd Tree Planting Program. In 1990, he received OU's highest honor, the Distinguished Service Citation, and a statue of Banowsky joins those of all OU presidents in niches fronting Evans Hall.

Perhaps even more lasting is the mark that OU has left on the heart of its tenth president. "To think that I was the president of the University of Oklahoma . . . it was stunning, it was surreal, it was romantic, it was heavenly. I loved it," Banowsky said. "I think the reason I could make six speeches a day was that I was on fire. I feel that the greatest honor of my life was to be president of the University of Oklahoma."

MARTIN CHARLES JISCHKE
February–September 1985

 ON DECEMBER 16, 1984, the day William S. Banowsky announced his resignation as president of the University of Oklahoma, OU Regents Elwood Kemp and Charles Sarratt called Engineering dean Martin C. Jischke to confer with him about the appointment of an interim president. They asked Jischke if he had any advice about appointing an interim president. Jischke, a seventeen-year veteran of the OU faculty and former director of OU's School of Aerospace, Mechanical and Nuclear Engineering, had served as chair of OU's Faculty Senate. He had also worked closely with President Banowsky while planning OU's future Energy Center. Jischke's name had been mentioned frequently as a candidate for provost when J.R. Morris became executive vice president to Banowsky.

That same evening, Jischke attended a party at Boyd House attended by OU Regent Julian J. Rothbaum, where he advised the Regent that the board should move quickly. Hours later, Jischke received a phone call from Regents chairman Dan Little, who summoned the engineering dean to a meeting with the entire Board of Regents, which had been in executive session at the OU Foundation. There they asked the forty-three-year-old to serve as OU's interim president.

"You could have knocked me over with a feather," Jischke said in a 2013 interview. "I had absolutely no idea that was in the offing." Before Jischke could respond, Rothbaum asked frankly, "Would you like to be permanent president?" Jischke hardly knew how to reply, but after a phone conversation with his wife, Patty, he agreed to serve as interim president. Jischke assumed leadership of Oklahoma's flagship university during one of its most volatile and difficult periods. Although his time as president was brief, Jischke would strive to keep OU moving forward and to make important steps toward recovery from an economic downturn that held Oklahoma in a crushing grip. The experience changed both his path and that of the University of Oklahoma.

PLUGGING THE DIKE

The next day Jischke told reporters that he was still "reeling" from the unexpected appointment and that his primary job was "to keep the ship pointed in the right direction." Given Oklahoma's precarious finances, some believed that the ship was sinking.

While the national cost of living continued to increase, OU faculty and staff had not received a raise in three years. OU's budget had been slashed by more than $12 million since 1982, and enrollment had dropped by thirteen hundred students in 1983 alone. Library hours had been limited, and seventy-six faculty positions had been cut. On the administrative level, OU was seeking a president, a provost, and two deans. There was even discussion about canceling summer school at the OU College of Law due to budget shortfalls.

Department chairs told Jischke that many faculty members were sending out copies of their curricula vitae and scheduling interviews at other universities. "In our department they assume that the situation is so bad that anyone with any self-respect would be looking for another job," said one professor quoted in the *Daily Oklahoman*.

Faculty members were happy to hear that one of their own would serve as interim president and made no secret of the fact they would support him to serve as permanent president. Jischke held a doctorate from the Massachusetts Institute of Technology. He was known to be well read and knowledgeable about a wide range of academic disciplines, including the arts. Music professor Kerry Grant, chair of OU's Budget Council and a member of the Faculty Senate, called Jischke's appointment "a real boost for the faculty" and said that Jischke was widely respected "for the quality of his mind and for his vision of what can be done here."

By necessity, much of that vision began and ended with funding. While the presidential search committee began its work, Jischke prepared himself to make OU's case before the State Legislature and Oklahoma State Regents for Higher Education. He crafted a message about OU's promise and dire need, and he delivered it to audiences statewide.

Interim president Martin C. Jischke, a popular OU professor of engineering, talks to the media during his introductory press conference. *(OUCT 2086)*

"If Oklahoma's educational support falters, future generations of Sooners will pay the price. They will starve for the best educational diet when they need it the most," he told members of the Norman Chamber of Commerce. Jischke was also honest about the fact that other universities were poaching OU's finest young professors. "We need some additional money," he said, "or the good Lord himself will not be able to turn it around."

"This is a pivotal period for OU," Jischke told reporters. "For the past two years, we've stood still or gone backwards. We've got to make progress now. That progress has to be both real and symbolic . . . and we can't wait until a permanent president is aboard."

Jischke set out a three-step plan: increase enrollment, increase private giving, and request a $22 million increase in state appropriations. In addition to the obvious benefits, he hoped attention to these three areas would improve campus morale and help steer the university away from a self-destructive path.

An OU committee, the President's Task Force on Enrollment, spent months analyzing the university's enrollment patterns and announced its findings in spring 1985. While national demographics played a role in decreasing numbers of college-age students, the task force concluded that OU needed to offer more scholarships, improve admission procedures, widen the university's recruiting territory, promote its unique offerings, and expand degree programs for adult students.

Even more serious was the fact that OU had gained a reputation for not caring about its undergraduate students. Ironically, the university's pursuit of Association of American Universities membership—considered the gold standard in higher education—had backfired with some prospective undergraduates and their families. Another public perception was that OU faculty members resented teaching large freshman courses; thus, the task force encouraged the recruitment of award-winning teachers for freshman instruction.

STATING THE CASE FOR OU

Based upon the task force's recommendations, the Board of Regents offered $250,000 in OU Associates funds to provide scholarships for undergraduates and grants to encourage innovation in undergraduate teaching. Money was also set aside for student recruiting and admissions.

The Associates fund came directly from private giving, an area in which the university was having success despite the devastation of Oklahoma's oil economy. OU was on track to raise $19 million in 1985.

OU's faculty was also doing its part to bring money to OU's two campuses through $47 million in grants and contracts. At the Health Sciences Center, a $1.6 million gift from the Parry Foundation of Houston to the College of Nursing provided undergraduate scholarships and an endowed chair devoted to the study of gerontology nursing. The drive for OU's Energy Center was making headway on the Norman campus, with construction on Phase I scheduled for completion in spring 1986. Some $35 million had been raised for the center, with another $10 million yet to be committed. A major gift from Loyce Youngblood would provide a library for the Energy Center in memory of her late husband, Oklahoma City oilman Laurence S. Youngblood.

There was more exciting news at the University of Oklahoma: burgeoning partnerships that would benefit Oklahoma's economy and help the university establish a niche in weather research. OU's School of Meteorology was attracting more than $4.8 million in grants and contracts each year, and had joined Applied Systems Institute, Inc., a nonprofit group of state, federal, and private weather facilities collaborating on weather research. In April 1985, OU broke ground on the National Weather Center, a cooperative venture between the federal government, OU, and private industry. The center's projects include the Next Generation Radar (NEXRAD), a Doppler radar system aimed at improving weather forecasting.

NEXRAD, developed and tested on OU's North Base, helped attract yet another weather-related gem, the $10 million Earth Observation Satellite Company (EOSAT). Norman became one of fifteen ground stations across the world and the only station in the United States to collect satellite data providing crucial information for crop forecasting and oil and gas exploration.

By promoting OU as an innovator in the development of cutting-edge technology, Jischke helped state leaders understand the need to invest in higher education. He demonstrated that, with the proper support, OU could gain a national reputation in energy, the sciences, and biotechnology. "I've learned that economic development is education, and education is economic development," then-governor George Nigh commented.

"The quality of our universities is a key to our future," Jischke affirmed. He believed that budget increases were crucial and stated that OU's two top priorities were offering raises to retain faculty and purchasing research equipment to attract new faculty. "Not having seed money for new faculty members would be like recruiting basketball players without a basketball court," he said.

As OU's most prominent public advocate, Jischke diligently fought to keep "the ship pointed in the right direction." Nigh and other state leaders promised him an increase in appropriations, and faculty members awaited final word from the Oklahoma State Legislature. Moods lifted across campus as it became clear that OU was slowly turning a corner; many credited Jischke with the change and hoped

that he would remain OU's president. A member of the State Regents for Higher Education even introduced Jischke as the clear front-runner for president during a public event.

"The spirit of the place [OU] picked up," Jischke recalled of those days. "But it was also a tough time. The relationship with the Board of Regents was a very challenging one."

Jischke believed that the board was divided by partisanship, personality, and different perceptions about its role at OU. The schism, reflected in minor decisions, was most prominent in the search for a new president. While some members were focused on presidential candidates' fund-raising abilities, others stated publicly that OU's next president should be "non-political," referring to Banowsky's considered run at Henry Bellmon's U.S. Senate seat and rumors that he would be appointed U.S. secretary of education.

"A second set of strains, I think, was a group on the board who felt that they ought to run the place," Jischke said frankly. "[They felt that] the administration was not strong enough, tough enough, that the faculty was not being controlled properly, and that was exacerbated by the popularity of Banowsky."

OU Regent Elwood Kemp of Ada was among those advocating for a stronger hand. After his own children were denied entrance to the OU College of Law due to strict admission standards, Kemp appealed to the Oklahoma State Regents for Higher Education with a proposal that students with a 3.0 or higher grade point average be offered admission. Jischke countered that broader admission standards would only be possible if OU Regents increased funding for the college.

"There was a long-term issue of the tension of the university's ambitions played off against its resources," Jischke said. "There were aspects that were positive and hopeful, but it was against the backdrop of this kind of debate about who was in charge, who was in control, who would be chair of the Regents? All of that was in play."

The schism in the board widened as the presidential search dragged on. The initial July 1, 1985, timeline for announcing a selection came and went. Jischke learned that four of OU's seven Regents were in support of his becoming president; Kemp was not among them.

VICTORY AND DEFEAT

The OU community was jubilant and relieved in mid-July 1985 when the Oklahoma State Legislature announced that the university could expect $16 million in additional appropriations for the coming year. The new funding would allow OU to offer faculty a 9 percent salary increase and hire twenty new faculty members and sixty graduate student assistants. It represented the first faculty raise in three years, at a time when a full professor made an average of $39,000 per year. Staff members would also receive slightly smaller merit and cost-of-living increases.

The funding bill included a promised $5.3 million for the OU Energy Center, and some $290,000 would go toward equipment purchases and $250,000 for library acquisitions. "This is a shot in the arm," said Dr. Clayton Rich, OU Health Sciences Center provost. "Our faculty members need to be encouraged and optimistic about the prospects for this institution." OU Faculty Senate chairman David Levy called the raises "an important turning point in the history of the university. They are an important step in the direction of creating excellence at this institution." Jischke told OU Regents that the appropriations represented "a genuine turnaround in funding for the university."

While OU's faculty and staff celebrated, the Regents continued to struggle with their choice of a new president. The names of candidates were kept secret, though it did surface that Jischke was among five contenders. The board, divided into two camps, met on August 1, 1985, in executive session for five hours before admitting defeat. Reporters watched carefully as "individual regents emerged [from executive session] periodically and expressed frustration that they couldn't come to an agreement."

The Board of Regents scheduled a special meeting for the next week and vowed to make a decision. "We need to get a new president on board," Regent Tom McCurdy told the *Daily Oklahoman*. "The school year starts soon and we need to get someone."

The special meeting was held on August 5, 1985. At its conclusion, the board announced that it had unanimously chosen Frank E. Horton, chancellor of the University of Wisconsin–Milwaukee, as OU's eleventh president. Horton was known as a successful motivator and fund-raiser who administrated a campus of 26,000 students and had overseen $60 million in new construction.

Though his name had surfaced as a candidate for the presidency of Iowa State University, Jischke announced that he would return to his position as dean of the OU College of Engineering. He expressed excitement at his return to the classroom. Ever diplomatic, he said that serving as interim president had given him "a deeper appreciation for the richness of the university."

In 2013 Martin Jischke admitted, "To not become permanent president at the time was a huge disappointment. But it was a wonderful learning experience for me." He felt deep satisfaction for having helped OU survive a financial crisis, move toward its future, and rediscover a sense of pride. "People felt good about OU, they felt good about me. We did, in fact, accomplish what we set out to do.

"But," Jischke conceded, "I certainly didn't fix or solve the problem within the governance." He knew the divide in the Board of Regents would continue to affect his successor, Frank E. Horton. "You can't be a good president in the face of a very divided board who is questioning their relationship to the administration, no matter who is president."

Jischke would get more than one chance to use the wisdom and knowledge he had gained as OU's interim president. Six months after returning to the College of Engineering, he was named chancellor of the University of Missouri–Rolla at age forty-four. The school was one of four campuses in the University of Missouri system and focused on engineering education. His appointment came as no surprise to many at OU. "Those of us who know him have realized that he would move on to a position of great responsibility," said OU executive vice president J.R. Morris.

Jischke moved on to even greater responsibilities five years later as president of Iowa State University. And, in 2000, he was named president of Purdue University, where he served for seven years. There Jischke helped raise more than $1.7 billion—an unprecedented amount in Indiana public education history—and oversaw the construction of forty-three new buildings, including a $300 million interdisciplinary research center.

Now retired in Indiana and still extremely active in higher education and private industry, Jischke remembers fondly his nearly two decades as an OU professor, director, dean, and interim president and expresses gratitude for the OU years that shaped his future.

"I think it has turned out pretty well," he said wryly.

FRANK ELBA HORTON
1985–1988

AFTER AN EXHAUSTIVE EIGHT-MONTH search, the Board of Regents announced in August 1985 that it had selected OU's eleventh president: Frank Elba Horton, a forty-five-year-old administrator and innovator who had ushered in a new era of vitality as chancellor of the University of Wisconsin-Milwaukee. During his five years of service there, the Chicago native was credited with starting the school's private foundation, increasing its number of federal grants and academic programs, developing international study programs, and building stronger relationships with area high schools. An urban geographer with a Ph.D. from Northwestern University, Horton had also initiated a major building program that combined $60 million in new construction with a campus beautification initiative.

When Horton met the OU community for the first time it was with Governor George Nigh and the seven Regents at his side. Exuding quiet confidence as he introduced his wife Nancy and their four daughters, Horton acknowledged OU's economic woes and pledged to help the university succeed despite these preexisting limitations. "My definition of a university is 'more ideas than money,'" he declared. "There is never going to be enough money."

During the next three years, Horton guided OU through some of its most wrenching financial times and relentless internal power struggles, as both president and Regents strove to assume greater direct control over university affairs. A crisis within OU's nationally lauded football program would add fuel to the fire. Despite these difficulties, and the constraints they posed for his ambitions, Horton's leadership kept the university afloat and helped it grow in remarkable ways, with many of his improvements sustained to the present day.

FINANCIAL WOES AND PERSEVERANCE

From the start of his presidential tenure, Horton, his faculty, and the Board of Regents attempted to respond to the dearth of funding caused by the oil bust. As the later years of President Banowsky's administration had shown, cuts to this crucial stream of revenue sent shockwaves throughout the state. For the University of

Newly named OU president Frank E. Horton meets the public at his first press conference. *(OUCT 2021)*

Oklahoma, that meant monies earmarked by the legislature for public education took successive hits, with reductions every fiscal year. New plans had to be crafted to keep the university solvent, and success depended upon tried-and-true tactics as well as innovative approaches.

Horton personally advocated new initiatives to staunch the wound left by the oil crisis. He joined the Oklahoma Council of Science and Technology, adding his voice to those who encouraged the state to expand its industrial base beyond energy and agriculture and thus shield it from the vagaries of the global market. He also used the President's Fund to establish the Office of Business and Industrial Cooperation, or OBIC, which operated as both an information clearinghouse for businesses in need of guidance and as a way to attract new businesses. Finally, Horton took his case to the people of Oklahoma, penning newspaper columns that noted OU's accomplishments and developments, from $47 million in research grants and contracts in 1985 to a record $51.7 million in external grants and contracts in 1987.

Despite his best efforts, each year of Horton's presidency began with proposed legislative cuts that required immediate redress, even as reserve funds dwindled. Although it was less than the 1982 reduction imposed on state colleges and universities, Governor Nigh's fall 1985 call for a 3.5 percent budget decrease would still cost the university approximately $3.8 million in funding. Acknowledging that the cuts held "serious implications" for OU, Horton vowed to make the necessary reductions without hiring freezes or furloughs. The following January when Nigh formally announced further budget cuts—the largest in state history—reducing OU's appropriations by

President Horton visits with Oklahoma governor George Nigh. The largest budget cuts in state history meant that Horton faced a financial emergency at OU throughout much of his tenure. *(Courtesy* Sooner Magazine)

$12 million, it became clear that Horton had to revise his plan.

OU's president instructed department heads to identify areas where costs could be reduced by 15 percent. In response, the Faculty Senate recommended that once cuts exceeded 10 percent or led to faculty dismissal, the university should declare a "state of financial emergency," which would allow OU to prioritize firings based on core needs and bypass the tenure process. Officials also encouraged early retirements for faculty and staff, and although layoffs were avoided, supplies, travel, maintenance, and equipment on all three campuses were drastically reduced. When further cuts loomed in 1987, Horton was able to avoid furloughs and layoffs, as well as the elimination of OU's dentistry college and the Tulsa medical school, but he had to raise tuition rates in order to do so. Although undergraduates ended up with a 21 percent increase in tuition costs, the university's rates still remained the most affordable in the Big 8.

President Horton also had to balance these successive financial crises with the needs of his faculty. Cuts from 1982 continued to reverberate alongside current funding concerns, as the number of unfilled faculty positions climbed to two hundred, class sizes increased with growing enrollment numbers, and classrooms and laboratories across campus fell into further disrepair. As national statistics painted a dismal picture for current and future professors—Oklahoma ranked fiftieth in funding increases for higher education, with a 20 percent salary gap—loyalty to the university vied with fears of what was yet to come. "Faculty are really worried about what the future holds," Faculty Senate chair Peggy Hopkins had stressed in 1986, a sentiment that only became more prescient as other

President Horton addresses an audience of one thousand during his October 1985 inauguration. "The days have long since passed when universities were walled away from the greater society, set apart from the issues and concerns of the world," he told the gathering. *(OUCT 2070)*

universities began to actively recruit OU professors. But most faculty stayed with OU despite the harsh conditions, leading Horton to exult, "I have never seen loyalty to an institution such as being displayed here." Their determination ushered forth a slew of scholastic advances, as the number of National Merit Scholars at OU rose from twenty-two to thirty-eight between 1985 and 1987 and the Honors Program, with new director Nancy Mergler at its helm, revamped its program guidelines and planned a new honors residence hall in Cate Center.

Despite their differences, President Horton and the Regents came together at the president's house in 1987 to celebrate the achievements of National Merit Scholars, two of whom are flanked here by Regent Mickey Imel and the president. *(OU EMP 87653)*

As in previous administrations, private giving remained the university's best solution to ongoing fiscal problems. Nothing exemplified OU's determination to maintain excellence amid financial adversity more than the November 1986 launch of the OU Centennial Campaign, a $100 million drive to fund professorships, research, scholarships, and facilities construction. Under the experienced direction of Vice President for University Affairs David Burr, the Centennial Campaign made an immediate impact and raised a $50 million during Horton's tenure.

RELATIONSHIPS WITH
THE REGENTS

"Dr. Horton has an enviable record of success in university administration," OU Regents vice chairman Tom McCurdy told the press when Horton's presidency was announced. Colleagues had noted his cordial relationship with Wisconsin's Regents, and Horton had hoped to experience the same during his presidency at OU. These illusions were swiftly shattered, as the new president found himself entangled in preexisting political currents centering on the Board of Regents' roles and responsibilities within the university.

First and foremost was the Regents' ability to audit the finances of various university organizations and their respective funds. Two weeks after Horton's arrival, the board held a special meeting in which it asked for routine audits of the president's office, with findings reported directly to the board. Horton conceded to the audits but insisted that the president be responsible for presenting university finances

to the board. The meeting established a tone of conflict and discord that would resonate throughout Horton's presidency. The Regents next sought greater disclosure of expenditures from the President's Fund, the discretionary monies first set aside under President Sharp and disbursed by the OU Foundation, an independent nonprofit organization benefiting the university. While the foundation eventually allowed the Board of Regents to audit its holdings, the outcome led to still more controversy: while all the spending analyzed fell within foundation policies, the results were somehow leaked to the *Daily Oklahoman*, even though they contained private donor information and were not a matter of public record.

Investments compounded the problem of financial transparency, as once again the Regents demanded a greater presence in negotiations and became increasingly dissatisfied with the president's explanations and compromises. When the university agreed to sell sixty-nine acres of land southeast of campus to Hitachi Ltd. for the construction of a $9 million manufacturing plant, several Regents were unhappy that they had not been consulted on the deal before being asked to approve the land purchase. Horton's response—that he had first learned of the opportunity just three weeks before and had been asked to maintain confidentiality—only created more hard feelings. The board's initial partial divestment of stock holdings in three South African companies failed to satisfy the Faculty Senate and OU Student Association, both of which had joined the movement against apartheid that swept the U.S. through much of the 1980s. At Horton's urging, the Board of Regents soon voted for full divestment. They did not, however, agree with Horton's endorsement of the sale of higher education bonds to a Japanese commercial bank, maintaining that the proposition was too risky.

As they expanded their involvement in the university's finances, the Regents also sought greater influence in other aspects of the university. In summer 1986, the board asked for an unprecedented change: instead of hearing hiring recommendations after completed searches, they wanted one or more Regents to serve on every administrative search committee, with the ranking Regent acting as chair. Strong faculty backlash led the Board of Regents to withdraw their request, instead asking Horton to keep them closely informed during those searches. They also sought to expand their purview with respect to athletics, seeking greater involvement in athletic director searches and the power to instruct President Horton on how to vote on major athletic issues when he represented the university at the annual NCAA convention. The Board of Regents also reinstated expelled wrestler Joe Brett Reynolds, the future 1990 NCAA Division I champion, despite his admission of academic fraud and in spite of Horton and the faculty's insistence that Regents stand by his expulsion. The board did, however, cede control of the Sooners' nonconference football schedule to the president and athletic director in 1987.

Events came to a head when an audit scandal at Rose State College led to the filing of criminal charges against its president and chief financial officer, sending shockwaves through Oklahoma higher education. Regent Elwood Kemp stepped to the forefront of this debate both behind closed doors and in the public eye, to the dismay of Horton and university faculty alike. Despite an internal audit three years earlier that had found no evidence of fraud or improper use of funds, Kemp asked that all of OU's twenty-seven auxiliary units be audited once again.

Furthermore, Kemp got the media involved, predicting in front of reporters that OU's inevitable discrepancies would make the Rose State scandal look like "a kindergarten affair." Horton's proposal to form a Regents committee that would work in concert with auditors became yet another failed compromise, as a split vote among the Regents led Kemp to repeat his request and expand the image of a potential scandal. "If this was my corporation that was in this shape, I'd shoot myself," Kemp declared, once again in the presence of media.

Not all president-Regent dealings were so antagonistic. In May 1987, when Kemp charged Horton with receiving illegal compensation through the President's Fund, Chairman John Imel reprimanded Kemp for his "irresponsible allegation" and demanded an apology. Nonetheless, by the end of Horton's tenure the tone between OU's president and the Regents was generally one of discord, despite Horton's repeated attempts to provide compromises and maintain cordial relations. As the *Daily Oklahoman* would later declare, "Depending on who's doing the talking, Frank Horton is either a tireless president who skillfully guided the University of Oklahoma during tough times or an ineffective leader whose poor chemistry with some OU Regents doomed him to failure."

THE RISE AND FALL OF SOONER FOOTBALL

As financial woes and relations with the Regents provided persistent sources of conflict, OU's athletic accomplishments at first provided a welcome respite. "Athletics are followed nationally in a way that allows OU to be recognized," Horton declared in 1987, and for the most part he was correct: the Sooners' various teams racked up multiple

With its win over Penn State in the Orange Bowl on January 2, 1986, the football team secured the 1985 National Championship for OU. Here Barry Switzer gets a ride across the field from players Tony Casillas (*left*) and Jeff Tupper (*right*).
(*AP photo by Mark Foley*)

accolades during his tenure in office. But even in this neutral arena, storm clouds threatened, as scandals and infighting at all levels threatened to overwhelm OU's athletic achievements.

Fresh from their 1985 national championship, the Sooner football team enjoyed a wave of national publicity in early 1986. Standout players lauded in the media included Jamelle Holieway, Keith Jackson, Tim Lashar, and Tony Casillas, although linebacker Brian "The Boz" Bosworth, with his outrageous personality and mohawk haircut, received the most press. OU continued to dominate the Big 8, and won both the 1986 and 1987 Orange Bowls.

Politics intervened, though, in the tumult over who would fill the position of OU athletic director after Wade Walker's resignation in mid-1986. Leon Cross, a longtime associate athletic director and former All-American under Coach Bud Wilkinson, and Donnie Duncan, a former coaching assistant for Barry Switzer who had become executive director of the Gator Bowl, vied for the position, and lines were swiftly drawn in the sand. Switzer escorted Duncan to a private, unofficial meeting with the university Regents, while Cross's supporters targeted alumni and the media with an intensive letter-writing and phone campaign. Winning the competition by a narrow margin in September, Duncan subsequently promised to "represent the school with style and class, in good times and bad times." During the Horton years, he had plenty of opportunities to prove his word.

The increased media focus on Brian Bosworth became

more of a hazard, as the linebacker provided ample controversy. Although he apologized after publicly insulting UCLA's team following a Sooner victory, Bosworth's damaging, off-the-cuff remarks in a *Sports Illustrated* article left a bad impression. Then came the next blow: one week before the Sooners played Arkansas in the fifty-third Orange Bowl, the NCAA notified Coach Switzer that Bosworth had tested positive for anabolic steroid use and was thus ineligible to play. Despite a more recent, negative test and Bosworth's insistence that he had used steroids only a year prior under physician's orders, the NCAA held firm. Indignant, Bosworth ignored warnings from Switzer and Duncan to keep his opinions private and instead appeared on the Sooners' sideline in a "National Communists

The OU men's basketball team enjoyed rousing successes throughout the 1980s under head coach Billy Tubbs, winning the Big 8 Conference title four times and becoming NCAA national runner-up in 1987–88. *(OUAth 496)*

The Sooner Schooner takes part in the campuswide celebration held in 1985 when the football team won the national championship. *(OU EMP 8637)*

Catlett Music Center during phase I of its construction, November 1985. *(OUFA 30)*

Against Athletes" T-shirt. Although he acquiesced to officials' demands to remove the shirt and issued a public apology within days, Bosworth's antics blazed across national television and newspaper headlines, leading both to Bosworth's dismissal from the team and to heightened national media attention that followed him into the National Football League.

NCAA regulations provided chronic challenges to OU's football program, as internal audits and the organization's own investigations turned up repeated infractions. First there was a report that OU had more academically ineligible freshman players than any other football team in the Big 8. While Duncan swiftly corrected the meal allowance process to maintain compliance after an internal audit revealed NCAA policy violations in basketball, these infractions, combined with Bosworth's positive steroid test and subsequent behavior, led NCAA investigators to make a "routine" visit to Norman in January 1987. Just over a year later, the investigation closed with a Letter of Official Inquiry from the NCAA rife with alleged rules infringements, including major recruitment violations. Its repercussions would last beyond Horton's presidency, diminishing the OU Sooners' star just when it had seemed to shine brightest.

RESIGNATION AND LEGACY

On May 30, 1988, President Frank Horton shocked the OU campus with his resignation. While he had expressed his desire to return to teaching, no explanation was given for his departure, although Regent Charles Sarratt admitted to reporters that "the chemistry of the board isn't in Horton's favor" and expressed doubts that the board would have voted for Horton when his contract came up for renewal.

Despite Sarratt's comments, Horton remained above the fray, simply saying, "The important thing is that the University of Oklahoma continues to move forward in a positive direction." Even Elwood Kemp, possibly his greatest opponent amongst the Regents, made a laudatory public statement, commending Horton for providing strong leadership for the university during difficult economic times and into the future. "The Regents will build upon these contributions, initiate others, and seek similarly strong leadership for the university's second century," Kemp declared. As *Sooner Magazine*'s Carol Burr revealed, however, the university community was well aware of the drawbacks of the job, made abundantly clear during Horton's tenure as president. "Cardiac and/or ulcer patients need not apply," she quipped, adding, "All you have to do to keep this job is please almost all of the people all of the time. For Frank E. Horton . . . that price may have become too high to pay."

Horton briefly served as a paid consultant for the Oklahoma State Chamber of Commerce and Industry before being chosen from a national pool of one hundred candidates to be president of the University of Toledo. He would serve there for a decade before forming his own higher education consultant firm and later assuming interim administrative positions in Illinois and Kansas City,

FRANK ELBA HORTON ❋ 149

and then traveling to Africa on behalf of the U.S. State Department to develop strategic planning for Namibia's national university. Currently, Horton lives in Durango, Colorado, with his wife, Nancy. Their daughter, Kelly, is a proud 1989 OU alumna.

Despite the turmoil of his brief presidency, Horton's legacy endures in the numerous additions to the university's facilities and the expansion of its academic repertoire during his time in office. His administration oversaw the completion of the first phase of OU's Energy Center as well as the Stanley B. Catlett Sr. Music Center, both iconic campus buildings that support science and the arts at OU. The Carl Albert Congressional Research and Studies Center in Monnet Hall also opened under his aegis, as did the Office of International Studies, offering unprecedented travel-study opportunities for students and faculty. Horton himself has expressed no regrets about his time at OU, then or now: "I've enjoyed Oklahoma, even though these years haven't been easy for anybody in Oklahoma," he stated in a *Daily Oklahoman* interview given shortly before his departure. "There's a kind of inner strength to the people here; they can move through adversity."

DAVID SWANK
1988–1989

 DAVID SWANK HAD, BY May 1988, served a quarter-century at the University of Oklahoma as professor, legal counsel, and dean of the OU College of Law. The last thing he expected was to be asked to serve as the university's interim president after the resignation of President Frank Horton.

Before agreeing, Swank decided to visit each of OU's seven Regents to gauge their expectations of an interim president. One of his primary goals would be to rebuild the relationship between the Office of the President and the Board of Regents, a link that had grown increasingly strained. "My agreement with the regents was that I would not seek to become the [permanent] president," Swank said recently. "But on the other hand, I said that if I am going to be president of the university, I will not be a caretaker. I will make all the decisions that a president of the university would make."

Swank's determination to take full responsibility for OU would lead him through a series of scandals that attracted the national spotlight and a wrenching decision that made him the target of death threats. The university emerged whole—but forever changed.

BUILDING BRIDGES

A Stillwater native and Oklahoma State University alumnus, David Swank earned his OU law degree in 1959. He entered his family's private law practice before being named Payne County Attorney, and he was offered a position as OU's legal counsel and assistant professor of law in 1963.

Swank thrived at OU, becoming a full professor and director of clinical education. He began a decade as associate dean of the OU College of Law in 1975 and was promoted to dean in 1986. But becoming OU's interim

president two years later was entirely different. Swank recalled realizing that he had suddenly gone from overseeing one college with a budget of less than $10 million to administering an entire university with three campuses. He turned to his wife, Ann, and asked, "What do we do now?"

His first step was to carry out the Regents' request to strengthen relations between the board and the president. Swank met with key presidential staff members to smooth issues that had rankled relations during previous administrations; he also learned how to get along with several Regents who wanted to take a strong hand in the university's daily business.

"I found that I could work with them pretty well, as long as you kept them advised of what you were doing and you recognized where they were coming from," Swank said. Two Regents were independent oil men accustomed to running every detail of their companies. "They sort of wanted to run the university, and you had

to control that and make sure they didn't, but you had to do it with a velvet glove," he explained.

After establishing improved relations with the board, Swank enjoyed the chance to work closely with faculty and staff from each of OU's colleges. President Horton was temporarily in residence at the presidential home on Pickard Avenue, so David and Ann used their private residence for entertaining. Their unique home—known locally as "The Teepee House"—was soon crowded with faculty, staff, alumni, and donors. "We really had a glorious time," Swank said of the experience.

The university seemed to be returning to glory days after long years of struggle. While a sixteen-member presidential search committee composed of faculty, staff, and students went to work, Swank proudly announced in September 1988 that OU had received a $1 million gift from the Kerr-McGee Corporation to commemorate the university's upcoming centennial.

OU was also celebrating the enrollment of an unprecedented forty-five freshman National Merit Scholars, ranking the university first among Big 8 schools in Merit Scholars and thirteenth in the nation among public universities. The scholars, touted as the "best and brightest," received full scholarships, and Swank called each of the scholars to welcome and encourage them.

In addition to helping attract top students, Swank oversaw other efforts to raise OU's profile. In October 1988, the university welcomed the installation of the first Next Generation Radar (NEXRAD) unit on North Base. The national NEXRAD program was designed to replace World War II–era radars with new Doppler radar to provide more detailed storm models, which would save hundreds of lives and prevent millions of dollars in damage each year. "It is this effort and science that will take Oklahoma to the future," U.S. representative Dave McCurdy said at the system's dedication. "Norman will be Oklahoma's high-tech capital."

OU's focus on technology and scholarship came as Regents Chancellor Hans Brisch advocated raising the minimum ACT score required for freshman entering OU from 18 to 19 and limiting admission to students who ranked in the top third of their high school classes. These suggestions met strong opposition in populist Oklahoma, but Swank supported the effort. "To be honest, I was a little ambivalent. I looked at the university as a place for people from Oklahoma to go to school," Swank said. "But I eventually decided to push for it because it improved the quality of OU."

IT STARTS WITH SANCTIONS

Swank was soon called upon to deliver on his promise to the OU Regents to make hard decisions. An avalanche of allegations came from the National Collegiate Athletic Association. OU had received an NCAA Letter of Official Inquiry one month before President Horton resigned, and that letter was among the first correspondence Swank read upon moving into the president's office. The Sooners were accused of eighteen NCAA policy violations, most between 1984 and 1986 under coach Barry Switzer. The allegations included improper benefits to student-athletes, such as payment for jobs with no documented work hours, airline tickets, and season football tickets that were often sold for cash.

Following an October 1988 meeting with NCAA investigators, athletic director Donnie Duncan reported that OU expected sanctions to include a reduction in athletic scholarships. Swank, who had served as OU's faculty athletic representative to the Big 8, believed more than scholarships would be at stake. "I knew we were in trouble," he said. "They had a lot of evidence about things we had done that were clearly violations." In his autobiography, *Bootlegger's Boy,* Barry Switzer denied he had ever paid a player. Other actions he attributed to the program's culture of family loyalty; Switzer admitted to buying a coat and shoes for one impoverished student-athlete and to paying for airfare so another could attend his father's funeral.

While awaiting the NCAA's verdict, the OU Board of Regents announced a set of athletic policies designed to place OU in compliance. Written by Swank, the rules included an NCAA policy education program for all student-athletes, Athletic Department staff members, and boosters. Any athletic staff member who knowingly violated Big 8 or NCAA rules was subject to immediate firing, and any student-athlete who knowingly violated rules would be barred from competition.

In mid-December 1988, the NCAA issued its ruling: the OU Sooners football program was barred from bowl-game competition for two years and from live national television for one year. The university also lost seven football scholarships and thirty-five paid recruiting visits. The penalties would cost OU an estimated $1 million in revenue.

Swank and other university officials were stunned by the ruling's severity. But when the NCAA demanded that OU "take appropriate disciplinary action," by firing staff members, or "show cause" why the university should not receive even greater penalties, Duncan and Switzer refused. Feeling they stood little chance of success, Swank and Duncan did not appeal the rulings.

Despite intense media attention focused on the NCAA sanctions, OU was getting on with the daily business of educating students. A record $50 million in research grants to faculty on the Norman and Health Sciences Center campuses was encouraging news, and OU was on track to raise the remaining $19 million needed to complete the Energy Center. A $250,000 gift from Conoco/DuPont to fund OU's first endowed professorship in chemical engineering was among hundreds of gifts to the Centennial Campaign, which attracted nearly $24 million in donations in 1989–90, marking the highest level of private support in university history. But donations and grants could not cover all of OU's rising costs.

The tuition hike that Oklahoma State Regents were considering at OU and OSU was expected to increase tuition by 14 to 22 percent, to as high as $43 per credit hour for in-state students. Students reacted swiftly to the announcement, telling reporters they were "screaming mad" at the possibility of paying higher prices yet again.

Swank expressed concern that OU "might be pricing itself out of the market" for minority students and for out-of-state students, who paid considerably higher tuition than residents. Members of the Oklahoma State Legislature also protested, yet the State Regents were committed to making students share a greater portion of their educational costs. After authorizing Swank to appoint a task force to study ways to enhance minority participation at OU, the university's Board of Regents voted to support the plan.

TRYING TIMES

In little more than four weeks at the beginning of 1989, the OU community, state of Oklahoma, and entire nation were shocked and saddened by a shooting, a gang rape, and a drug arrest involving members of the OU Sooners football team. The events shook the university to its core and led Swank to an almost unthinkable decision.

On January 13, an OU football player shot his friend and teammate, then attempted suicide. Just eight days later, a twenty-year-old woman reported she had been sexually assaulted multiple times while visiting Wilkinson House, a residence hall for athletes. Three OU players were charged with first-degree rape.

The news rocked Oklahoma, and national media descended on Norman in droves. Athletic director Donnie Duncan vowed to do whatever was necessary to clean up the program, but he assured supporters that Barry Switzer's job was not in jeopardy.

The OU Board of Regents adopted a new discipline code for athletes, including a stronger drug-testing policy and stricter monitoring of class attendance and grades. Female visitors were prohibited from entering Bud Wilkinson House, and extra security personnel were added to all athletic residence halls. A new assistant athletic director was hired to ensure student-athletes met OU's academic standards. Swank introduced the policies to the media, saying, "The win-loss record on the athletic field is important, but much more important is the student's education."

Newspapers and television broadcasts exploded with more bad news for OU on February 13, when Sooner quarterback Charles Thompson was arrested for selling cocaine to an undercover FBI agent. Thompson's arrest would prove to be part of a larger investigation.

Coach Switzer resented media implications that he was personally responsible for the crimes, but the public wanted answers and accountability. After a sensational exposé of the program in *Sports Illustrated,* the three largest papers in the state began calling for Switzer's resignation. Even Oklahoma governor Henry Bellmon weighed in, saying he was "surprised and disgusted" by the crimes.

Swank encouraged the faculty and staff to carry on, but it was not easy. "The faculty is very concerned," Swank told the *Daily Oklahoman*. "They go to national meetings, as I do, and the first question that is always asked is, 'What's wrong with your university?'" Swank also assured reporters that OU had not yet experienced a decrease in private giving as a result of the athletic scandals. "Right now people have some confidence we are going to do something. They are still very supportive," he added before cautioning, "We have to do something, or we're going to lose [that support]."

Twenty-five years later, Swank confides that he was berated by alumni and donors. While supporters respected and held great affection for Coach Switzer, they were worried about the reputation of OU and Oklahoma and wanted meaningful change. Members of the 1949 football team announced they would not hold their reunion on campus unless Switzer was removed.

Asked in February 1989 if he planned to fire Switzer, Swank told the *Daily Oklahoman:* "At the present time, I am not going to ask for the termination of Mr. Switzer's contract. I am going to rely upon the athletic director and the football coach to get these problems solved. Now, if they can't, then we'll have to look at other solutions."

Swank wrote an open letter to the people of Oklahoma. Published in state newspapers, the letter assured Oklahomans that OU had implemented a "comprehensive plan of action to address problems in the athletic program." Swank continued: "We at the University have found no simple answers to these deep human tragedies. . . . But the fact is that five players do not make up the whole athletic program or the whole university. Perspective has been shattered. OU's Norman campus is a community of more than 21,000 students. . . . Your community has been touched by someone who was educated, gained experience and maturity, and prepared for a profession at the University of Oklahoma."

While in New York on business in March 1989, Swank picked up the *New York Times* only to see a bold headline announcing the weekend arrest of an OU basketball standout. The student had been charged with public intoxication, deepening OU's reputation as an "outlaw school."

Swank had his turn in the headlines when he was asked to speak before newspaper executives in Texas. When asked how long Barry Switzer had to clean up his program, Swank replied, "I think actually within this next year we have to see signs of major changes in the program, or changes will have to be made."

Swank faced an immediate backlash from Switzer supporters and others who felt it was inappropriate for him to make such remarks in Texas—Oklahoma's archrival state. Swank apologized for creating more media attention and conflict for the university.

Endless speculation about the future of OU football taxed the university community, and at least half the candidates for OU's presidency withdrew their names from consideration. "We may have lost some good candidates because of foot-dragging," OU Regent Charles Sarratt admitted to the *Daily Oklahoman*. "We need a new president as quickly as possible. We need top management in place to get stability

After a harrowing eight months, David Swank takes a light touch in celebrating his final day as OU's interim president in July 1989. *(OU EMP 89620)*

at OU." Sarratt and Regent Elwood Kemp told reporters that Swank was considered an attractive presidential option. But Swank reminded the board of his promise that he would not seek the post. "A deal's a deal," he said.

On May 7, 1989, the OU Board of Regents announced they had chosen Richard L. Van Horn as the university's next president. Van Horn, president of the University of Houston, would transition to OU in July. The end of David Swank's long, difficult interim presidency was within sight. But he would have one more hardship to endure.

NO WAY BACK

In early June 1989, Swank received a phone call from a U.S. attorney based in Oklahoma City who informed him that former OU assistant football coach Scott Hill had been the focus of the FBI drug investigation that targeted former quarterback Charles Thompson. Hill's investigation was now complete, and he would be charged in federal court with distributing cocaine.

Although Hill was no longer a member of OU's athletic staff, Swank felt certain that the university had reached the absolute limit of wrongdoing and bad publicity it could stand without drastic change in the football program. "That's when I said, 'It can't go on. That's the end of it,'" Swank recalled.

Swank contacted incoming President Van Horn, and then placed a phone call to Las Vegas, Nevada, where Barry Switzer was on vacation. He asked Switzer to return to Norman for a meeting with Duncan, OU legal counsel Fred Gipson, external counsel Andy Coats, and Board of Regents chairman Ron White. When Switzer arrived at Evans Hall, the group "discussed all that had gone on," Swank said.

Although Swank's recollection of the meeting differs from memories detailed by Switzer in *Bootlegger's Boy*, the result was the same. On the afternoon of June 19, 1989, an enormous crowd of reporters, OU administrators, Athletic Department staff members, student-athletes, friends, and family looked on in the Jack Santee Lounge of Oklahoma Memorial Stadium as an era ended with Barry Switzer's resignation from his position as OU's head football coach. Switzer thanked his current and former players, the university, and "Sooners everywhere" for their support. "But I have finally decided the time has come for new leadership." He expressed pride in the Sooners' record of 159 wins, 29 losses, and four ties—the finest in college football. During sixteen years as OU's head coach, Switzer had led OU to twelve Big 8 Conference titles and three national championships. "But," he added, "my greatest pride is in the young men who have come through this program and who have worked so hard to accomplish those achievements which made me proud and made you proud."

Having returned to his duties as dean of the College of Law, former interim president David Swank greets incoming president Richard L. Van Horn and his wife, Dr. Betty Pfefferbaum. *(Courtesy* Sooner Magazine*)*

Switzer accepted responsibility for OU's 1988 NCAA sanctions. However, he concluded with a plea to amend NCAA regulations to allow programs to meet the "basic financial needs" of student-athletes, so buying them coats and shoes or a plane ticket to a family member's funeral would not result in sanctions. Two days later, thirty-six-year-old Gary Gibbs, a former linebacker at OU and Switzer's hand-picked successor, was named head coach.

Swank was confident he had done the right thing for OU, even as he had received death threats at his home and had faced two enormous stacks of letters on his Evans Hall desk—one stack supporting Switzer and the other calling for his dismissal. Swank felt saddling a new president with that choice, involving arguably the most famous and popular man in Oklahoma, seemed unfair. "I decided it was better for me to do it," he said.

OU's athletic nightmare slowly lifted, as justice was served for the 1989 crimes. The players and coaches charged in various investigations stood trial, and most were convicted and faced prison time.

The university moved beyond the scandals, as did Swank. He returned to serve as dean of the OU College of Law and continued his involvement with the NCAA. He became vice president of the NCAA in 1991 and served as chair of the NCAA Committee on Infractions for seven years. In 1994, Swank was named one of the fifty most influential people in college athletics by *College Sports* magazine.

Dean Swank had a front-row seat in 1991 for one of the decade's most volatile news stories, that of OU law professor Anita Hill and Supreme Court nominee Clarence Thomas. Swank's stand for his faculty member would contribute to his resignation as dean in 1992, though he continues to teach law at OU in semi-retirement. In 2011, David Swank was inducted into the Oklahoma Higher Education Hall of Fame.

Looking back on his eight months as interim president, Swank acknowledges that time as among the most painful in OU history. But he finds satisfaction in the fact that he helped lead OU forward; as always, the University of Oklahoma persevered and prospered. "We came out of a very dark time," Swank said, "and I think we were headed in the right direction."

RICHARD LINLEY VAN HORN
1989–1993

THE UNIVERSITY OF OKLAHOMA was eager for a fresh start when Richard Linley Van Horn was named OU's twelfth president in May 1989. No stranger to the challenges of higher education, Van Horn was welcomed by a campus hungry for stability. The Indiana native held a bachelor's degree in industrial administration from Yale University, a master's in industrial management from the Massachusetts Institute of Technology, and a Ph.D. in system sciences from Carnegie-Mellon University. A former chancellor of Carnegie-Mellon University, Van Horn had served as president and chancellor of the University of Houston and had keen insight into OU's current problems. Months before OU's athletic troubles emerged, the University of Houston's athletic department had faced an NCAA investigation.

"If the University of Oklahoma Regents hadn't been so enthusiastic or so determined a group, I might still be at the University of Houston," Van Horn said. "But I'm very glad they were." OU also gained a professor of child psychiatry when Van Horn's wife, Dr. Betty Pfefferbaum, former vice president of the University of Texas Medical Center at Houston, accepted a position in the OU College of Medicine in Oklahoma City.

During his introductory press conference, Van Horn

met what *Sooner Magazine* editor Carol Burr called "the media preoccupation with things athletic" head on. As an audience of OU faculty, staff, and students watched, Van Horn was questioned repeatedly about OU's NCAA probation, criminal activity involving former football players, and Switzer's resignation the previous month. "It's terrible for OU not to have a model athletic program," Van Horn stated emphatically. "OU can win and follow the rules." When one reporter suggested the coach at OU had more to say about what goes on than the president, Van Horn replied, "That says more about the president than it does the coach."

"The university set out to identify a president who would have impeccable academic credentials, excellent managerial skills, and the vision to lead the university into its second century," Board of Regents chairman Ron White said. "Richard Van Horn meets all of those criteria."

President Van Horn meets "the media preoccupation with things athletic" during his first press conference in Evans Hall.
(*Courtesy* Sooner Magazine)

FRESH STARTS AND FAST BREAKS

President Van Horn revealed his vision for the university in short order. "First we need to be good," he said, "then we need to communicate that quality." The president established a series of goals for OU. Increasing faculty salaries was a top priority, along with a new general education curriculum.

Van Horn announced his intent to make OU one of the top seventy research universities in the United States by 1993. The university had earned $17 million in research funding in 1988, and Van Horn was aiming for $35 million annually. To reach this goal, OU would need to expand its endowed chairs and professorships program with support from the OU Centennial Campaign, which raised $24 million in 1989–90 alone.

The endowed chairs were key to attracting nationally recognized scholars to OU. One notable 1989 addition to the faculty was Admiral William J. Crowe, Jr., retired chairman of the U.S. Joint Chiefs of Staff, who came to OU as a professor of geopolitics. An OU alumnus, Crowe had been president of his freshman class in 1943.

Again the Oklahoma State Regents for Higher Education called for a tuition increase at OU and OSU, marking the eighth increase in ten years at Oklahoma's two comprehensive universities. Tuition had nearly doubled in the previous five years. Although tuition increases helped ensure academic quality for students, the hikes had taken a toll on OU's enrollment, which declined for the second consecutive year. OU students expressed anger at another increase, and Van Horn empathized with them. "The students have a legitimate complaint," he said, adding that any tuition hike should be matched

by an increase in state appropriations.

Tuition faded from the headlines in March 1990 when the OU Athletic Department announced plans to eliminate the women's basketball program and reallocate its $280,000 budget to other women's sports. The decision followed a player-requested review of the program after the 1989–90 season, which recorded six wins and twenty-one losses.

"We wanted an evaluation of the program to see if we could find out why we weren't winning," said OU player Tammy Rogers. "We had no idea it would go this far." Later it was revealed that players might have been seeking the removal of head coach Valerie Goodwin-Colbert. If so, their plans had backfired.

OU assistant athletic director Don Jimerson told reporters that eliminating women's basketball could allow OU to begin a women's soccer team. "I understand Oklahoma is a big women's basketball state, but for whatever reason, the program hasn't caught on at the University of Oklahoma," Jimerson said.

The public outcry was immediate and impassioned. The president's office received dozens of phone calls, and women's basketball players held a protest outside Evans Hall. Team members filed a grievance claiming the university was in violation of Title IX, the federal law mandating equal opportunity in public education. But athletic officials maintained that an equal number of opportunities were still available for OU women.

Members of the OU Faculty Senate stepped in, publishing an unflattering report contrasting grades of OU women and men basketball players. The Oklahoma State Senate passed a resolution "deploring the elimination of women's basketball" and calling OU's decision "an embarrassment" to Oklahoma. And an attorney with the National Trial Lawyers for Public Justice in Washington, D.C., announced his intent to file a sex-discrimination lawsuit on behalf of the OU women's basketball team.

The most visible stand came during the 1990 NCAA Women's Final Four tournament in Knoxville, Tennessee, where hundreds of women's basketball coaches wore red ribbons to protest the OU decision. The protest was led by revered North Carolina State University coach Kay Yow, who called the program's closing "disgraceful."

Conceding to the outpouring of support, OU reinstated women's basketball just nine days after the team's elimination. "The broad interest in the program expressed during the past week is most encouraging, and hopefully will translate into financial support and increased attendance in the years ahead," Van Horn said.

Academic excellence was Van Horn's focus in 1990. That April he predicted OU's annual budget would grow from $387 million to $1 billion by the year 2000, and that federal research support would increase from $17 million to $100 million by 1995. In June, the OU Board of Regents approved the largest budget in OU history, based on a $409 million increase in state appropriations. Part of the money would go toward a 5.3 percent raise for faculty, though Van Horn argued that larger raises would be necessary to retain OU's faculty and staff. OU's funding still lagged far behind peer institutions, and Van Horn challenged the Oklahoma State Legislature to approve increases of 19 percent or more for two consecutive years. "We still have a major challenge ahead of us in the next several years" he said.

In July 1990 the promised Earth Observation Satellite Corporation (EOSAT) established its ground station on OU's North Base. Receiving digital images from the LANDSAT 6 Satellite, the station would assist in oil exploration and agricultural research. EOSAT's presence would also provide cooperative research opportunities for students in meteorology, geology, and geosciences.

OU was widely considered a solid choice for science and medical education in 1990, but Van Horn recognized that it lacked the endowment and funding necessary to become a national research university. OU administrators also realized that, on average, only one-third of incoming freshmen would eventually graduate. The university was, however, making great strides in attracting students who had unlimited potential for success. Among the three thousand students entering OU in August 1990 were ninety-five National Merit Scholars, an increase of nearly 50 percent in just one year. OU led the Big 8 in National Merit Scholars and students in the affiliated National Achievement and National Hispanic minority scholarship programs.

For the second year in a row OU student leaders attempted to change the Student Code to ban discrimination based upon sexual orientation, but the changes were rejected by the OU Board of Regents, who feared alienating conservative Oklahoma taxpayers. In April 1990, Van Horn attempted to meet students halfway by issuing a policy requiring limited protection from sexual orientation discrimination.

That fall, 150 students demonstrated outside Evans Hall to demand a new policy against racial harassment at OU. The protest grew from two incidents during one month, when members of OU fraternities reportedly threw bottles at the Jim Thorpe Multicultural Center parking lot and yelled derogatory remarks at black students. Matters deteriorated when an Oklahoma City skinhead group posted racist fliers on OU buildings after learning of the students' protest.

These actions flew in the face of OU's ongoing efforts to recruit minority students. The university's 1988 "Strategy for Excellence" set a goal of increasing minority recruitment by 25 percent, and OU's minority enrollment had grown by roughly 2 percent in two years. The year 1990 was the most successful in university history in terms of recruiting freshman minorities, yet fewer than two thousand of the university's nineteen thousand students were minorities.

Van Horn appointed a task force to draft a racial harassment policy and asked OU's white students to extend a hand of friendship to minority students. His gesture was

OU's new president quickly laid out his vision for the university: to make OU one of the top seventy research universities in the nation, to institute a new general education curriculum, to increase faculty salaries, and to grow OU's endowed chairs and professorships. *(Courtesy Sooner Magazine)*

interpreted as patronizing, and one minority student leader accused the president of "making a mockery of the whole issue." Van Horn encouraged students to become involved in "OU Together," a program aimed at cross-cultural understanding.

Student demonstrations continued until OU unveiled its racial harassment policy in November 1990. Racial harassment was defined as "conduct directed at others because of their race, religion, or national origin which could cause violence or property damage." The policy stipulated punishment for using "fighting words" against minorities, including racial slurs, insults to incite violence, obscene language, libel, and slander. Offenses were subject to review by a seven-member panel of students, faculty, and staff, and OU's administration retained the right to exact penalties ranging from reprimands to expulsion. "It puts us in a position so that everyone knows what we mean when we say 'racial harassment,'" said OU Director of Minority Student Services Norris Williams.

A CENTURY OF GREATNESS

On November 16, 1990, OU jubilantly dedicated the Sarkeys Energy Center. In development since 1984, the $50 million, 340,000-square-foot facility was constructed with the help of federal and state funds and more than 170 individual donors, foundations, and corporations, including a $3.3 million gift from the Sarkeys Foundation of Norman. Hundreds gathered for the dedication, which featured a keynote address by U.S. Secretary of Energy James Watkins. "I can't think of any better way to celebrate the University of Oklahoma's Centennial than with the opening of this center," Watkins said. "There's very little like it in the world, and you should be proud."

During the dedication OU announced a new research program and partnership with the Chicago-based Gas Research Institute. The $17 million project enabled OU to build an experimental facility to study the behavior of fluids used under pressure to extract oil and gas from natural rock, the practice known today as hydraulic fracturing, or fracking.

On December 19, 1990, OU rolled out the largest celebration in its history when the university officially turned one hundred. Dubbed "A Time for Greatness," the centennial was preceded by a yearlong series of more than forty special events, exhibits, lectures, and symposia. A black-tie dinner

Richard L. Van Horn accepts the official symbols of OU's presidency during his inauguration, held in conjunction with the centennial commencement ceremony in May 1990. *(Courtesy* Sooner Magazine*)*

for eight hundred guests featured a rare gathering of five living OU presidents: Van Horn, Frank E. Horton, William S. Banowsky, Paul F. Sharp, and George Lynn Cross. The dinner was held on the eve of OU's May 1990 commencement exercises, which also served as the stage for Van Horn's investiture as OU's president.

December 19 marked the culmination of OU's Centennial Campaign, begun in 1986 under the late, beloved vice president for university affairs David Burr. OU had harnessed the energy of hundreds of alumni and friends to serve as members of the Centennial Commission. Their efforts garnered 29,000 donations, large and small, including thirty-one gifts exceeding $1 million, for a grand total of $111,821,000 in four years. The Centennial Campaign surpassed OU's goal by nearly $12 million.

The majority of centennial funds would provide endowed faculty positions, and another $42 million was dedicated to general academic support, $8.5 million to scholarships, and more than $17 million to capital projects. Van Horn underscored OU's focus on education: "OU's goal is for every student to gain the knowledge and skills needed for leadership in the twenty-first century."

Students, faculty, staff, and alumni also gathered that day to break ground for the Centennial Arches, which today welcome visitors to OU's south entrance at the Van Vleet Oval.

Despite such celebrations, Van Horn faced the harsh reality of declining enrollment. As Oklahoma State University was in the same straits, the two traditional rivals chose to launch cooperative initiatives, including joint courses at local community colleges, to turn the tide. Efforts to streamline efficiencies between OU and OSU included collaborative research between OU's meteorology and OSU's agriculture program and televised courses between the two campuses.

In spring 1991, with the support of Governor David Walters and State Regents Chancellor Hans Brisch, higher education leaders asked the Oklahoma State Legislature to approve a $300 million capital improvements bond issue and a $100 million increase in state funding, with an additional $92 million requested for each year through 1996. The education bond issue, the first since 1968, would provide funds for renovation and construction at each of Oklahoma's twenty-five colleges and universities. Funds would also support endowed faculty positions, salary increases, computers, laboratory equipment, and library acquisitions. Even so, $300 million would address less than one-third of Oklahoma's higher education needs. Tuition hikes were part of the proposal, with State Regents asking for 5 to 10 percent increases each year through 1997.

Van Horn warned legislators that OU was in danger of "going backwards," and he worried about the university's ability to maintain student-teacher ratios and attract and retain outstanding faculty members. "Much has been asked of faculty and staff who have remained with OU," he said, adding the university was in "a very vulnerable position." The legislature voted down the bond issue; however, it soon approved a $54.9 million increase in education funding that allowed OU to offer a 6.4 percent raise to faculty and 4 percent to staff. The increase was the largest among Big 8 schools that year.

But a study released in spring 1991 showed significantly lower graduation rates for OU basketball, baseball, and wrestling team members than national and Big 8 averages. Men's basketball graduated only two of sixteen entering freshmen, and OU's football program graduated 45 of 128 players who enrolled between 1981 and 1985. Van Horn called the graduation rates "completely unacceptable" and said OU's Athletic Department and coaching staffs had already instituted changes to promote graduation and academic excellence.

A study of OU women's athletic guidelines was also released. A sixteen-member commission called for the addition of a female assistant athletic director, separate training rooms for female athletes, stronger marketing of women's sporting events, and higher salaries for women's coaches.

Restating OU's academic goals, Van Horn announced the university was seeking funds for two hundred endowed faculty positions by the year 2000. OU added fifty-six endowed professorships, raising $18 million in private funds and $15 million in state funding in only three years.

Focused on excellence at the Health Sciences Center campus, OU proposed a $39.4 million biomedical research tower. But state funds for the tower depended on a new higher education bond issue. In summer 1991 the first sustained effort to organize a labor union at OU arose when Communication Workers of America representatives declared that OU faculty and staff were dissatisfied with inadequate state funding and low salaries. Van Horn welcomed staff commitment to increasing funding, but thought a labor union might not be the best answer for OU. Faculty and staff reaction to the union was tepid, but it caught the attention of the Oklahoma State Legislature. A new higher education bond issue was under development by early 1992.

In the meantime, OU did what it could to contain costs, recruit students, and increase private giving. A record number of gifts were recorded in 1990–91, totaling $27.5 million—a one-year increase of $3.6 million. The university's endowment stood at $136 million, as compared to $50 million in 1981. For the first time, private giving approached the same level of university funding as tuition, and Van Horn set a $400 million goal for endowments by the year 2000.

Van Horn joined a rare gathering of five living OU presidents at the black-tie dinner celebrating OU's centennial in May 1990. With him from left are George L Cross, Paul F. Sharp, William S. Banowsky, and Frank E. Horton. *(Courtesy* Sooner Magazine*)*

Reaching Van Horn's "optimal enrollment" of 22,000 students on its three campuses in 1992, the president insisted that OU was "as large as we can be with our existing faculty and facilities." Nonetheless, OU was able to reach an expanded audience by offering degree programs at the University Center at Tulsa. UCAT, a consortium created in 1990 between OU, OSU, Northeastern State University, and Langston University, enabled OU to establish the Oklahoma Research Institute at Tulsa. The institute would include the OU College of Medicine–Tulsa, and the National Resource Center for Youth Services, with all teaching and research conducted by OU faculty members.

AT THE EPICENTER ONCE MORE

The campus news in October 1991 was staggering: National Public Radio had broken an investigative report revealing that OU law professor Anita Hill had accused Supreme Court nominee Clarence Thomas of sexual harassment. Thomas, a conservative federal circuit judge from Georgia and the second African American ever nominated to the Supreme Court, had less than two years of judicial experience and his appointment was already a political lightning rod for special-interest groups. Regardless, Thomas's confirmation was considered a certainty; now the word of an OU law professor could derail his future.

Within a day, the NPR report was the top national news story. Summoned to testify before the Senate Judiciary Committee, Hill responded to a swarm of national and state media during a press conference in the College of

Law faculty lounge. More than 150 law students, faculty, and staff members crowded the room, and OU law dean David Swank served as moderator. Swank had issued a public statement supporting Hill, expressing "the greatest confidence" in her honesty and integrity. "I have found that she is always truthful and I can believe what she tells me without question."

On October 11, Americans were riveted to their TVs as they watched Hill testify before the Senate Judiciary Committee. The Oklahoma native and Yale law graduate declared that she had endured multiple incidents of sexual harassment while working for Thomas between 1981 and 1983 at the U.S. Department of Education's Office for Civil Rights and at the Equal Employment Opportunity Commission. Thomas also testified before the committee, refuting each of Hill's claims.

A week later, the Senate narrowly confirmed Thomas's nomination, and Hill returned to OU. But the national reaction to Hill's testimony was visceral. Phone calls, either supporting or condemning Hill, poured into OU. The university was caught in the middle. Oklahoma representative Leonard Sullivan called for Hill to be fired due to her "left-wing extremist" influence. But Van Horn refused to fire Hill, maintaining that "Anita Hill's teaching ability is not being questioned; her scholarship is not being questioned, so therefore there is no basis for any action against her."

OU's rank and file was decidedly supportive and protective of Hill, who reimmersed herself in teaching and eventually granted one national interview to CBS news magazine *60 Minutes.*

SAVING OKLAHOMA'S TREASURES

OU celebrated when Norman voters approved a $5 million bond issue in November 1991 to provide a new Oklahoma Museum of Natural History. The museum was a crucial step in saving Oklahoma's natural treasures, many of which had long been stored in horse stables from OU's World War I era.

Again the university requested an increase in funding from the legislature. A budget sent to the State Regents requested $22.7 million in new funds for the 1992–93 academic year, which would allow OU to add fifty-five faculty positions and fifty graduate assistants, offer an 8 percent raise to faculty, and increase library acquisitions by 30 percent.

Facing similar financial challenges, the OU and OSU Boards of Regents met jointly for the first time in history in December 1991. Their focus was to "expand cooperative efforts" and establish a legislative wish list for increased funding. The meeting also focused on admission criteria proposed by the State Regents that would require students applying to OU or OSU in 1992 to score 21 on the ACT or finish in the top third of their graduating class and have a 3.0 or better grade point average.

Though tightened admission standards helped improve the preparedness of OU students, Van Horn believed the proposal would be unfair to students from small towns. He proposed a broader-based admissions standard. Students would be able to enter OU summer courses under a "right-to-try" policy, and once they had earned a minimum 2.5 GPA, they would be admitted to the university. "We need flexibility," Van Horn argued.

OU boasted seventy-three new National Merit Scholars in 1991, maintaining its top spot in the Big 8 and ranking ninth among public universities nationwide.

The university's academic mission was strengthened further with the naming of a new provost. College of Geosciences dean Jeff Kimpel had long been a member of OU's faculty and served as director of the OU Weather Center. Kimpel, who had played a major role in attracting a $12 million National Science Foundation grant to OU, would oversee twelve colleges, including the newly elevated College of Continuing Education.

A RAINY DAY SAVES OU

Oklahoma higher education was experiencing its worst financial crisis in two decades in spring 1992. The legislature announced that less than $4 million in funding increases might be available to OU. "We are going to be underwater," Van Horn told reporters. He advocated a one-time, $19 million allocation from the state's Rainy Day Fund, saying that if the money was not available, OU might be forced to cut 111 faculty and staff positions.

The financial strain came just as the university was expanding. OU's Board of Regents assumed control of Cameron University in June 1992, and OU was cooperating with Cameron on a series of nursing courses, business initiatives for southwestern Oklahoma, and computer simulations of weapon systems for the U.S. Army's Fort Sill in Lawton. Van Horn looked for ways to minimize costs and recommended to the OU Board of Regents that the university cap enrollment 10 percent below current levels—no more than eighteen thousand students. But the board did not approve Van Horn's request.

The president was also facing criticism from the faculty union that had affiliated with Communications Workers of America. Faculty members disputed Van Horn's budget priorities and demanded higher salaries.

The university community was relieved at this time to learn that a new bond issue was working its way through the Oklahoma State Legislature. The bonds, to be paid through a tax on nontribal bingo games, were subject to a public vote as State Question 649 in November 1992. The bond package contained $66.7 million for OU, including $15 million for the Oklahoma Museum of Natural History.

OU President Richard L. Van Horn and First Lady Dr. Betty Pfefferbaum. (*Courtesy* Sooner Magazine)

Professor Anita Hill again became the focus of headlines when she requested and was granted a year's sabbatical. Conservative legislators took umbrage with Hill's plans to write a book, "organize an interdisciplinary conference focusing on issues of race and gender," and work with a group of academic administrators and businesswomen to establish "an institute or center to focus on issues of policy affecting black women." State representative Tim Pope opposed her sabbatical, stating that Oklahomans should not pay Hill's salary, since her intentions were to "further her notoriety with the public" and "her own agenda." Referring to faculty sabbaticals, Pope told the *Daily Oklahoman*: "We're paying for professors not to be there. And higher education officials are crying about how hard up they are for money."

Legislators complained that the university was shielding Hill, and Dean Swank came under attack again for supporting his faculty member. By August 1992 Swank announced his retirement as dean and his intent to return to teaching in the College of Law. Following the sabbatical she was granted, Hill requested a leave of absence from OU. In 1996, she returned to OU to teach, but she soon left for an appointment at the University of California, Berkeley, and later went on to Brandeis University to teach social policy, law, and women's studies.

While the College of Business Administration welcomed Dean Richard Cosier, the College of Geosciences began to search for a new dean. The College of Architecture selected OU's first female college dean, Deborah Dalton, and Arts and Sciences was now led by David A. Young, who had served as associate dean and OU professor of botany and microbiology.

The OU Health Science Center campus welcomed as its new provost Dr. Jay H. Stein, former U.S. assistant secretary of health under President Ronald Reagan. Stein called OU's health complex "Oklahoma City's gem" and vowed to turn the HSC into a nationally recognized center for patient care and medical research. He was the first to recommend that OU establish a national cancer center, an effort that would be realized two decades later.

Turnovers in university leadership had caused disruptions in OU's administration. Now alumni and supporters were questioning the university's decision to retain OU Sooner football coach Gary Gibbs, who was in his fourth season. Regents credited Gibbs and athletic director Donnie Duncan with making progress in cleaning up OU's football program, but the Sooners were underperforming, with the team posting a 5-4-2 season. It had also lost four consecutive games to the rival University of Texas Longhorns.

But OU reveled in good news when a $350 million bond issue, with $258 million for Oklahoma's colleges and universities, was passed by voters in November 1992. This victory provided funding for the first significant capital projects in Oklahoma higher education since 1958. "No longer is the construction crane an extinct species on Oklahoma's college campuses, and it is our children who will benefit," Governor David Walters wrote in *Sooner Magazine*.

As 1992 wound down, the state faced a $51 million revenue shortfall, and Governor Walters called for a 9 percent cut to all state agency budgets. OU could lose $13 million in funding. Ironically, the university had requested an increase of $24.7 million for "mandatory increases," including utilities, employee health insurance premiums, and retirement funds. Now OU might need to cut as many as five hundred classes and seventy-five faculty and three hundred staff positions.

"Can we afford a nationally competitive university?" Van Horn asked frankly. "Clearly, any plan for the future of higher education should address the apparent paradox of the increasing importance of and decreasing support for higher education." Oklahoma's legislature funded higher education at 66 percent of the national average.

The president resurrected the possibility of enrollment caps, pointing out to State Regents that OU had gained three thousand students in three years despite more stringent admission criteria. OU now had the highest student-teacher ratio in the Big 8, and the budget picture was bleak.

In May 1993 the Oklahoma State Legislature tapped the Rainy Day Fund for $28 million and held higher education cuts at 3.3 percent. Legislators also approved a 10 percent tuition increase. To stave off future funding shortages, OU and President Van Horn cultivated private donations for capital campaigns. Since $15 million of the $28 million in bond funding meant the university could begin plans for the new natural history museum, a fund-raising drive had been kicked off in April 1993 with the dedication of the museum's site at Chautauqua Avenue and Timberdell Road. OU pledged to raise $20 million for the museum and announced that $6 million was already in place, including a $1 million donation from the McCasland Foundation of Duncan, Oklahoma. Construction was scheduled to begin in 1994.

But May 1993 also brought division to OU when more than one hundred faculty and staff members signed a letter to Van Horn and Regents chairman E. Murray Gullatt requesting an investigation of and potential disciplinary action for "several high administrators" in OU's Office of Administrative Affairs. An internal audit examined compensation for university travel and staff members' "improper acceptance of gratuities from vendors."

Following internal review, the audit was provided to the Oklahoma state auditor and inspector. OU's student newspaper, the *Oklahoma Daily*, also requested the audit results, but OU could not release the findings, which dealt with confidential personnel issues that were not a matter of public record. The university's refusal lit a fire among local media, and the audit quickly became the focus of hostilities aimed squarely at Van Horn.

Soon conflicting versions of the audit's outcome filled the news. Van Horn said that the state auditor's review found no prosecutable activity, but the state auditor told the *Daily Oklahoman* his office had uncovered "possible violations of state law." In September 1993, the OU Regents issued a statement that the board had been advised by legal counsel to the effect that all personnel matters had been resolved. No further public action would be taken.

OU's student newspaper reacted by calling for Van Horn's resignation. "Our position is that his contract should not be renewed," wrote *Oklahoma Daily* editor Diane Plumberg. "Release the audit on your way out the door."

Oklahoma City's *Daily Oklahoman* also called for the audit's release, and Oklahoma representative Leonard Sullivan called for a grand jury investigation and asked the OU Board of Regents to fire President Van Horn. OU journalism professor Bill Loving, who held a law degree and headed the nonprofit Freedom of Information Oklahoma, Inc., also joined the fight, filing a lawsuit to force the audit's release.

WINS AND LOSSES

By fall 1993, OU had returned to the daily business of education and proudly announced that 140 new National Merit Scholars would attend the university that year, ranking OU third among all public colleges and universities. OU now boasted 454 National Merit Scholars. "National Scholars enrich OU's academic environment," said Lisa Vaughn, director of the scholars program. "Their enthusiasm for learning inspires and challenges faculty and students to reach farther and do more. Oklahomans have made a wise investment in these leaders of tomorrow."

The university broke ground for a new Family Medicine Building on the OU Health Sciences Center in Oklahoma City. The $7.75 million project included a 67,000-square-foot space to train primary care physicians, including many who would serve Oklahoma's rural communities.

OU's externally sponsored research and training were at an all-time high, topping $89 million, as compared to $17 million when Van Horn had taken office, and well beyond the $35 million goal he had initially set. The university's endowment had also grown significantly under Van Horn's leadership, from $102.4 million to $187 million. Enrollment declines and minority recruitment had been addressed. OU's athletic programs were firmly in compliance with NCAA rules, and academic performance had improved among student-athletes.

Despite these achievements, on October 15, 1993, Van Horn announced he would resign the OU presidency and

President Van Horn saw OU through times of difficulty and celebration, from battles over funding and recovery from the university's athletic troubles to record growth in fund-raising and external research and the shattering success of OU's $100 million Centennial Campaign. *(Courtesy* Sooner Magazine*)*

return to teaching. "This is very emotional for me," he said. "I've become very fond of the University of Oklahoma."

"By the end of my five-year contract, OU had achieved the things I had set out to help it do," Van Horn said in 2013. "After six years as president and chancellor at the University of Houston and five years at OU, I felt a desire to return to an academic role."

Ironically, one of the most significant achievements of Van Horn's administration came four months after his decision to resign. The largest private gift in OU's history was made in February 1994 when family and colleagues of former OU Regent and Oklahoma oilman Sam Noble gave

$9 million to construct what would be named the Sam Noble Oklahoma Museum of Natural History.

As winter wore on, the university began a selective search for a new president that focused on a law alumnus, former governor, and U.S. senator. OU would turn to longtime faculty member and administrator J.R. Morris as interim president until David L. Boren was free from his Senate commitments.

True to his word, Van Horn joined OU's Management Information Systems (MIS) program in the College of Business Administration, where he taught from 1994 to 2006. He served as the first head of OU's Management Division and helped establish the university's Center for MIS Studies. An enthusiastic private pilot, he also served as the Clarence Page Professor of Aviation and helped redesign OU's aviation curriculum. "I had a great time," Van Horn said of his years on OU's faculty. "That was a really enjoyable period of my life."

Van Horn retired from full-time teaching in 2006 but continued as an adjunct instructor for the OU Department of Psychology and Behavioral Sciences. He coauthored several publications and research grants, and served as project director for the university's Center for Terrorism and Disaster Studies. Looking back over his years as OU's president, Van Horn says he is most proud of his efforts to enhance student education. "All of the effort that went into our work," he recalled: "I think of it as maximizing the value of an OU degree."

JOHN RANDOLPH MORRIS
August–November 1994

 WHEN DAVID L. BOREN was named president designate of the University of Oklahoma in April 1994, he realized it would be eight months before he could leave the U.S. Senate. OU needed a trusted and committed leader to guide the university in his stead.

The choice was obvious. No one was more knowledgeable about the university's inner workings than J.R. Morris, a retired administrator who had made OU his life for more than four decades. The Shawnee, Oklahoma, native had come to OU in 1954 as a doctoral student in clinical psychology and served as an assistant professor of psychology during his graduate years.

After graduation, Morris took a job at Norman's Central State Hospital until University College dean Glenn Couch asked him to return to OU as assistant dean. In 1963, Morris helped establish OU's University Scholars Program, working with director Stephen Sutherland to recruit forty-seven students during its first year. Although students did not receive scholarships, the Scholars Program quickly doubled in size and laid the foundation for OU's Honors College and National Scholars Program.

When Dean Couch died in November 1966, President George Lynn Cross named Morris as dean. Morris soon began coaching students for the GE College Bowl, a long-running quiz program on NBC. OU's team—Ed Balsinger, Ralph Doty, Steve May, and Stephen Wilson—studied rigorously and commuted between Norman and New York City each weekend for six appearances. Morris prepped the team and traveled with them as chaperone and coach. OU's team went undefeated and won $10,000 in student scholarships for the university, and Morris played a pivotal role in the team's success.

"The team, to a man, had class. It won with élan,"

wrote *Sooner Magazine* editor Paul Galloway in 1966. "And though winning a television quiz show doesn't automatically make the University of Oklahoma a great institution, it's nice to remind the people of the state and the country that OU is primarily a center of learning."

Among Morris's lasting legacies is Project Threshold, a minority recruitment and support program. Many black OU students were struggling academically in 1966, because black and white public schools were poles apart when it came to financial resources. Many black students had not received an education equal to that of most white students and had significantly lower American College Testing (ACT) scores upon graduation.

"It was obvious that they didn't have the preparation for college work that our average students had," Morris said. To bridge this gap, University College offered academic advisement, counseling, and tutoring at no cost to black freshmen with identified needs. The program

later attracted federal funding and expanded. Morris said Project Threshold received federal support longer than any program of its kind in U.S. history. Today the program encompasses first-generation college students and those from economically disadvantaged backgrounds.

Morris supported black students again in 1968 when he became chairman of the Norman Community Relations Commission, which settled discriminatory housing and employment disputes. "J.R. was one of the leading university voices calling for justice," said Regents Professor of Education and Human Relations Jerome C. Weber, who began his OU career working for Morris as assistant dean of University College.

In 1968, Morris helped produce President Herbert J. Hollomon's sprawling strategic plan, *The Future of the University.* And when OU erupted in protest following the 1970 Kent State tragedy, Morris was a key figure in keeping the peace between demonstrators, Army ROTC students, and law enforcement called in by Governor Dewey Bartlett during the May 12 Field Day demonstration. "That was the most tension-filled day on the university campus in all the years of demonstrations," Weber said. "It was brought off without any violence whatsoever. J.R. Morris was the perfect person in place at that time."

After Hollomon resigned in 1970, Morris was tapped by President Paul F. Sharp in 1971 as OU's vice president for university community to support all areas of nonacademic student life and serve as go-between for students and the university administration. Morris also helped oversee the construction of the west top deck of Oklahoma Memorial Stadium and the Lloyd Noble Center.

Morris became a spokesperson for OU, delivering hundreds of speeches promoting the university and higher education. He was one of OU's most familiar and credible authorities. "When one had any sort of dealings with J.R., one could be absolutely certain of two things," said OU David Ross Boyd Professor of History David W. Levy. "First, you were talking to someone whose loyalty to the university was absolute and whose only ambition was to see the institution do the right thing; and second, that he was telling you the truth."

When Sharp resigned in 1978 and Williams S. Banowsky became president, Morris served as both vice president for university community and interim provost for OU. Named provost in 1979, Morris briefly served as provost and interim president when Banowsky resigned in 1982. Banowsky soon returned to the university and Morris to his provost duties, which included managing the university's operations while the president traveled the state and region raising unprecedented levels of private donations. "George Lynn Cross once said that Bill Banowsky was the 'outside president' and I was the 'inside president,'" Morris recalled with a grin. Morris was proud of helping OU maintain its teaching mission despite the funding shortages of the early 1980s. He also played a part in bringing federal and state agencies together to support the development of OU's Energy Center and today's National Weather Center. But Morris was ready to return to the classroom.

In 1986, Morris retired as provost and was awarded the titles of provost emeritus and Regents Professor of Psychology and Educational Leadership. He split his teaching duties evenly between the College of Education and the

Department of Psychology until May 1993, when he retired to conduct research and write in his Bizzell Memorial Library office.

BACK TO EVANS HALL

J.R. Morris was no stranger to David L. Boren. As provost he made annual trips to Washington, D.C., and regularly visited Boren's U.S. Senate office. Still, he never expected Boren to ask him to serve as OU's interim president for a third time. "Although I was a bit shocked at his request, I didn't hesitate too much. David is hard to turn down," Morris said wryly.

Morris began his third interim term on June 1, 1994, but he knew how long his job would last, because Boren had set a timeline for leaving the Senate. "That alone created a sense of stability," Morris said.

There was plenty of work to accomplish in eight months. The fund-raising campaign for the Sam Noble Oklahoma Museum of Natural History was in full swing, and Morris was frequently called on to make speeches about the university's progress and goals. "In some ways," he said, "there wasn't much of a change."

One new challenge was an ongoing demonstration by Stephen Selkirk, the twenty-four-year-old president of OU's American Indian Student Association who had embarked upon a "spiritual fast" on the steps of Evans Hall June 27, 1994, to protest the university's handling of a dispute with members of the Phi Kappa Psi fraternity.

Each year, students celebrated OU American Indian Heritage Week by erecting a teepee and holding overnight vigils in front of Bizzell Memorial Library. On March 14, 1994, Selkirk was one of five students in the teepee when a naked man attempted to enter. The Native American students emerged from the teepee to see a half-dozen naked, intoxicated young men running in circles around the teepee, slapping its sides and knocking over a support pole. American Indian students contended that they also heard someone urinating on the teepee.

A shouting and shoving match ensued between the American Indian students and fraternity members. The OU Police Department was summoned, but the fraternity members ran away before officers arrived. No criminal charges were filed at the time.

OU's American Indian community was outraged. Students filed a racial harassment claim with the university's Office of Affirmative Action and considered a civil lawsuit. The six OU fraternity members were identified and charged with multiple violations of OU's Student Code, and the university suspended all Phi Kappa Psi social fraternity activities, but due to federal privacy laws under the Buckley Amendment the offending students' names could not be released.

A week later, vandals spray-painted the words "Navajos go home" on OU's iconic statue of President William Bennett Bizzell. American Indian students protested OU's perceived lack of action against the fraternity members and Phi Kappa Psi. OU law professor Anita Hill was a featured speaker at one rally.

The fraternity members pled guilty to violating OU's Student Code and accepted sanctions. The terms of their punishment could not be revealed, and no criminal action was taken.

On July 4, Selkirk staked a spot directly in front of Evans Hall. Partaking of "fasting tea," he pledged to fast "as long as I feel it is appropriate." "I want to call attention to the recurring pattern of dismissal of Native American concerns and the tapestry of racism against minorities," Selkirk told a *Daily Oklahoman* reporter. He issued a letter requesting records of any racial incidents having occurred at OU since 1983. The university agreed to comply by releasing all that were legally allowed.

Morris did what he could to bridge the conflict. He introduced himself to Selkirk and offered to discuss OU's policies. The university issued a public apology to American Indian students, and Morris met weekly with Oklahoma tribal leaders. "We are committed to having a campus environment that enhances the learning and living experiences of all students, and I am prepared to begin the process of defining issues and addressing concerns," he stated.

Still, tribal leaders expressed frustration. "How can we assure Indian recruits that they will be safe at OU and their human rights will not be violated?" asked Jacob Tsotigh, an OU Indian Alumni Association member.

The meetings were highly productive and fostered OU's current Native American Studies program. Regardless, Selkirk fasted throughout July, and student rallies continued on campus.

When Boren came to OU late that month, he stopped to talk with Selkirk and credited him with bringing attention to the issue. He expressed concern for Selkirk's well-being if the fast continued but chose not to intervene. OU dean of students Rick Hall shared Boren's worries. "I don't think there is any question that the university community is concerned for Stephen and the issues he has addressed," Hall said. "Stephen has been nothing but a gentleman during this fast and a lot of people respect him."

Selkirk's fast stretched into late August, and concerned calls flooded OU's Jim Thorpe Multicultural Center. Finally, after fifty-eight days without food, Selkirk agreed to end his protest, but he did not give up his fight. He hired attorneys and established a legal defense fund to force OU to release the names of fraternity students involved, but the university declined the request under threat of losing federal funding for violating the Buckley Amendment.

RETIREMENT, TAKE TWO

Morris readied the campus to formally welcome its thir-teenth president, and quietly left Evans Hall when David L. Boren took office November 15, 1994. Morris returned to his Bizzell Memorial Library office, nicknamed "the bunker," where he worked until 1998. His continued presence on cam-pus meant that Morris's priceless experience and institutional knowledge were close at hand.

In 1996, J.R. Morris was inducted into the Oklahoma Higher Education Hall of Fame. Another award reflects Morris's career and passion for students: The J.R. Morris Campus Life Award recognizes OU students who have been deeply involved in and have given outstanding service to the university community.

Yet awards and honors—or even the long list of titles he has carried over four decades—cannot fully relate what J.R. Morris has meant to OU. "In all the years that I've been at the University of Oklahoma, I have never heard anyone in any context, formal or informal, speak other than glowingly of J.R. Morris," Weber said of his colleague and friend. "In a time of great transition . . . J.R. was universally seen to be the epitome of good judgment, fairness, openness, and honesty."

J.R. Morris, seen with his wife, Barbara, in 1982, was incoming president Boren's first and only choice as OU's interim president. *(OU EMP, J.R. Morris)*

DAVID LYLE BOREN
1994–PRESENT

ON SEPTEMBER 15, 1995, more than six thousand guests gathered on Parrington Oval to witness the inauguration of David L. Boren as the thirteenth president of the University of Oklahoma. Under a canopy of umbrellas, the crowd of spectators listened with anticipation to the new president's inaugural speech, their enthusiasm undampened by the rainy weather. As he began his speech, Boren acknowledged the formidable achievements of his predecessors—courageous leaders like David Ross Boyd and George Lynn Cross. He applauded the previous contributions of OU's students, teachers, and administrators. And he outlined a clear vision for the future of the university, where administrators, faculty, researchers, and students would together embark on a "quest for excellence."

Even as his notes melted in the rain, Boren identified both teaching and research as significant areas of concentration in OU's pursuit of excellence. In particular, he called for a return to great teaching as a priority for the university, where students would learn and thrive through more direct interaction with faculty. He also emphasized the need to internationalize the curriculum and student experience to prepare OU graduates for the increasingly global environment. To reach these and other goals, he would immediately launch the landmark Reach for Excellence fund-raising campaign, which became the largest private fund-raising campaign in state history.

Yet even as he brought forth an ambitious plan for OU's future, Boren also called for a renewal of "old-fashioned" community values on campus, where faculty would not only function as leaders in the classroom but personally nurture students to help them achieve their hopes and dreams. By encouraging engaged dialogue and mutual respect among all members of the OU community, the university would serve as an example to other American institutions of higher education and to the nation at large. Boren also made it clear that he could not fulfill this mission alone. The institution "has been placed in the care of all of us," he explained. Faculty, staff, administrators, students, alumni, and all citizens of Oklahoma would bear the responsibility of moving Oklahoma's flagship university into a more promising future. As "stewards" of the university, Boren observed, "it is our turn to love it, nurture it, preserve it, revitalize it, and prepare it to serve the next generation even better than it has served us."

OU's first couple on President Boren's inauguration day. *(Courtesy Sooner Magazine)*

The inauguration ceremony gave Boren the opportunity to introduce ideas that would become signature themes of his administration. In truth, he had already been hard at work for months laying the foundation for the fulfillment of his goals. Major changes began occurring at the university as soon as he and his wife, First Lady Molly Shi Boren, assumed its leadership on November 17, 1994. When the Borens moved to campus that fall, their arrival set off a virtual explosion of activity. Within weeks, Boren was immersing himself in meetings with faculty, staff, and administrators to begin planning for the programs and initiatives that would make his expansive vision for the university a reality.

The new president was no stranger to such an intense work pace, as he had worked in prominent government positions for much of his adult life, having served the state of Oklahoma as state legislator, governor, and most recently, U.S. senator. During his fifteen years in the U.S. Senate, from 1979 to 1994, Boren served on both the Senate Finance and Agriculture Committees and was the longest-serving chair of the Senate Select Committee on Intelligence. When Boren decided to leave the Senate, he had a 91 percent approval rating among his constituents.

During their years of living in Washington, D.C., the Borens enjoyed the many cultural opportunities offered by the nation's capital and its surrounding region. Molly Boren, who admits she had never visited an art museum until the age of twenty, experienced a kind of cultural awakening, visiting architectural monuments and historic homes and traveling with her husband to many countries all over the world.

Along with her newly expanded appreciation for art and cultural diversity, Mrs. Boren brought significant professional experience to her role as OU's first lady. A former educator and attorney, she was, like her husband, an OU graduate, having obtained both a master's degree and law degree from the university. One of the first woman judges in Oklahoma, she was serving as special district judge in Pontotoc County when she married then-governor Boren. And, after arriving with her husband on campus in 1994, she would soon establish a reputation as OU's "first volunteer," helping to spark a renewed spirit of volunteerism among OU students. Through her unwavering dedication to beautifying the campus and other projects, she played a pivotal role in realizing Boren's dream of creating a more communal and uplifting atmosphere on campus. David and Molly Boren's tenure at OU would be a true presidential partnership.

The Borens also shared a common bond from the past. Both had strong Oklahoma roots and both had grown up in small-town environments. David Lyle Boren was a native of Seminole, and Molly Shi Boren hailed from Stratford. Each was highly influenced by the family values instilled in them during childhood. To bring that sense of family unity to the OU campus became David Boren's overriding goal. He was determined not to come across as a detached administrator. From the start, he and Molly took frequent walks on campus, greeting students along the way and engaging in friendly conversation. "I'm old-fashioned," Boren said unapologetically. "In some respects the university president and first lady should be kind of like Mom and Dad." As Mrs. Boren pointed out in a 2014 interview, Boren's desire to build a "shared community" at OU would be at the core of all his initiatives as president of the university.

In addition to cherishing the institution of family, David Boren had never forgotten his love of education. He came from a family of teachers and taught political science at Oklahoma Baptist University before becoming the state's governor. A graduate of Yale University with a ranking in the top 1 percent of his class, he was selected as a Rhodes Scholar, earning a master's degree in politics, philosophy, and economics from Oxford University in 1965. He earned his law degree from OU in 1968. While attending law school, he served as a resident advisor for freshmen in the OU residence halls.

Boren's commitment to reform, to making government

First Lady Molly Shi Boren has provided invaluable support to the president's office in addition to her many other contributions to the university. *(Courtesy the president's office)*

Statesman: The Life of David Boren, the senator explored the idea further by meeting with a group of key OU faculty members at the home of then–OU chief legal counsel Fred Gipson. Boren left that meeting deeply impressed by the passion and commitment the faculty expressed for OU's educational mission. As one professor told him, "We just want a president that will be a part of the university family and love this place as much as we do."

The most influential voice of encouragement belonged to legendary OU president emeritus George Lynn Cross, who had served as president longer than any other and had also been a member of the selection committee that had nominated Boren for a Rhodes Scholarship. "The university is at a critical crossroads," Cross told Boren during a series of phone calls. During one such call, he plainly asked Boren to take the job for the good of the university and Oklahoma.

The OU Board of Regents met with Boren in March 1994 and unanimously offered him the presidency. He promised the board a swift answer, then returned to Washington, where he conferred with his wife. He also spoke with colleagues, Oklahoma corporate leaders, and such respected OU mentors as Savoie Lottinville, former director of the University of Oklahoma Press, who had also served on Boren's Rhodes committee. Two weeks later, Boren accepted the OU presidency. "When the opportunity came to impact the next generation, I grasped it with all the enthusiasm I could muster," he later said of his decision.

A formal announcement was made on April 27, 1994, when a thousand OU alumni, students, faculty, staff, and supporters packed Holmberg Hall to greet their future president. Boren had specifically chosen the site because of the building's long history and his own experience of performing there while still a member of his high school band and debate teams. On that stage, the senator explained why he was leaving one of the most influential jobs in the nation to become OU's leader: "Public service is not about power but is about where you can do the most good."

work better for all American citizens, fueled his desire to serve in public office. By the early 1990s, however, his feelings toward his work in the Senate had undergone a sea change. During his years as a senator, Boren had worked fiercely to champion campaign finance reform and to work cooperatively with Democrats and Republicans alike to relieve legislative gridlock. Despite his high approval rating, the senator found himself frustrated by the increasing levels of partisan bickering, which stymied progress on campaign finance reform and other causes he championed to help end corruption in government. He questioned whether remaining in the Senate would be the best way to continue to serve the common good.

Then, in 1993, OU president Richard L. Van Horn announced to the OU Board of Regents that he intended to retire within the coming year. OU Regent Steven Bentley approached Boren with the idea of succeeding Van Horn and, for the first time, Senator Boren began seriously to consider the possibility of becoming OU's president. Boren recalled having written in his college diary a list of ambitious goals for his life. A few of them he had already achieved. Another was to become president of his alma mater. Should he take this opportunity?

As author Bob Burke relates in his book *Oklahoma*

The Board of Regents has reappointed vice president for university governance Chris Purcell to her post every year since 1992. Since joining the OU staff in 1974, Purcell has served as assistant vice president for student affairs and as director of student development. Currently she is also executive secretary for the board and secretary of OU. *(Courtesy OU Public Affairs)*

The Borens embraced the new roles they had chosen: "There are seasons in your life. And for Molly and me this is the season in our lives for going back to our state, which has given so much to us, by investing our lives in the next generation. This is a great institution, worthy of being loved and cherished for itself. Worthy of a lifetime of commitment."

Despite his clear declarations of commitment to OU, Boren still needed to convince many people that he had come to stay. "One of the first things I faced when I came back to the university was a general skepticism about why I was here," Boren said in a 2013 interview. "Was it a stepping stone back into politics? How long would I be here? How long would I devote myself to the university? I tried to convey that this was a life's decision. I feel that this is what I'm called to do; it should be my life's work. I didn't come to OU to spend a year or two—I came to invest the rest of my life."

One of the first commitments Boren invested his energy in was raising faculty salaries and morale. Shortly after arriving, he learned that faculty members were outraged by recent administrative raises. The raises had been placed on the Board of Regents' agenda before Boren had taken charge at OU, and they were approved at his very first Regents meeting.

Boren asked to meet with faculty representatives in Evans Hall. During that meeting, he learned that OU's faculty members had not had a raise in several years. They felt unappreciated and without a voice. "I called you here because I'm in total agreement with you," Boren told the surprised group before pledging that "no administrator, including the president, will have a raise until the faculty has had a cumulative raise of at least 7 percent. We are all working together in this." His pledge took two years to fulfill, but Boren kept his word.

Within months of his arrival at OU, Boren was facing other challenges. One major concern was the enormous hidden cost of deferred maintenance in buildings across OU's Norman campus. "Holmberg Hall was just falling in," he recalled, adding that previous renovations of such treasures as Bizzell Memorial Library had destroyed much of the campus's architectural integrity.

Boren believed that other OU treasures were in danger of being lost, and with them the university's sense of history and community. Many students, alumni, and friends had no idea of the significance or scope of OU's past and present, and Boren made a point of telling them at every opportunity. "We had fallen into a habit of not believing in ourselves, what a special university we were and what we could become." His efforts turned into a publicity campaign titled "OU Excellence: Don't Keep It a Secret," a tagline printed on thousands of bumper stickers handed out at OU football games and events. The slogan soon spread statewide. "It was a challenge to start believing in ourselves and start believing that we can be competitive at the highest national level among public universities," Boren said. "Before you really can become that, you have to believe that you can be that."

CREATING A SENSE OF COMMUNITY

When he took the reins as OU president, Boren was well aware that the very idea of community had changed and, in some ways, had shattered since he was a child growing up in Seminole. But he had hopes that the university could play a role in putting communities—and America—back together. Boren often reminded students to "never underestimate the power of kindness. How we treat each other will largely determine our nation's future."

The president felt deeply that the breakdown of community posed one of the country's most serious challenges. The lack of shared experiences across social and economic boundaries had led to fragmented communities in which people separated themselves into groups with others just like themselves, rarely encountering new ideas or points of view. "We need a national intervention about forming diversity and community and being part of each other's lives.

As President Boren's first executive assistant, Ann Dubler aided both of the Borens in their efforts to guide the university to greater success. *(Courtesy the president's office)*

Executive assistant Sherry Evans handles day-to-day operations for the president's office. *(Courtesy the president's office)*

Longtime university presence and vice president for public affairs Catherine Bishop keeps relations strong between the university and the wider world. *(Courtesy OU Public Affairs)*

Re-creating the American community is a national priority," Boren said. "The greatest point of intervention is the university." He believed that OU and universities nationwide could and should intervene by purposely bringing together people of different races, religions, and economic backgrounds, both in the classroom and in residence halls.

The first point of intervention would be on-campus housing. The president learned that OU's longtime practice of allowing students to choose their residence hall, roommates, and suitemates had unintended consequences. Over the years OU's housing had become homogenous. In their segregated living spaces, students had little opportunity to experience and learn from other students outside their social and economic circles—from those who represented the diversity of nationalities, beliefs, and cultures embraced by the university community.

A new plan was born. While Boren agreed to allow students to continue picking their roommates, from that moment on, students could not choose which residence hall they would live in, or who their suitemates might be. Rather than flocking together according to hometowns, race, or interests, all students would become part of the OU community.

At first the idea met with some resistance. "I probably got three hundred calls from parents in protest," Boren said. But the formula worked. "The residence halls now are all equally diverse. It changed everything," he said. "I think that was one of my most important decisions."

Another key decision about university housing was on the horizon. In 1996, Boren established the OU Faculty in Residence (FIR) program. Spacious, three-bedroom apartments were constructed in each residence hall. Select faculty and their families were invited to enjoy a unique experience while living in student housing for one to three years and becoming mentors, friends, and neighbors to students.

The FIR program quickly became a huge success. Tom Boyd, OU's Kingfisher Chair in the Philosophy of Religion and Ethics, and his wife, Barbara, were the first FIR members. They took up residence in an apartment at Couch Center. Boyd said he soon realized that his greatest asset as a FIR was a listening ear, a set of comfortable armchairs, and two black cats. Students would drop by unannounced to visit with the cats and wind up sharing their concerns and stories with the Boyds. "You just want to listen to those students, listen to what they have to say and respond to them," Boyd said. He believes the program offers students an important taste of the home life they miss. "Anything that came up, we would just sit and talk about it."

By 1999, the FIR program had expanded to all Norman campus residence halls. FIR members became involved in every aspect of student life, organizing nature walks, cookouts, and study nights; baking giant batches of cinnamon rolls; and even hosting Thanksgiving dinner for students who chose to stay on campus over the holiday. Boren believes having a FIR within easy reach gives students a built-in connection to a teacher, mentor, and friend who has their best interests at heart. "It is so easy to knock on the door and ask for help," he explained. "I'm a great believer in intergenerational friendships."

To encourage more sophomores, juniors, and seniors to live on campus, OU announced plans in 2014 to develop residential colleges modeled after those long established at

Shad Satterthwaite—pictured here in 1998 with his wife, Valerie, and children, Pace, Megan, and Tanner—served as Walker Housing Center's faculty in residence from 1998 to 2001. A former assistant to President Boren, Satterthwaite is now OU's assistant vice president for university outreach, Continuing Education Academic Programs. *(Courtesy* Sooner Magazine*)*

Harvard, Yale, Oxford, and Cambridge Universities. Each college will have its own dining room and study area, along with intramural teams, crest, and motto. Ten faculty fellows will have offices in the colleges, and seminar rooms will also be included. Parking will be located nearby. "These residential colleges will make a huge imprint on the campus and will help strengthen the bonds of community," Boren said.

Hannah Morris, a Newalla senior and 2012 president of the OU Student Association, related one unique opportunity for community available to all OU students. When dignitaries visit the OU campus, Boren often invites members of the President's Associates support group to enjoy a special lecture and dinner. Every OU student is welcome to attend the event, at no cost, and is seated with OU Associates who can share their own university experiences. "When you understand the roots that you stand on, you know where to grow," Morris said. "One of the greatest gifts President Boren has given us is to open that dialogue."

Boren also wanted to make the university campus itself a gift to OU students, faculty, and alumni. Within weeks of arriving at OU in 2004, Molly Boren had taken on the task as her own and immersed herself in learning every aspect of the campus grounds. She formally educated herself in landscape design by auditing OU classes and soon knew all the gardeners on campus, becoming involved with OU garden designs from the ground up.

Among those she came to know best was Allen King, director of OU Landscape and Grounds, who shared Mrs. Boren's passion for beautifying the campus. "Creating and maintaining a beautiful campus is an invitation to prospective students to explore the opportunities that are going on beyond the lawns and gardens and within classrooms,"

explained the president. The Borens' vision has led to a virtual transformation of both the Norman and Oklahoma City campuses and has earned OU accolades and awards.

The Borens also wanted to make the campus more user-friendly. Soon after arriving at OU, they purchased six comfortable teakwood benches for visitors to enjoy. Molly Boren believed that the benches would serve two special functions: they fostered communication and interaction while affording individuals a space for solitude and contemplation. After the benches appeared around campus, the idea proved contagious, and more benches began popping up all across campus. To date, more than 175 benches have been installed as gifts from donors or corporations, and each bench carries a plate engraved with the name of the donor or honoree. The Borens also believed that they, and all OU students, had a civic responsibility to preserve and expand the number of trees and amount of green space on campus. Through Mrs. Boren's leadership and the collaboration of landscaping experts, roughly 25,000 trees have been planted on the OU campus since the Borens first arrived at OU. To help encourage the planting of these trees, Mrs. Boren spearheaded the return of the Arbor Day Tradition, which originated during David Ross Boyd's presidency. Each year on Arbor Day, students work together on the planting of trees. The thousandth Arbor Day tree, planted in 2012 near the Jim Thorpe Multicultural Center, is a water oak—a large, majestic species that will serve as a symbol of OU's mission for up to a century.

Molly Boren says that her most gratifying experience at OU occurred in 2007 after the city of Norman suffered a devastating ice storm. With financial support from Jon and Dee Dee Stuart, a cleanup and reforestation campaign was initiated on campus. Approximately one thousand students showed up on a Saturday morning and worked in teams on the cleanup effort. Mrs. Boren believes that this was the students' way of taking ownership in the recovery efforts, to "claim their community."

Outdoor sculpture and fountains have also enhanced the campus for both students and visitors, with more than two dozen art pieces thoughtfully placed in academic areas, gardens, and passageways. Five sculptures, including *Moonscape Beach* by Jesús Moroles, line the Stuart Walk connecting the Fred Jones, Jr., Museum of Art with the Fine Arts Center, the pathway named in recognition of the Stuarts' outstanding commitment to the university. Several of the best-known and beloved works are sculptures by the acclaimed Chiricahua Apache sculptor Allan Houser. *May We Have Peace,* a dramatic, eleven-foot bronze of a Native American man holding a peace pipe aloft, became the centerpiece of the North Oval, home to President Boren's Evans Hall office. Another Houser sculpture, *Homeward Bound,* is placed in the garden between Bizzell Library and Adams Hall. Molly Boren recalled a day when she and her husband encountered a young Asian student standing by the sculpture shortly after it had arrived. He told them that he had been back to visit the spot four times that day in the midst of studying for finals. "He knew nothing about American Indians, didn't realize that the woman herding her sheep was Indian," Mrs. Boren explained, "but there was something so universal about that piece of art that it spoke to him."

The *Seed Sower,* the icon on the university seal, is rendered in bronze on the South Oval and on both the OU-Tulsa and OU Health Sciences Center campuses. It is perhaps the most visible work of OU Artist in Residence Paul Moore, an Oklahoma native who returned home from Santa Fe, New Mexico, to revive OU's figurative sculpture program, inactive since 1969.

Additional sculptures have found homes in a variety of locations on campus. A grassy area between the fine arts buildings is home to *Pastoral Dreamer,* by OU MFA 1984 graduate David L. Phelps. The bronze of a giant man reclining on the grass is especially popular with children, and small visitors can often be seen clambering over its head and shoulders. Four-legged visitors have their own spot on OU's campus. Bailey's Fountain, located behind Evans Hall, is a replica of a fountain in a five-hundred-year-old Italian villa. This lovely little fountain, offering a watering bowl for creatures great and small, was a gift to the university community from Mrs. Boren in remembrance of their beloved West Highland terrier. In 2014 the Norman campus was named one of America's twenty-five most beautiful college campuses by a national digital media group.

The benches, gardens, sculptures, and fountains soon spread to OU's Health Sciences Center in Oklahoma City, where some were duplicated to underline the connection between the two campuses. Having set a goal of helping to design a garden oasis that would inspire medical students and patients alike, Mrs. Boren wound up creating the largest landscaping project in Oklahoma's history. A highway running down the middle of the Health Sciences Center campus was replaced by a giant green space, funded by private donations. Across campus, the Peggy and Charles Stephenson Oklahoma Cancer Center offers the Healing Garden, a lush, below-street landscape with a huge, flowing fountain where families, patients, and medical staff can retreat to calm and reinvigorate their spirits and better face the realities of fighting cancer.

As on the Norman campus, much of the vision and detail now enriching the OUHSC campus began with First

The iconic *Seed Sower* statue, here holding flowers to celebrate the Sooners' appearance in the 2003 Rose Bowl. *(Courtesy Robert Taylor)*

Pastoral Dreamer plays host to some of the University's younger visitors. *(Courtesy Robert Taylor)*

Lady Molly Shi Boren. The first lady's vision and hard work were recognized when OKC Beautiful presented its top honor for outstanding beautification to the OUHSC in 2002.

To ensure that campus beautification will last beyond the present generation, endowments were established to provide for the care and maintenance of gardens on both campuses. Today the university has raised more than $3 million to maintain its gardens in perpetuity. "Even in bad times—especially in bad times—we will have beauty around to inspire us," President Boren said, pointing out that the Norman campus's two ovals were designed by Vernon Louis Parrington, who was one of OU's original professors and its first football coach. "He often said that you elevate the quality of what goes on in a place by making it beautiful and special, by making people feel you're in a special place that calls forth your best efforts. You create a high standard of excellence. Why do you build cathedrals or beautiful places of worship? Something in them is sacred, lifts it up. At OU, you cannot go into the Great Reading Room, or walk across campus, or sit on a bench by a garden with the sculpture and fountains, and not feel awed or inspired by the beauty of it."

Likewise, Mrs. Boren looked to the great gardens of the United States and Europe for her inspiration. She hopes her investment in creating beautiful and uplifting natural spaces will spread to OU's students, faculty, and staff. "I believe one's environment has a huge impact on them, and we've had countless students and faculty say that the landscaping was a major part of their decision to come to OU," the first lady said at the 2012 Arbor Day event. "I believe it also helps make people more productive and consider this beautiful space sacred ground."

Among the unique aspects of the Peggy and Charles Stephenson Cancer Center is the Healing Garden, where patients and staff alike can enjoy a respite. *(Courtesy Robert Taylor)*

While the university's external surroundings create an atmosphere of learning and peace, President Boren has worked equally hard to ensure that its interiors encourage unity and a feeling of family. Among the first projects in his sights was remodeling the Oklahoma Memorial Union, which was attracting as few as six hundred students a day when the Borens came to OU in 1994. One of Boren's first observations about the 1990s student union was a literal ringing silence. The chimes that sounded from the Union's clock tower during his OU law studies had been broken for approximately fifteen years. "I asked, 'How much will it cost to fix them?' and I was told $18,000," the president remembered. "I said, 'Go ahead and fix them. I'll find the money or I'll write a check myself.'"

Twelve months later, a comprehensive, five-year renovation of Oklahoma Memorial Union began. Among the changes were a return to the Union's original Gothic style, an expansion of the food court, and a new student learning center with a twenty-four-hour computer lab. The most apparent change was the addition of a leadership wing, housing offices and meeting rooms for more than twenty-five of OU's student organizations.

Students also need places to study and relax, and these were made possible through the addition of beautiful and comfortable furnishings. Leather couches, Mission-style furniture, and southwestern art were added throughout the union, and it became common to see students studying or even catching a quick nap between classes, while surrounded by rushing crowds on their way to talk over lunch at the food court or en route to the offices of student organizations. The sight of all this activity was a source of joy for the Borens. As David Boren explained, "If you're going to be a real community, you have to have a place that substitutes for the town coffee shop, a place where everyone passes through in a day and exchanges ideas," he said.

Students passing through the union walk by dozens of historic photos highlighting the university's first century. The early photos were replicated and placed all across campus, along with historical markers installed throughout the grounds. Their images and words serve as important reminders of OU's past, helping to create a sense of continuity and giving current OU students an implicit understanding that they have joined a vast university family.

When the Oklahoma Memorial Union renovation was completed, the president felt the financial investment was well worth the effort. After all, the ultimate goal had been quite simple: to return the student union to the students. The former count of six hundred students passing daily through the Union grew steadily, exploding to as many as twelve thousand students actively using the facility each day. Students were leaving their mark on the union once again—in some cases, for good. In 1998, Boren began an

Night and day, the Oklahoma Memorial Union provides a haven for student life and activities.
(Courtesy Robert Taylor)

OU annual tradition borrowed from his alma mater at Yale. The new Clark Anderson Room in the union was outfitted with solid oak "leadership carving tables." Every year organizations and clubs of every stripe, including athletic teams, are invited to attend a carving party, during which they carve their names or initials into one particular table. A group photo, taken to capture the experience, is displayed above the table.

Faculty, staff, students, alumni, and supporters were given a second special gathering spot in the union when renovation of the University Club was completed in 2013. Former union activities director Jan Marie Crawford of Denver made the gift in the name of her late husband, Richard J. Crawford; in thanks, the space is now named the Jan Marie and Richard J. Crawford University Club.

Yet another campus landmark that benefited from the Borens' passion for community was Boyd House, the grand neoclassical mansion built in 1906 that had served as home to OU presidents from David Ross Boyd to George Lynn Cross. Boyd House had sheltered OU's most distinguished guests, including former U.S. president Harry S. Truman, former first lady Eleanor Roosevelt, and poet Carl Sandburg. Boren launched a $2 million private campaign to renovate the home, which was brought back to its former glory under the hand of architect Hugh Newell Jacobsen and the supervision of Mrs. Boren. The newly expanded Boyd House now provided living areas for OU's first family and spaces for meetings and academic and social functions. The completed renovation of Boyd House was celebrated in November 1996 with a weeklong open house, during which

Freshman students display Sooner spirit at Camp Crimson as they sing the OU Chant. *(Courtesy Robert Taylor)*

The OU Ring Ceremony.
(Courtesy Robert Taylor)

every student and faculty and staff member was invited to tour the home. Within three days alone, 10,000 visitors accepted the invitation.

President Boren's efforts to build OU's community also included drawing on its history by reviving OU traditions that had faded in the decades before he became president. The OU Chant, written in 1938 by Jessie Lone Clarkson Gilkey, made its way back to prominence—sung by students, athletes, and supporters at OU athletic events, including football games, and at other events, such as the university's commencement exercises. Soon every student knew the thrill of thousands of voices calling, "Live on, University." Commencement was moved outdoors and celebrated with style, concluding with a giant fireworks display. A new tradition, the OU Ring Ceremony, was introduced in 2000. All OU seniors are invited to purchase a common, gold class ring emblazoned with the interlocking OU symbol and the university's Cherokee Gothic arches. The rings are presented each spring during a special ceremony led by President Boren.

In addition to these time-honored rituals and customs, David and Molly Boren established brand-new traditions for OU. In 2005 they created a competition called the President's Trophy. The purpose of the competition is to encourage students and their organizations, such as sororities, fraternities, and residence halls, to excel in four areas of emphasis: academics, campus activities, volunteerism, and multicultural participation. The winners of the competition are recognized with cash prizes and large trophies presented by the president at an annual ceremony.

To further extend the spirit of volunteerism among students, David Boren initiated the Big Event, which became the university's official day of community service. Every year, on a single day, thousands of OU students devote their time and energy to working at different job sites in the Norman and Oklahoma City metro areas. As expressed by its mission statement, the Big Event strives to unify campus and community through one big day of service and gratitude.

The many efforts in the name of community—from the residence halls to the Ring Ceremony to the Big Event—share the goal of establishing and maintaining an environment of true belonging and service at the University of Oklahoma. "The sense of family is one of the things that touches me most at OU," said Boren, who delights in the nickname "D-Bo" given him by students. "I feel it among our students, faculty, and staff. The students are like my own sons and daughters; you care about them all so much. I just don't find that feeling at very many universities. At OU, people make eye contact, they speak to each other, they like each other, they relate to each other across disciplines. You can feel it, and if you're here even a week, you know that the 'OU Family' is not a slogan—it's a reality."

REWARDING GREAT TEACHING AND ATTRACTING GREAT STUDENTS

"If you want to pick just two things that produce an outstanding university," President Boren has said, "it is great teachers interacting with great students." This goal was foremost in Boren's mind even before he formally became OU's president. Throughout his long career in the U.S. Senate, Boren mentored students who served as summer interns in his Washington, D.C., office. He made an effort to get to know each student and often asked questions about their education and life goals. When he inquired about exciting developments at the University of Oklahoma, Boren repeatedly heard one name mentioned: the OU Honors Program.

The Honors Program had been in continuous operation at OU since 1962, making it one of the oldest programs of its kind. When Boren became OU's president in 1994, the program was headed by Nancy Mergler, who helped shepherd more than a thousand students each year through small-group, honors-designated classes and colloquia taught by faculty drawn from five colleges across campus. At that time, OU faculty members were not allowed to teach honors courses in addition to their normal class load, which severely limited the variety and availability of courses. Faculty who agreed to teach an honors class had to give up one of their "regular" teaching sections, which caused problems for their departments and constituted a disservice to students outside the Honors Program.

This situation ran counter to OU's reputation as an institution attracting outstanding students, a reputation growing in large part through the establishment of the Oklahoma Academic Scholars (OAS) program in 1988. The OAS provided full-ride scholarships for students who qualified as U.S. Presidential Scholars, National Merit Scholars, or National Merit finalists. Only three students were drawn to enroll at OU when the university's efforts to recruit National Merit Scholars began in 1984, under the leadership

Since 1987, Regents Professor Nancy Mergler has worked tirelessly to promote the Honors College and the university. She has directed the Honors program and is now senior vice president and provost emerita. (Courtesy Nancy Mergler)

of program director Stephen Sutherland. Sutherland steadily increased OU's National Merit numbers through a combination of dogged determination and OAS resources. A decade later, in 1994, OU boasted 161 National Merit Scholars.

Boren was impressed, but he wanted to do more. "He wanted to set a high academic bar for OU as he began his presidency," said Nancy Mergler, who served until 2014 as senior vice president and provost for the Norman campus. "His basic impulse was to send a message to alumni, donors, faculty, and staff that he cared deeply about academic rigor and wanted us to aggressively recruit honors students and provide them with small, wonderful classes."

At Boren's request, Mergler conducted an in-depth study comparing OU's Honors Program to honors colleges across the nation. In her report, Mergler championed the idea of an honors college with its own dean and a faculty free to control the college's curriculum. This study became the cornerstone of Boren's plan to elevate OU's Honors Program to a college, providing it with a private endowment, faculty, and programs rivaling those of Ivy League schools. In 1995, the new president received a resounding vote of confidence for the idea through a $1.5 million grant from Norman's Sarkeys Foundation. Soon after, an anonymous pledge of $5 million made it possible to establish an endowment for Honors College programs. That pledge was later disclosed as coming from Helen Walton, an OU graduate and the wife of the late Sam Walton, the founder of Walmart. A generous philanthropist, Helen Walton had cochaired the search committee that brought the Borens to OU in 1994. Her gift, along with a $500,000 gift from the Carol Elizabeth Young Foundation of Oklahoma City, resulted in a $1 million fund to support an endowed chair for the college's new dean.

The Honors College was part of Boren's larger vision to attract outstanding students and recruit and retain excellent faculty. These concerns were the president's top priority. Morale had been declining among OU's educators, and the university was in danger of losing some of its most promising young faculty to institutions that did more to foster and support teaching and research. OU's student body was declining in numbers as well. These factors concerned Boren, who feared that OU was on the verge of losing its reputation as Oklahoma's flagship university. He believed that attracting quality faculty and rewarding the university's most celebrated teachers and researchers were crucial steps toward fulfilling OU's educational mission.

Boren valued the mission of teaching so strongly that he insisted on teaching a course each semester as a condition of his acceptance of the OU presidency. "I wouldn't have come if the regents had said, 'No, we don't want you to teach,'" Boren said in 1995.

Boren's first educational initiative on campus was to establish the Presidential Professors Program. The program

Dean Emeritus Andrew Coats continues to teach in the College of Law as a Samuel Roberts Noble Foundation Presidential Professor and the Arch B. and Joanne Gilbert Professor of Law. Both the Law Center building and its fountain are named in his honor. *(Courtesy College of Law)*

Dean of the College of Law and director of the Law Center Joe Harroz also holds the office of university vice president. He was the longest-serving general counsel in OU history. *(Courtesy OU Foundation)*

recognizes and rewards top faculty members through annual, four-year salary stipends. The awards and nominees are selected through a highly competitive process, with approximately fifteen new awards each year. Presidential Professorships, among the most coveted faculty awards on campus, are made available through the generosity of OU donors. "This program has made a real difference in faculty morale and compensation, because it truly rewards merit," Boren said.

Boren's commitment to expanding the quality of teaching on campus took further shape when he initiated the Retired Faculty Program in 1995. He believed that full professors who had retired still had vast wisdom and talent to offer students, especially by teaching introductory classes and mentoring freshmen. The renewed involvement of these senior professors would help maintain and enrich the quality of undergraduate education at OU.

OU's commitment to legal education was also a focus of the new president, who himself was a 1968 alumnus of the College of Law. OU had come under increasing scrutiny by the American Bar Association, which warned that the college's accreditation was endangered by overcrowded facilities, low faculty pay, and funding issues. Boren responded first by luring acclaimed attorney and former Oklahoma City mayor Andrew Coats, of Oklahoma City's Crowe and Dunlevy law firm, to serve as dean of the OU College of Law. Together, Coats and Boren launched a successful campaign to build a $17 million law school expansion that was later named Andrew M. Coats Hall. The expansion included the 350,000-volume Donald E. Pray Law Library, the largest of its kind in Oklahoma, and the Dick Bell Courtroom for mock trials; it doubled the law school's square footage. Upon Coats's retirement in 2010, Boren convinced OU 1989 alumnus Joseph Harroz, Jr., the longest-serving OU legal counsel,

President Boren publicly announces OU's landmark Reach for Excellence campaign in 1995. *(Courtesy Robert Taylor)*

to return to the university as its twelfth dean of law. Harroz doubled the college's endowment; today, the Thomas M. Cooley Guide ranks the OU College of Law among the top fifteen law schools in the country.

The university's landmark Reach for Excellence campaign, launched in tandem with Boren's inauguration, was critical for the mission to strengthen OU's faculty. This campaign also provided for major capital improvements, increased research funding, and improved student resources, including $36 million in endowed and annual scholarship support.

The campaign aimed to raise $200 million in five years—twice as much as any fund-raising project in state history—and it garnered $110 million in the first year alone. President Boren acknowledges that $200 million was at that time an audacious goal; the largest educational funding campaign in Oklahoma history to date had raised $100 million. His new campaign was also launched in an untraditional fashion. Rather than hewing to the formalities of establishing a committee and entering a silent phase of fund-raising, Boren jump-started the campaign with a public announcement on the steps of Evans Hall. Waiting crowds had already gathered when Boren found vice president for university development David Maloney in the president's office, fingering a string of rosary beads. "This is not how it's done," the veteran fund-raiser told Boren nervously. Maloney's concerns were valid, but unnecessary. "The biggest pleasant surprise of my presidency has been how ready our alumni and supporters were to give to the university," Boren said, adding that the Reach for Excellence campaign would go on to raise $500 million. "I think they were just waiting for a plan that would show them that giving to OU was a good investment."

Annual giving rose from $10–$15 million in the 1980s to an average of $110 million during the early years of the Boren presidency. And when Tripp Hall, as vice president of development, took over leadership of the campaign, annual giving rose well above this amount to approximately $150 million. In addition to the leadership of Tripp Hall and David Maloney, the university has also benefited enormously from the fund-raising talents of Paul D. Massad, former executive director of the OU Alumni Association, who currently leads planned and major gift activities. Boren is grateful for the efforts of these dedicated leaders of university development, and he is overwhelmed by the generosity of the university's friends and alumni. "Because of their help we have reached a new level of excellence," he said.

With the wheels now firmly set in motion to attract the best students and faculty, President Boren announced his intention to dramatically raise OU's admission standards, making them the most rigorous in Oklahoma higher education. "We're sending a strong message to high school students that you have to be academically ready if you want to get into the University of Oklahoma," Boren told the OU Board of Regents in September 1998. He hoped higher standards would challenge high school students to work harder and take more core academic courses. "OU deserves to be a university of national stature, and we're going to get there," he declared.

In fall 1998 Oklahoma's statewide ACT average was 20.5 (on a scale of 1 to 36), while the national average was 21. OU already expected incoming freshmen to exceed both averages, requiring students to have an ACT score of 22 and rank within the top 33 percent of their high school graduating class. The new 2002 academic standards required students to have an ACT of at least 24 and be ranked in the top 30 percent of their graduating class, making OU's enrollment policy the most academically rigorous of all universities in the state. In 2014 the incoming freshman class had an average ACT score of 26.4, exceeding the national average. OU did continue to offer an alternative admissions program that allowed up to 8 percent of incoming students to be admitted on a probationary status without meeting the new criteria.

The university posted its biggest enrollment of the decade in fall 1999, with 21,120 students on the Norman campus alone. Alumni and friends shared in the excitement of this renaissance. OU's new vitality translated into exponential growth in the number of donors—from 17,000 individuals in 1994 to more than 71,300 by 1999. Attracted by the university's focus on excellence, alumni and friends of the university heeded President Boren's call to invest in OU's faculty through the Oklahoma State Regents Endowment Program. Established in 1988 by the Oklahoma State Legislature to help retain nationally and internationally recognized researchers and enhance existing faculty, the program allowed university donors to support an endowment in perpetuity and double their investment through dollar-for-dollar matching funds at the state level. When Boren first focused on what the Regents program could do for OU, the university had slightly fewer than one hundred endowed faculty positions. President Boren convinced OU alumni and donors that the state endowment program was a golden opportunity to double their help to the university and, within one two-month period in 1996, OU raised $61 million in pledges. From 1993 to 2014, the number of endowed positions at OU grew from 92 to 580, an increase of more than 500 percent.

The Reach for Excellence campaign also attracted donors for new student scholarships, university programs, and infrastructure. An $18 million gift from Wall Street manager and 1973 alumnus Michael F. Price doubled the size of OU's business college. A $5 million commitment from OU alumnus and Broadway producer A. Max Weitzenhoffer established the university's new musical theatre program, which grew to become OU's Weitzenhoffer School of Musical Theatre. A $22 million gift from the Edward L. Gaylord Family ensured that OU would have the new, state-of-the-art Gaylord College of Journalism and Mass Communication. A $5 million gift to the OU School of Social Work from the Anne and Henry Zarrow Foundation provided a new, 30,000-square-foot home for the school. And an $11.2 million gift from the Donald W. Reynolds Foundation helped create the OU Health Sciences Center's Department of Geriatric Medicines.

The impact of Reach for Excellence was clear as the campaign drew to a close in 2000. Some said that OU had made more rapid progress in five years than any other public university. Thanks in large part to Molly Boren's dedication to beautifying the campus, OU had been transformed physically, and the university now led the Big 12 in research growth. OU had also attracted outstanding students through the millions raised for scholarships intended for students with disabilities and for children of victims of the 1995 bombing of Oklahoma City's Alfred P. Murrah Federal Building.

Believing the time had come to balance student enrollment with the size of OU's faculty, classrooms, and residence halls, President Boren made the difficult decision to increase admission standards yet again. This time, the standards would be raised solely for out-of-state students, who now made up 25 percent of OU's total enrollment. The university's improved reputation for academic achievement and the fact that its out-of-state tuition charges were among the lowest in the Big 12 drew greater numbers of nonresident students to OU.

While selective admissions helped raise OU's standards for academic excellence, its resources were being stretched thinner and thinner. State allocations for higher education had been declining for decades. Indeed, state support had fallen from 50 percent of OU's total operating budget in the 1970s to below 30 percent by the mid-1990s. Boren reluctantly asked for increases in student tuition and fees to keep pace, but he knew the burden on families would mean that

George Henderson is Sylvan N. Goldman Professor Emeritus, David Ross Boyd Professor Emeritus, and Regents Professor Emeritus of Human Relations, Education, and Sociology. A recipient of numerous teaching awards and honors, Henderson joined OU as associate professor of sociology and of education in 1967. Both the Henderson Scholars Program and the Henderson-Tolson Cultural Center on the Norman campus bear his name. *(Courtesy OU Public Affairs)*

fewer and fewer deserving students could afford the quality education OU was working so hard to provide. The funds raised through the Reach for Excellence campaign would not be sufficient for addressing the increasing tuition burden placed on students and their families, so in April 2006 OU launched a $50 million, five-year campaign to ensure that no qualified student would ever be turned away from the university due to financial need. The campaign's top priority was to raise unrestricted scholarship dollars, which gave the university the most flexibility in helping students on all three campuses. OU alumni and donors responded through gifts large and small. President Boren decided to extend the scholarship drive indefinitely, and by 2014 the campaign topped $250 million and is still growing.

The Campaign for Scholarships launched an unprecedented period of support for students. The amount of available scholarship funds has tripled since 1994. As of 2014 nearly two thousand need-based scholarships have been offered to students, reflecting an increase in annual awards from $8.1 million in 2005 to $13 million in 2012. Alumni and friends of the university alone have provided more than $190 million.

While the endowed chairs and professorships program had rolled along for years with the support of OU donor generosity, funding for the state matching side of the budget equation had slowed and finally stalled when the Oklahoma State Legislature's initial $15 million appropriation was outpaced by successful fund-raising at OU and other universities. State matching funds for the program had ceased by 2003 and were not renewed by the legislature, leading to a backlog of more than $230 million in unmatched commitments. Boren expressed concern that the freeze in matching public funding would discourage donors and affect OU's overall progress—including the university's momentum in research and new projects.

In 2008, the Oklahoma State Legislature finally passed a

Students in an Honors College reading group tackle Lucretius's *The Nature of Things* with the help of Dr. David H. Ray, dean of the college. *(Courtesy Robert Taylor)*

$100 million bill to address the huge backlog. "It sends a strong, clear message to private donors that their gifts are deeply appreciated and that commitments made to them by the state will be kept," Boren said upon passage of the bill. With the final appropriation in place, the State Regents Endowment Program came to a highly successful end, having contributed to more than 340 OU endowed positions and having provided some $240 million in matching funds. The entire OU community could look back on the years from 1994 to 2014 with a deep sense of pride and gratitude, knowing that the Campaign for Scholarships, the endowed chair and professorship program, and the Reach for Excellence campaign—all results of the university's hard work and success—were undertaken in the spirit of serving OU's outstanding faculty and students. As President Boren had hoped, these efforts enabled the university to become a home for the best and brightest.

Still leading the way toward student excellence is the Honors College, which provides OU's premier learning environment for high-achieving students. The Honors College has nearly tripled the size of its student body since 1994 and features ten faculty members, all either endowed chairs or professors. Today's Honors College students are offered the benefits of a fine, small liberal arts college within the setting of a large, state-supported national research university.

Honors College dean David Ray has said that before the college grew into its current form, OU's most academically talented students sometimes had difficulty finding their way at the university—but that has changed. The Honors College offers targeted activities, groups, and opportunities for students to shape a community of scholars. "We've made progress in creating an atmosphere where OU's most motivated students can find each other," said Ray, a recipient of the UOSA Award for Outstanding Teacher and the Regents Award for Superior Teaching.

Students in the Honors College receive close, personal attention from faculty members. In 2014, OU received a $1.6 million gift from Will and Helen Webster to fund an endowment for the new Presidential Faculty Fellows Program, which provides annual stipends to university professors who excel at teaching and mentoring students and allows them to teach exclusively in the Honors College. Students in the college can also take advantage of special presentations and programs, including the Outdoor Adventure First-Year Trip, a six-day backpacking experience for students new to the Honors College, and Honors in Oxford, which features a three-week course on the Norman campus followed by an intensive three-week travel-study experience at Oxford University in England.

One of the Honors College's most popular programs began with Dean Ray's simple suggestion that students get together to discuss great books. From that idea blossomed the Honors College Reading Groups, which pair an OU faculty member or student moderator with ten to fifteen students for an informal reading and discussion program one hour per week. Students are asked to read approximately fifty pages each week and attend the group as frequently as they can. Books are provided at no cost to students through the support of private donors. More than one thousand honors students have met in as many as eighty different reading groups across OU's campus since the program began in 2010, tackling such works as *John Adams* by David McCullough, *Cat's Cradle* by Kurt Vonnegut, and Dante's *Inferno*. "The reading groups have become the college's signature program. The students have taken to it like ducks to water," Ray said proudly. "They aren't receiving a grade, they're doing it on their own time, and some of the books are extremely challenging. Yet here you have ten students reading *Ulysses* because they want to." By 2014, Ray had led ninety-three of these informal reading groups. That year forty-six informal reading groups on campus were satisfying students' intellectual curiosity.

It comes as no surprise that many of the Honors College's most outstanding students are National Merit Scholars. OU's success in attracting Merit Scholars has grown dramatically since President Boren joined the university in 1994, when OU had 161 Merit Scholars and ranked fourth among all public universities in attracting them. That number rose steadily to an all-time high of 311 incoming National Merit Scholars in 2014. Currently, OU ranks first among all public universities in the enrollment of freshman National Merit Scholars.

The university's excellence has been recognized well outside the boundaries of Oklahoma, and OU boasts a number of firsts when it comes to student excellence. OU students achieved the best graduation rate in state history for a public university—a record high of 67.8 percent for the freshman class that entered in 2005. And in 2012, the university's student body had the highest academic ranking of any public university in Oklahoma history. The *Princeton Review* now ranks OU among the best in the nation for academic excellence and cost to students. The number of international students enrolling at OU has also continued to rise, with more than 2,200 students from 120 countries enrolled in 2012, marking a 22 percent increase since 2009.

Thanks to its ability to attract outstanding students and faculty, OU is considered to be among a small group of the very finest public universities in the country. The university has produced twenty-eight Rhodes Scholars; no other university in Oklahoma has had more than three. Seven OU students have been named Truman Scholars since 1990 for their leadership potential and intellectual ability. Thirty-five students have been selected as Goldwater Scholars for excellence in mathematics and science since 1994, and forty-two OU students have been chosen as Fulbright Scholars since 1997. In addition, OU has achieved the Carnegie Foundation's highest tier of research activity classification, the first time a public institution in Oklahoma has received this recognition.

Overall, more than thirty new programs and initiatives were started during the Boren years, including five new colleges: Honors, International Studies, Atmospheric and Geographic Sciences, the Mewbourne College of Earth and Energy, and the Gaylord College of Journalism and Mass Communication. A new Religious Studies program was initiated. New institutes were developed as well, including the Center for the Creation of Economic Wealth under current Price College of Business dean Dan Pullin. Among the center's achievements is an interdisciplinary internship program

that pairs OU students with technology inventors in the private sector. OU's Institute for the American Constitutional Heritage was founded to promote the study of American constitutionalism from legal, historical, and philosophical perspectives. A new Confucius Institute, designed to foster understanding between China and other parts of the world, was established at OU in 2006. And in 2010 the College of International Studies added the Arabic Flagship program, which offered to students an innovative five-year curriculum in Arabic language and culture, the first program of its kind in the state of Oklahoma. The Institute for Quality Communities, formed in 2011, is the outgrowth of an idea that originated with Molly Shi Boren. Housed in the School of Architecture, the IQC provides a forum for students, researchers, practitioners, and Oklahoma community leaders to collaborate on making places that support habits, activities, and lifestyles that lead to whole and healthy people. The importance of interdisciplinary learning was further reinforced through the creation of the Peggy Helmerich Collaborative Learning Center at Bizzell Memorial Library, where students and faculty from different disciplines work together in cooperative teams.

Boren believes the many changes made over the past two decades have coalesced into something wonderful that has affected the university's core identity. "These last couple of years, I have really felt the intellectual vitality of the campus go up dramatically. You can't measure it. All of these things have come together as building blocks, as catalysts, to bring all these disparate pieces together from the past eighteen years, sort of like a thunderclap."

That thunderclap is reverberating. A retired OU professor wrote to President Boren that he had been listening to student conversations as he walked across campus. "I cannot tell you how impressed I am by what's being talked about, the excitement about ideas, about learning, about experiences. I am overjoyed to hear the kinds of conversations I am hearing students have," the professor wrote. "It was a wonderful, heartwarming letter," the president said with a broad smile, "because this is what we were trying for."

INTERNATIONALIZING THE EDUCATIONAL EXPERIENCE

Two years before becoming OU's president, then-senator David Boren sounded the call for the internationalization of higher education. While delivering a commencement address at American University in Washington, D.C., Boren drew on his experience as the longest-serving chairman of the U.S. Senate Select Committee on Intelligence to warn of a "new isolationism" that he believed would threaten U.S. national security. "How in the world can we relate to this new international environment if we do not understand

President Boren takes the wheel for a hayride at the annual OU Cousins Barbecue and Western Party. *(WHC)*

the world's cultures or speak their languages?" Boren asked, pointing out that seven times as many international students came to the United States to study as the number of U.S. students who studied abroad. "How can we expect to play a role when we do not even attempt to understand other people?"

Boren felt strongly that American education at all levels had become too provincial and failed to equip students for a world far more international in scope than the one their parents and grandparents had experienced. Today's students anticipated being involved in a global world that affected every aspect of their daily lives. Learning foreign languages would no longer be a luxury but a necessity. Interacting with people from around the world was not a nicety but an important preparation.

As a member of the U.S. Senate, Boren had worked hard to influence international education. He authored the 1991 National Security Education Act, which provided funding for the new National Security Education Program (NSEP). The program was aimed at colleges and universities seeking to improve their foreign-language and international studies offerings, especially in areas of critical importance to U.S. security. Scholarships for study abroad were also provided through the legislation, which Washington, D.C., policy makers deemed the most important higher-education initiative in more than thirty years. The NSEP launched a variety of initiatives promoting study abroad and foreign languages nationwide and encouraging thousands of U.S. students to take advantage of international learning opportunities. The program initiated by Boren was the largest federal international exchange agreement enacted since the Fulbright Scholarship program. By 2014, 4,474 students had been named Boren Fellows or Scholars.

Boren led the same growth in international studies at

OU after taking the university's helm. OU established the International Programs Center in 1996 under the guidance of former U.S. ambassador to the United Nations Edward J. Perkins, who served as the center's first executive director. Opportunities to study and understand other cultures grew exponentially on campus. In an effort to show OU students what they were missing and encourage them to seek opportunities to study abroad, President and Mrs. Boren established the OU Cousins program the same year, which pairs international and exchange students with American students during social events at the university. Still active today, the program culminates with the annual OU Cousins Barbecue and Western Party held at the ranch of late OU law professor Leo Whinery and his wife, Doris. All OU students, faculty, and staff are invited to join international guests and enjoy hayrides, country music, and dancing.

As a result of such initiatives, more students began selecting international relations as a major, and program enrollments rose by as much as 20 percent over the following fifteen years. The number of study-abroad offerings exploded, growing to nearly two hundred opportunities in more than fifty countries, and Presidential Study Abroad Scholarships, established in 1997, made funding to study abroad possible for every student who desired to do so. Students majoring in the College of International Studies were now required to participate in a minimum of four weeks of international experience. The Price College of Business and the College of Arts and Sciences also began to require students to study abroad for majors such as international business and modern languages, including Chinese, Italian, and German.

By 2001, OU's international offerings had coalesced into the School of International and Area Studies, an academic unit within the College of Arts and Sciences. In its early stages, the school had a handful of dedicated faculty and attracted approximately fifty students. It grew to include OU's Institute for U.S.-China Issues, which supports research and outreach activities to improve U.S.-China relations, and the Center for Middle East Studies, whose goal is to enrich students' Middle

Students participating in the Arezzo program demonstrate their Sooner spirit on a visit to Seville, Spain. *(Courtesy Suzette Grillot)*

As dean of the College of International Studies, Suzette Grillot has guided recent renovations to the Arezzo campus and contributed vitally to the growth of international studies at OU. She also holds the William J. Crowe, Jr., Chair in Geopolitics and serves as the university's vice provost for international programs. *(Courtesy Suzette Grillot)*

East experiences at OU through visiting speakers and special events. Despite these advances, President Boren believed that more OU students should take advantage of education abroad, and in 2009 he challenged the university community to double the number of students studying abroad within five years. To strengthen that effort, OU expanded its study-abroad scholarship program and renamed it the Presidential International Travel Fellowship. Eighteen years of encouragement left a mark on the university: the number of students embarking on study-abroad opportunities increased by more than 1,300 percent from 1994 to 2012 and the percentage of undergraduates studying abroad rose from 1.5 percent to 27 percent in the same period.

Kimberlee Davies, an OU student from Tulsa and 2012 international studies–environmental studies graduate, spent the spring semester of her junior year abroad in France and Senegal, West Africa, pursuing her dream of a career in international development. She said the experience opened more than a career path. "It made me a stronger person," said Davies. "I developed self-discipline. Being able to step outside of my comfort level and take classes in another language helped me to be prepared to not always be in control and to just enjoy my time." Davies earned a position as a Fulbright Scholar to study small-scale farming in Malawi and plans to take these lessons back to Africa while researching why some farmers have successfully adopted imported farming methods and others have not. "But the biggest change was personal," Davies said of her study abroad. "You learn more about yourself, how to be both alone and interact with other cultures. That prepares you for whatever job you get—in whichever city or country that might be."

In 2011, OU announced a $2 million leadership gift from L. Francis and Kathleen Rooney to establish the College of International Studies, which now includes the School of International and Area Studies, Education Abroad, and International Student Services. The College of International Studies has been highly successful in

attracting OU students since it was first created. In the decade after the School of International and Area Studies was formed, its enrollment grew more than tenfold to include many of the university's best and brightest students; in fact, it became a top choice among OU National Merit Scholars. "Students voted with their feet immediately," Boren said. "They have been pouring in."

Through the NSEP program, OU students could also apply for a variety of scholarships and fellowships, including the NSEP David L. Boren Graduate Fellowship. Recipients receive a stipend of up to $20,000 to study abroad and are assured a job within the federal government upon graduation. More than forty OU students took advantage of the program within its first few years.

The success of the College of International Studies inspired a $14 million campaign to support new faculty positions

Four-star general and former secretary of state Colin Powell and former British prime minister Margaret Thatcher have been among the campus's distinguished guests during the Boren years. At the 2000 Big Event, Powell encouraged students to volunteer in their communities. Thatcher headlined the university's second annual Foreign Policy Conference on February 25, 1999. *(Courtesy Robert Taylor and Western History Collections)*

and renovations to an eighteenth-century monastery that is now home to OU's signature education-abroad program in Arezzo, Italy. The 2012 purchase of the monastery made OU the only American university with a permanent presence inside the city walls. The University of Oklahoma boasts the largest number of U.S. students studying in Arezzo each year, and one in five OU students who study abroad will go through the Arezzo campus. "The programs have grown in response to student interest and the critical need for knowing what's going on in the world," said Suzette Grillot, dean of the College of International Studies. During the 2011–12 academic year, Grillot spent ten months as a faculty-in-residence at the Arezzo campus. "Cultural literacy is important," she said. "Any student will find that kind of education gives them an advantage, an additional skill that is useful to them in the workplace, no matter what they do."

Boren also sought to bring internationally renowned speakers to OU to enrich the student experience, including some of the world's most prominent political leaders, authors, and dignitaries. Campus guests have included former U.S. president George H. W. Bush, former Soviet premier Mikhail Gorbachev, former chairman of the Joint Chiefs of Staff Colin Powell, former British prime minister Margaret Thatcher, five former Central Intelligence Agency directors, Nobel Peace Prize–winner Archbishop Desmond Tutu, and ambassadors of nations ranging from China to Great Britain to Mexico. Many OU students have had the rare opportunity to learn directly from these experts through lectures, roundtable discussions, and classroom visits.

Because of his experience in foreign relations, Boren's perspective on international affairs is in demand, and his views on international issues have been published worldwide. Boren is the author of *A Letter to America*, which addresses the country's standing as a global superpower in a changing world, and coeditor, with Ambassador Perkins, of *Preparing America's Foreign Policy for the Twenty-First Century*. Boren was also one of three former U.S. senators named in 2001 to cochair a special bipartisan taskforce on U.S.-Russia relations. In the political science course he teaches each semester, President Boren shares with OU students the lessons he has learned through these experiences. "The University of Oklahoma has been front and center in increasing global opportunities for our students," Dean Grillot said. She credits Boren's work as an innovator and leader in international affairs and believes it has made all the difference for OU students. "He brought with him a commitment to internationalizing the curriculum for all students at the University of Oklahoma." Boren is highly aware, however, that he was not alone in building up this program. Particularly notable are the contributions of Millie C. Audas, faculty member in the Jeannine Rainbolt College of Education for Higher Education Administration. During her thirty years

of service to the university, Audas worked on establishing 174 university agreements of exchange worldwide and developed numerous programs to help international students and scholars integrate themselves into the life of the OU and Norman communities. "Millie Audas has truly built the foundation of excellence in international exchanges at the University," said President Boren.

FOSTERING EXCELLENCE IN RESEARCH

Although the University of Oklahoma has a long-held reputation as one of the state's leading research institutions, no one could have predicted the explosive growth in research that would take place during the new president's tenure, or how the private and public sectors would intersect to change research at OU.

Funding for research at the university had been steadily increasing by 10 to 20 percent annually since the early 1990s. But OU research experienced a watershed moment when the National Science Foundation awarded $4.9 million in funds to establish the OU Center for the Analysis and Prediction of Storms (CAPS) in 1989. Called "the Manhattan Project of weather prediction," CAPS brought researchers together to explore the scientific principles that govern weather. To attract the NSF grant, OU invested seed money and assigned faculty to work and research under the umbrella of a cooperative project. OU's place in the international weather research community was further strengthened through the hard work and determination of President Boren, Oklahoma's congressional delegation, and such leaders as former Oklahoma State Senate President Pro Tempore Cal

The National Weather Center's atrium houses Science on a Sphere, whose six-foot-tall fiberglass surface shows visitors the global movements of weather patterns.
(Courtesy Robert Taylor)

Vice president for research Eddie Carol Smith also served as graduate dean from 1993 to 1999. The Eddie Carol Smith Scholarship is awarded biannually to a graduate student whose research creates or expands an area of scholarly endeavor. *(Courtesy Sooner Magazine)*

Hobson, all of whom spent several tumultuous years putting together a funding package for the $67 million National Weather Center. Their work culminated in the Weather Center's dedication on the OU Research Campus in 2006. The center "literally makes Norman the weather capital of the nation," Boren said, "and establishes OU as the nation's academic leader in meteorology."

Winning the CAPS funding represented a collaborative shift in how OU would approach future applications for research grants. That cooperative change was compounded soon after Boren arrived at OU, when the new president expressed a commitment to making OU a national research university recognized for excellence. Boren met with Eddie Carol Smith, then vice president for research administration, along with faculty members and administrators, to conceptualize a strategic plan. During one of these meetings, Smith suggested that OU should strive to become a Research I university—the designation then offered by the Carnegie Foundation to universities reaching the highest tier of research activity. Boren agreed, and Smith helped develop an incentive program that allowed faculty who participated in interdisciplinary research to receive nearly twice as much funding; the additional monies would come from grantors to cover overhead expenses for these new collaborative projects. What followed was a natural evolution in the history of OU research. Faculty members who pursued their work aggressively emerged as the university's research leaders, playing to OU's strengths and allowing the university to focus its resources where they could do the most good.

OU's research strengths were revealed in energy, meteorology, the social sciences, life sciences, and engineering. Each field of study could bring outstanding researchers and scholars to the university, as well as critical research dollars from state and federal government programs. Perhaps more important, OU's new research programs held the promise of reshaping Oklahoma's economy. Oil and gas production would always be a vital part of the state's fiscal health, but enriching the economy with new technology and biomedical research would provide both greater economic balance and greater opportunity for all Oklahomans.

In January 1998, the OU Board of Regents called for a change in the way the university and its faculty approached research. Along with officials at Oklahoma State University, the board asked the state legislature for $1 million in new funding to open technology spin-off offices at OU and OSU. That same week, Norman state representative Laura Boyd introduced legislation to allow state universities and faculty members to keep an ownership interest in businesses developed from their research findings.

OU also asked for increased funds for research patents. That year the university had received only $40,000 to spend on research patents, which meant that work having commercial potential often went unprotected and could be exploited by virtually anyone. OU's intellectual property had repeatedly been published and commercialized without any financial compensation to the university or its researchers. President Boren and Dean Smith recommended that a new Office of Technology Management be created to evaluate OU research discoveries for commercial value and help faculty members patent their findings. Discoveries would be developed for the commercial market, and the new technology management office would help establish and finance any spin-off companies. By February 1998, several legislators had offered versions of the bill that would allow universities and professors to profit from creative research. Oklahoma governor Frank Keating offered his own bill and backed $1 million in funding for OU's and OSU's proposed technology spin-off offices. Later that month, Keating appointed retired Kerr-McGee Corporation chairman and CEO Frank McPherson to oversee a statewide technology transfer program within the Oklahoma Department of Commerce.

Later in 1998, funds from OU's Reach for Excellence campaign were used to purchase land near State Highway 9. Envisioned as a center for technology firms and developed

As executive vice president and vice president of administration and finance, Nicholas "Nick" Hathaway directs the university's financial affairs and acts as a senior policy advisor. *(Courtesy OU Public Affairs)*

Vice president for research Kelvin Droegemeier is also a Regents Professor of Meteorology and Weathernews Chair Emeritus. *(Courtesy OU Public Affairs)*

in partnership with OU researchers, the property soon became home to the National Weather Center.

A new neighbor for the National Weather Center was assured when Charles Stephenson, an OU graduate and the chairman of Tulsa-based Vintage Petroleum, and his wife, Peggy, gifted $6 million to build a multipurpose research facility on the south campus research park. Named the Stephenson Research and Technology Center, the 93,000-square-foot facility provides a unique interdisciplinary environment for biologists, computer scientists, engineers, and physicists. A few years later, the Stephensons pledged $15 million more for a new Life Sciences Research Center. The new Stephenson center houses thirty life sciences research groups working in such areas as cancer therapies, diabetes, and Alzheimer's disease, as well as alternative energy sources.

The promise of cooperative research and development opportunities has improved retention of outstanding teachers and researchers at the university and helped bring about additional facilities and programs. To offer engineering students the same kind of facility as athletes benefit from at Everest Training Center, President Boren and other campus leaders envisioned a $10 million structure to be built on Jenkins Avenue that would include computer labs, offices for student engineering groups, and a large space for students to test new inventions.

Oklahoma brainpower was tapped when OU received a five-year, $17 million grant to join the Engineering Research Center for Collaborative Adaptive Sensing of the Atmosphere. OU partnered with other universities and federal and private entities—including the National Oceanic and Atmospheric Administration, Oak Ridge National Laboratory, and IBM—to develop technology that increased warning times during severe weather and climatic events.

Research at OU received another boost in 2004 when the Center for Applied Social Research (CASR) was created to foster multidisciplinary research encompassing the many

fields within OU's College of Arts and Sciences. CASR works to solve complex problems, and among its earliest projects were studies for the National Institutes of Health and the National Science Foundation to help researchers better understand ethical decision making in the sciences.

Recognition for what OU was doing came in early 2011, when the university achieved the Carnegie Foundation designation for Very High Research Activity. Formerly known as Carnegie Research I, the designation placed OU in the same ranks as Harvard, UCLA, Stanford, the University of North Carolina at Chapel Hill, and the Massachusetts Institute of Technology. After the retirement of Dean Eddie Carol Smith, Vice President for Strategic Planning Nicholas Hathaway, working with Vice President for Research Kelvin Droegemeier and Daniel Pullin, dean of the Price College of Business, spearheaded renewed efforts that included the rapidly growing Research Campus.

A REVITALIZED OU HEALTH SCIENCES CENTER

For seventeen years, students and faculty at the OU Health Sciences Center had been waiting for the construction of a student center. In September 1994, months before his inauguration, David Boren met with students and faculty from the colleges of medicine, nursing, allied health, pharmacy, dentistry, and public health. Before walking away from the Oklahoma City meetings, Boren pledged that the student center would be built soon after he became president and would feature a common area, exercise space, study rooms, a food service court, and retail shops. "It is time to redeem that promise," he said. "Such a facility is essential to building the spirit of family and community that I hope to see prevail on all of our OU campuses."

Boren was good to his word. By August of the following year, ground was broken for the student center that Senior Vice President and Provost Joseph Ferretti called "the new heart of our campus" and that spearheaded President Boren's vision for the campus. It was one of many facilities built and programs developed in transforming the OUHSC during Boren and Ferretti's seven-year collaboration. Later, in August 1995, ground was broken for the Biomedical Research Center, a highly anticipated enterprise that would make OU the first university in Oklahoma to encourage its faculty to bring laboratory discoveries into the open market. A month later, Children's Hospital at the OUHSC unveiled a new addition: the third-floor Jimmy Everest Center for Cancer and Blood Disorders in Children. The treatment center focused on improving the experiences of children and families facing cancer. Named in honor of Jimmy Everest, who had died at the age of seventeen after a yearlong battle with Ewing's Sarcoma, the center was made possible through the generosity of Jimmy's parents, Jim and Christy Everest of Oklahoma City. The Everest Center, along with the OUHSC's new student center and biomedical research center, became part of a massive health complex already known as the Oklahoma Health Center.

From the beginning of his presidency, Boren sought to tie the OUHSC closer to the Norman campus. According to a 2004 *Sooner Magazine* article, when Molly Boren "first saw the collection of stark health-related buildings, separated by a six-lane thoroughfare and crisscrossed by huge electric high lines, she pronounced the urbanscape 'so sterile.'" In September 1999, inspired by his wife's vision for a more inviting Oklahoma City campus, Boren asked the OU Board of Regents to approve a $5.5 million landscaping plan to create a pedestrian mall in the core of the OUHSC campus. More than two thousand trees, fountains, stone benches, brick-paved sidewalks, flowerbeds, and outdoor works of art transformed the campus with a beautiful pedestrian mall closed to automobile traffic and linking the OUHSC's main academic buildings.

A hundred miles away in Tulsa, OUHSC degree programs had no centralized home. In fact, OU's degree programs were spread across a dozen different locations in Tulsa. In December 1999, news headlines announced that OU had signed a $24 million contract to purchase the BP Amoco Technology Center, to be transformed into a new home for the OU-Tulsa programs. A $10 million grant from Tulsa's Schusterman Family Foundation was paired with $17 million from the OU Foundation to cover the purchase and necessary upgrades. Dedicated on November 2, 2001, the Schusterman Center soon became home to more than one thousand OU graduate and professional students in sixteen degree programs, including the College of Allied Health, College of Medicine, College of Nursing, College of Pharmacy, and College of Public Health. Another new building, the OUHSC Physicians Center, dedicated in April 2002 on the Oklahoma City campus, became the medical hub for the largest and

most diverse concentration of health care practitioners in Oklahoma. The College of Allied Health celebrated the opening of its new, $25 million home in September 2009. The facility replaced a building dating to 1928.

Sustaining excellence was the focus of a new, five-year strategic plan to target and enhance the OUHSC's existing research strengths. The plan's goals included propelling Oklahoma to regional and national prominence in medical research and development, translating medical discoveries into new treatments, continuing to meet the health care needs of the state, and promoting further economic development. As provost, Ferretti took justifiable pride in the fact that the OUHSC had become an economic force in Oklahoma. He credited the 1998 passage of State Questions 680 and 681, whose campaign President Boren helped lead. The new laws allowed state universities to participate in commercializing intellectual property developed by researchers and helped produce more than a dozen technology transfer companies. More than one hundred NIH-funded scientists obtained patents for their work at the OUHSC.

While the Schusterman Center at the University of Oklahoma–Tulsa was being renovated, plans went ahead for the largest project in OUHSC history: a comprehensive cancer center. Oklahomans had long called for a cancer center of their own. Although good cancer care was available at hospitals and clinics across the state, the nearest available Phase I clinical trials had to be obtained at the M.D. Anderson Cancer Center in Houston, Texas, more than four hundred miles away. At that remove, many cutting-edge drugs were physically or financially out of reach for most of Oklahoma's 3.7 million residents. Provost Ferretti, dean of medicine M. Dewayne Andrews, and Dr. Robert J. Mannel were determined to develop a major cancer research facility within the state. Mannel had developed one of the top gynecologic cancer programs in the country.

When construction of the cancer center, which began on November 12, 2007, became more expensive than first anticipated, fund-raising efforts received a boost from the center's first-ever grant from Susan G. Komen for the Cure in October 2008. Then, in January 2010, Peggy and Charles Stephenson pledged $12 million to complete the center and fund two endowed chairs in cancer research in what was the largest gift in OUHSC history. It proved a turning point in the quest for a comprehensive cancer center in Oklahoma. Some $5.5 million of the total was devoted to completing construction of the seven-story cancer center. An additional $500,000 was set aside for a healing garden, and the remaining $6 million endowed faculty positions in perpetuity. "This is very special to me," said breast cancer survivor Peggy Stephenson, who serves as executive director of the Stephenson Family Foundation. The OU Board of Regents named the cancer center in honor of the

Dr. Gerard P. "Gerry" Clancy, MD, has served as OU-Tulsa's president since 2006. He also holds the Morningside Health Care Foundation Endowed Chair in Leadership and was previously dean of the OU College of Medicine in Tulsa. *(Courtesy OU Public Affairs)*

The June 2011 dedication of the Stephenson Cancer Center featured Pulitzer Prize–winning author and physician Siddhartha Mukherjee as guest speaker. Pictured left to right are professor and then-provost Dr. Joseph J. Ferretti, the Borens, Charles and Peggy Stephenson, Mukherjee, Alex Fields, Cynthia "Cindy" Stephenson Fields, and Steven Stephenson. *(Courtesy Robert Taylor)*

Stephensons' long history of giving so generously to OU.

The grand dedication of the Stephenson Cancer Center took place in June 2011 as dignitaries from across Oklahoma joined to celebrate the largest public-private biomedical partnership in state history. Generous donations from across the state, both public and private, large and small, made the center a reality. Of special note were the many young people who gave to the campaign, including students from nine Oklahoma high schools that each raised more than $10,000 to purchase naming rights to examination rooms. Molly Shi Boren worked tirelessly in concert with Oklahoma City designer Steve Callahan—with whom she had collaborated earlier on Boyd House—in enhancing the cancer center's interior spaces, and with Bobby Jackson on its landscaping. OU artist Roger Sprague (who died shortly before the center was completed) gave nearly two hundred paintings for display in the center's rooms and hallways.

Cancer is not the only disease that threatens the health of many Oklahomans. In 2012, an estimated 296,000 adult

M. Dewayne Andrews, MD, MACP, is senior vice president and provost and executive dean of the College of Medicine at the OU Health Sciences Center in Oklahoma City. A David Ross Boyd Professor of Medicine who holds the Lawrence N. Upjohn Endowed Chair in Medicine, Dr. Andrews has chaired the National Commission on the Certification of Physician Assistants, as well as the Section on Medical Schools of the American Medical Association. *(Courtesy OU Public Affairs)*

Oklahomans were diagnosed with diabetes, according to the Henry J. Kaiser Family Foundation. In response to this growing health problem, Boren called for establishing a national diabetes center on the OUHSC's Oklahoma City and Tulsa campuses. In March 2007, Harold Hamm of Enid responded, ultimately giving more than $20 million toward providing diabetes programs, facilities, and faculty endowments. The newly created Harold Hamm Diabetes Center then received an $11 million grant from the National Institutes of Health to improve interdisciplinary diabetes research and intervention among Native Americans, 40 percent of whom are at risk of developing diabetes.

The University of Oklahoma and the University of Tulsa formed a partnership to establish the new School of Community Medicine, due to open as a four-year medical school in Tulsa in the fall of 2015.

Through teaching, research, creative activity, and service to the state and society, both the OU Health Sciences Center and the OU School of Community Medicine could now focus on training a new generation of health practitioners whose mission will be to improve the lives of all Oklahomans.

SHOWCASING OKLAHOMA'S TREASURES

When President Boren came to OU in April 1994, he walked into the midst of a passionate campaign to save Oklahoma's heritage. The Oklahoma Territorial Legislature had established the Department of Geology and Natural History in 1899 under Professor Albert Heald Van Vleet to collect and preserve Oklahoma's natural record. In 1943, J. Willis Stovall became the longtime director of the museum that would carry his name for decades. Since then, the museum's collections had greatly outgrown their home at a former Army ROTC administration building, where storage was provided in wooden gun sheds and stables dating from World War I. Less than 1 percent of the museum's holdings were on exhibit. In fact, many of the museum's six million items, including rare dinosaur fossils, tens of thousands of birds and insect specimens, and artifacts from the ancient Spiro culture, were warehoused in buildings scattered across the campus.

With the OU Board of Regents' endorsement, plans for a new museum worthy of housing these treasures began in 1988 and continued into the early 1990s. A site on sixty acres at Timberdell and Chautauqua Avenues was designated. The museum fund-raising campaign received its largest gift just a few months before Boren arrived at OU, when the family of late philanthropist and oilman Samuel Roberts Noble of Ardmore pledged $7.5 million from his foundation. Noble's company, Samedan Oil Corporation, offered an additional $1.5 million in funding. In response, OU officials proposed that the new museum be named in Noble's honor. His family agreed, with one request: that the museum's name should be the Sam Noble Oklahoma Museum of Natural History.

President Boren helped raise the last of the museum's funding needs. After decades of waiting, the museum's staff began preparing for its future in a new facility and the chance to showcase the museum's artifacts, including many that had been hidden for more than fifty years, such as the museum's future star attraction—the world's largest specimen of an apatosaurus, formerly known as a brontosaurus.

In October 1996 the spotlight shifted to the Fred Jones Jr. Museum of Art when it was announced that the university had purchased one of Oklahoma's finest private art collections. The Fleischaker Collection, composed of more than four hundred major art pieces, included nineteenth- and twentieth-century paintings, sculpture, pottery, basketry, and Native American artifacts that had been privately held by the late Richard H. and Adeline J. Fleischaker of Oklahoma City. Spanning the 1870s to early 1990s and

Following his graduation from Yale University, Dr. Eric McCauley Lee served as director of the Fred Jones, Jr., Museum of Art for almost a decade. Among his numerous achievements, he oversaw the acquisition of the Weitzenhoffer Collection and the 2005 addition of the Lester Wing. *(Courtesy OU Public Affairs)*

including prints by Pablo Picasso, Henri Matisse, Marc Chagall, and Salvador Dali, the collection was one of the most comprehensive private holdings of works by artists of the Taos Society of Artists and the Santa Fe Art Colony. Although a national auction house was campaigning to sell the artworks, the Fleischaker children preferred to honor their parents by keeping the collection intact and within the state for all Oklahomans to enjoy.

Across campus, as construction of the natural history museum progressed, museum staff packed six million artifacts for a safe move to new quarters. When the transfer was completed, the entire collection was under one roof for the first time since 1903.

On April 12, 2000, President Boren, state dignitaries, supporters, friends, and staff all gathered for the official ribbon cutting and dedication of the Sam Noble Oklahoma Museum of Natural History. It had taken more than a decade of dreaming and planning and four years of construction to make the museum a reality. Boren presented a copper box that would be placed in the museum's cornerstone, to be opened a century hence. The box's contents included a dinosaur bank; newspaper clippings; letters from museum director Michael A. Mares and Boren to a future museum director and OU president; and Mares's book *Heritage at Risk*, which had been the genesis of the museum campaign. "The whole story of Oklahoma is preserved in your museum," Mares proclaimed to the audience.

In the following days, the Sam Noble staff bustled through preparations for a public opening on May 1, 2000. Free museum admission was offered through the end of June, and hopeful visitors quickly clogged the museum's telephone lines as they called to reserve opening-day tickets. More than fifteen hundred people thronged the museum on opening day, and huge crowds persisted throughout the summer. In little more than seven weeks, museum attendance reached an astounding 100,000 visitors, 35,000 of whom were children.

In addition to his work as director of the Sam Noble Oklahoma Museum of Natural History, an office he has held for more than twenty-five years altogether, Michael Mares also holds the position of Sam K. Viersen Presidential Professor and Research Curator for the museum's Collection of Mammals. *(Courtesy OU Public Affairs)*

Two months later, President Boren announced one of the most significant museum events in state history with the news that OU had received the largest and most important collection of French Impressionist paintings ever donated to a public university. The thirty-three-piece, $50 million collection had been assembled by Clara Rosenthal Weitzenhoffer, wife of the late Oklahoma City oil entrepreneur Aaron Weitzenhoffer and mother of OU '62 MFA alumnus and renowned Broadway and London theatre producer A. Max Weitzenhoffer. Clara had amassed dozens of works by Renoir, Monet, Gaugin, and other renowned artists in the private sanctuary of her home. The collection came to be housed in a new, unique area of the Fred Jones Jr. Museum of Art that mirrored Clara Weitzenhoffer's own home in Oklahoma City. Designed by internationally renowned architect Hugh Newell Jacobsen, the gallery re-created several rooms in the Weitzenhoffers' Nichols Hills residence. "When people go into the rooms, it will look as though the owners have stepped out," said Max Weitzenhoffer. "That's what Mother would have wanted." The Weitzenhoffer gallery was just one part of an extensive addition that Jacobsen designed for the Fred Jones Museum. The $14 million project was made possible through the generosity of foundations and individual donors, including a $1 million gift from the Fred and Mary Eddy Jones Foundation and a $2.5 million gift from native Oklahoman Howard Lester, then chairman of the board for Williams-Sonoma Inc. The museum's new auditorium would be named for Jones, and the entire west-wing addition would be named the Howard Lester and Mary Lester Wing in honor of its donors.

Boren believed the Weitzenhoffer Collection would have a deep effect on OU students, which was the most compelling reason for its presence on campus. "Exposure to the arts is a catalyst for opening up your mind; it expands your intellectual curiosity and broadens you. It is a university's duty to expose students to the greatest artistic traditions that we can," he said. Exposure to the Weitzenhoffer Collection

The campus's art scene also includes the Charles M. Russell Center for the Study of Art of the American West. Its director, Byron Price, also serves as director of the University of Oklahoma Press. (Courtesy OU Press)

More than a half-dozen couples have become engaged in the homelike setting of OU's Weitzenhoffer Gallery. (Courtesy Robert Taylor)

had some delightful side benefits that the president never predicted. Since the gallery's 2005 opening, more than a half-dozen young men have asked permission to propose marriage in the homelike setting of the Weitzenhoffer "living room." "That just shows we are expanding the sense of beauty and creative sensibilities of our students," Boren said with a smile, adding that each marriage proposal made in the Weitzenhoffer Collection has been accepted.

More exciting news for the Fred Jones Jr. Museum of Art came with the announcement in July 2007 that OU and Tulsa's Philbrook Museum of Art had entered into a partnership to share a private art collection valued at nearly $50 million. The Eugene B. Adkins Collection contained more than one thousand paintings, baskets, and pieces of jewelry and pottery. Adkins had selected only the very best artists for his four hundred–painting collection, which featured major representatives of the Taos Society of Artists. "The Eugene Adkins Collection further solidifies the Fred Jones Jr. Museum of Art as one of the leading university art museums in the entire nation," Boren said, adding that the collection's Taos pieces are "unexcelled by any art museum in the country. It really makes Oklahoma a destination."

With the museum's collections fast outgrowing even the recently built Lester Wing, planning began for a new top floor that would house the Eugene B. Adkins Gallery, a new photography gallery, and updated administrative offices. Soon that additional space would be in even greater demand. Private collector James T. Bialac of Arizona had learned of the educational programming, exhibits, and displays being accomplished through OU's Adkins Collection when he struck up a friendship with Rennard Strickland, senior scholar in residence at the OU College of Law. Strickland had given his own extensive collection of Native American art and artifacts to the Fred Jones Museum in 2009. Bialac called President Boren in 2010 and asked if OU would like to have the artworks he had gathered over nearly a half-century. Boren agreed to meet with Bialac and was astonished to learn that his collection included more than thirty-seven hundred pieces and was worth millions of dollars.

"I want to see that the paintings don't just sit in a basement," Bialac explained when he came to Norman to announce his gift before the OU Board of Regents. "This is the place where things can be seen and can be done." Bialac lovingly entrusted the museum with more than two thousand paintings and works on paper, one thousand kachina dolls, and one hundred significant pieces of Native American jewelry. According to Bialac's wishes, his artworks rotate each year within a permanent exhibition space designed to house the collection and are also displayed in campus locations where they can be appreciated by OU students, faculty, staff, and visitors.

Forty years after the Fred Jones Jr. Museum of Art first opened, the long-awaited Stuart Wing was dedicated in October 2011. The $13 million addition, named for OU Regent Jon R. Stuart and his wife, Dee Dee, in recognition of their $3 million lead gift, added 18,000 square feet to the museum, including a spacious gallery to house the Adkins and Bialac Collections. Other art collections came from William H. and Roxanne Thams and from Priscilla C. and Joseph N. Tate. Richard and Ellen Sandor donated a photographic collection. By 2014 the museum's combined holdings constituted one of the largest collections owned by a university. In terms of the value of its collections alone, estimated at nearly $1 billion in 2014, the Fred Jones ranks among the top three university art museums in the country.

In retrospect, the growth and development of collections at OU's art and natural history museums over the past two decades seems almost inconceivable. Today, the Sam Noble Oklahoma Museum of Natural History ranks third in attendance among national university-based museums. In 2014 the museum was one of five across the United States to receive the prestigious National Medal for Museum and Library Service, the nation's highest honor conferred on a museum for service to the community. First Lady Michelle Obama presented the award to museum director Michael Mares on May 8 at the White House. Museum founders Oscar Jacobson and J. Willis Stovall would hardly recognize the ventures they began more than a century ago. Yet they would no doubt be proud of the vital role their institutions now play in the university, state, and nation.

"Museums are very important. They are not extras that are optional for a university," Boren said. "If we are going to bring students a quality of life, give them the full human experience, then we need to minister not only to their minds and their physical bodies, but we need to touch their creative spirits. Our museums have become jewels in the crown."

REBUILDING THE SOONER ATHLETICS PROGRAM

The University of Oklahoma's outstanding tradition in collegiate athletics has helped shape not only the university's image but also the state's. Thus, from his very first day as president, David Boren faced some tough decisions. Reporters interviewing Boren on his inaugural day were eager to know if the presence of a new administration would signal a sea change for the OU Sooners football team, which had been under the direction of Coach Gary Gibbs since 1989. Gibbs, an OU linebacker and defensive coordinator under Barry Switzer, was credited with cleaning up the program following OU's devastating 1988 NCAA sanctions. The sanctions had limited the number of scholarships the team could offer during the first two years of Gibbs's tenure, adversely affecting the team's performance. The 1994 season had been especially tough, with a six-win, six-loss record. Gibbs deserved credit for taking the team through a difficult transition, but many criticized his coaching performance.

President Boren faced the issue head on, telling reporters, "Football is always important here, but it's not our central mission. We need to be number one in academics, and number one in football if we can be. I want to win like anybody else. But we need football players known for their character and integrity. We should have a proud tradition in athletics; we need to win, but we need to win the right way." Gary Gibbs offered his resignation on November 21, 1994, a change that had been agreed upon before Boren became president.

While the headlines featured OU football, President Boren focused his efforts on the university's overall athletic offerings, declaring that gender equity among athletic teams was a top priority. Under Title IX, the 1972 federal

Sherri Coale has become the winningest coach in OU women's basketball history and has led the team to multiple awards and Big 12 titles, as well as to the NCAA Finals. *(Courtesy Jared Thompson)*

In his more than fifteen years as athletic director, Joe Castiglione has guided the department to unparalleled success on and off the field. *(Courtesy Athletics Media Relations)*

As the winningest coach in Sooner football history, Bob Stoops has led his team to victory for seventeen seasons and counting. *(Courtesy Athletics Media Relations)*

law prohibiting sex discrimination in education, all universities and colleges receiving federal funds must offer equal opportunities for student-athletes. OU announced that, to achieve compliance, it would upgrade athletic programs and facilities for female student-athletes. To better achieve the goal of gender equity, women's soccer was added in early 1996 as OU's twentieth overall and tenth women's sport, and on April 26 OU hired a relatively unknown Norman High School women's basketball coach named Sherri Coale to coach the Sooner women. The team was in turmoil when Coale took over, but through her coaching talents and fierce dedication, she would build the Lady Sooners into what the *New York Times* later called a basketball "dynasty."

In 1998, the Athletic Department faced the new challenge of having to replace its beloved athletic director, Steve Owens, the former OU linebacker and 1969 Heisman Trophy winner. During his directorship, Owens had successfully spearheaded the five-year Campaign for Sooner Sports, which provided $12 million for capital projects, $10 million for scholarship endowments, and $3 million for annual programs. Upon Owens's resignation, Boren commended his service. "He's an Oklahoma hero," the president declared; "he deserves to be an Oklahoma hero. He loves this institution and represented it so well."

Soon after Owens's departure, OU officials traveled to Dallas to interview athletic director candidate Joe Castiglione. On April 30, 1998, OU welcomed Castiglione as its eleventh athletic director and vice president for intercollegiate athletics during a ceremony on the steps of Evans Hall. Castiglione, former athletic director at the University of Missouri, had developed a reputation as a hands-on manager. He was reputed to be someone who was not afraid to tackle tough issues and who paid personal attention to student-athletes, coaches, alumni, and supporters.

After Coach Gibbs resigned as OU's head football coach, two other coaches, Howard Schnellenberger in 1994 and John Blake in 1995–1998, took over the team's helm. The

team's win-loss records during those years were weaker than what OU fans had come to expect, and both coaches moved on to new positions at different universities following their brief tenures at OU. With Castiglione on board as athletic director, Boren knew exactly who he wanted to lead OU's football team into the future. He encouraged Castiglione to target Bob Stoops, a thirty-eight-year-old University of Florida assistant head coach and defensive coordinator. Considered one of the hottest prospects in the nation, on December 21, 1998, Stoops was introduced as the University of Oklahoma's twenty-first head football coach.

Stoops's performance exceeded all expectations. By the end of 1999, the new head coach had led the Sooner football team to its first bowl appearance in five seasons, against Ole Miss at the Independence Bowl. The game ended in a loss, but OU fans were thrilled to see their team back on the national stage. Sooner fans were also elated when the OU women's softball team won the Big 12 Conference championship in April 1999, marking only the second time in school history that the program had finished the regular season in first place. Men's gymnastics took the Big 12 title that year and, under Coach Mark Williams, has won five national championships. Also in 1999, the OU wrestling team won its first conference championship since 1986.

The Lloyd Noble Center became home to an emerging powerhouse in spring 2000, when the OU women's basketball team, under Sherri Coale's inspired leadership, won the Big 12 title and qualified for its first NCAA Sweet 16 appearance in fourteen years. In fact, the year 2000 proved to be what one sportswriter called "halcyon days for women's sports in Soonerland." The women's gymnastics squad broke five school records and set its all-time best score; it went on to win the national championship in 2014. The OU women's golf team won its first Big 12 Women's Golf Tournament since 1990. Then, the OU softball team won its second Big 12 regular season championship and made its first-ever appearance in the NCAA Women's College World Series—going

Often called the "Palace on the Prairie," the Gaylord Family–Oklahoma Memorial Stadium represents the very best of OU pride. Oklahoma weather permitting, the university's annual commencement ceremonies, pictured here, take place on its spacious field. *(Courtesy Robert Taylor)*

on to win the national championship, an accomplishment the team repeated in 2013.

Also cause for celebration, the OU Athletic Department announced in June 2000 that it would end the fiscal year in the black for the first time in a decade. But Castiglione's vision for OU athletics extended a decade into the future and included a complete renovation of the 1925 Oklahoma Memorial Stadium. The stadium plans called for overhauling all structures and amenities, replacing seating, adding twenty-two hundred club seats and twenty-seven sky suites, and covering the stadium's concrete walls in brick and cast stone. Castiglione acknowledged that his big dreams would come with a hefty price tag. "If you aren't moving forward, you are getting left behind. We want to be on the leading edge," he said. "Our stadium is somewhat of a Mecca for college football in this region; some of the best teams and some of the best games in college football history have taken place at our stadium. We need to make it a showplace."

In the fall of that same year, attendance at Memorial Stadium reached a six-year high as the football team experienced an electric season that included winning every game. Then, on January 3, 2001, OU won the Bowl Championship Series against Florida State University and become the 2000 national champions. Sooner fans were overjoyed.

The Sooner football team was not alone in achieving national prominence during the Boren years. In 2002 the women's basketball team reached an even higher level of performance, recording its best season in OU and Big 12 history by winning a third straight conference title and making it all the way to the NCAA Finals. This was a resounding statement about how far OU women's basketball had come since nearly being eliminated twelve years earlier. Coale had

revitalized the team, and she was careful to remind players what had come before. "Coach Coale would always say, 'Think of the players before you and what they had to go through to get us here,'" said OU junior Caton Hill.

As good news continued to mount in the Athletic Department, Joe Castiglione found a way to give back to the university's academic mission. In April 2002, the Athletic Department and OU Libraries announced a unique partnership that would provide $250,000 each year for four years to establish a $1 million library endowment to promote reading and academic achievement. The first year of funding sponsored an exhibit called "Books That Inspire," featuring titles recommended by OU faculty members, coaches, and Athletic Department staff members.

Stealing headlines later that year was the news that the Edward L. Gaylord family had made the largest gift in OU history. Their $12 million donation completed a $75 million

Sul Lee served as dean of university libraries for more than thirty years before his retirement on June 30, 2012. During his tenure, library holdings grew from 1.7 million to 5.5 million volumes and endowments rose from $300,000 to more than $25 million. *(Courtesy OU Public Affairs)*

expansion of OU's stadium, now named the Gaylord Family Oklahoma Memorial Stadium.

In 2008, the university celebrated Joe Castiglione's tenth year as athletic director. During that decade, the university had seen seven national team championships and forty conference championships. Even more important, the Athletic Department had achieved a decade of financial health. Castiglione had balanced every budget. No less significant, under Castiglione's leadership, OU's athletic teams had recorded their best-ever cumulative spring semester GPA and were graduating a record number of student-athletes. "It was kind of like turning a battleship; you can't wheel it around quickly," Castiglione said of the decade of work he and his staff put into making the Athletic Department thrive.

While Boren and Castiglione were thrilled with the program's successes, in 2010 they would face a new and serious challenge. The University of Colorado opted to move from the Big 12 to the Pac-12, and Nebraska left the Big 12 to join the Big 10 Conference. Then the University of Missouri and Texas A&M University joined the Southeastern Conference. Balance in the Big 12 Conference was now in question, and the conference's very existence was made even more uncertain after the Pac-12 issued an invitation to OU, Oklahoma State University, the University of Texas, and Texas Tech University to join that conference.

Boren and Castiglione spent many stressful days trying to decide whether or not OU should remain in the Big 12 Conference, which had lost a third of its members in fifteen months. Some OU supporters had seen enough and pushed for OU to leave the Big 12 for the Pac-12, but issues such as television markets, travel distance to games for players and fans, and university finances were all factors to be weighed. Another consideration was regional loyalties; the remaining members of the Big 12 had been part of the Big 8 or the Big 12 for fifty years, with six of the member schools having played one another since 1921. OU stepped up to save the conference by committing to stay in the Big 12. After a long series of negotiations, the Big 12 Conference held fast, recruiting Texas Christian University and West Virginia University to join its ranks in fall 2011.

As the 2012 Summer Olympic Games opened in London, a dozen current and former student-athletes represented the University of Oklahoma. The OU Athletic Department had still other achievements to boast in a year that had ended with six conference championships and more than fifteen hundred hours of community service by student-athletes, including a second trip to the Mission of Hope in Haiti.

The University of Oklahoma's achievements in sports, its deep love of tradition, and its drive to help form student-athletes who represent the best in competition, academics, and citizenship have brought an astonishing legacy to Oklahoma that includes more than 250 conference and 26 national championships. During President Boren's tenure alone, OU's teams have won more than 55 conference titles and 8 national titles. "The Athletic Department makes an important contribution to the spirit of our entire institution and our determination to be the best in every area," Boren explained. "OU seeks to be a role model for athletics, setting the highest possible standards for players, coaches, and staff. We seek to win the right way—by playing by the rules." As of 2014 President Boren, athletic director Joe Castiglione, and head football coach Bob Stoops had served together longer than any similar group of administrators in a U.S. college football program.

A VISION FOR OU'S FUTURE

As David Boren looks back over his two decades as president of the University of Oklahoma, he experiences a profound sense of satisfaction and pride in all that has been accomplished for tens of thousands of OU students and for the people of Oklahoma. But President Boren also sees a university that continues to challenge and inspire him every day. "The most fun part of the job for me is teaching and spending time with students," Boren says. "That's the joy, that's the connection. But you have to constantly struggle to put students first."

Foremost in this struggle is the continuing, yearly effort to keep OU affordable for future generations of students. "There have been ups and downs. We have worked very hard," the president said of his administration's efforts to secure state appropriations and private funding. Despite these efforts, Boren voiced concern that since 2010 the university has received only half of its average yearly percentage of state funding, so that state support amounted to only 16 percent of the OU budget in 2014, as compared to 50 percent in the 1970s and 1980s. Such devastating cuts have meant necessary increases in tuition and fees. "That is always the most heart-wrenching decision I have to make, because I have two essential goals that often come into conflict," he said. "One is achieving academic excellence, and the other is the need to keep an OU education affordable." Boren continues to seek ways to bridge the gap between OU's funding and its educational mission. Among those helping him are a legion of alumni and friends who have already provided $2 billion in private giving during Boren's presidency—an amount unprecedented in OU's history.

President Boren's efforts to put students first are also elevated by a stalwart Board of Regents, whose members have unanimously approved nearly every issue brought before them during his tenure. "That doesn't mean I always get my way," Boren cautioned, adding that his years in the U.S. Senate taught him valuable lessons about compromise. "You share ideas, you talk things out, you have to meet the other

President David L. Boren and President Emeritus George Lynn Cross share a moment of conversation at the dedication of Cross's statue in front of Evans Hall.
(Courtesy Robert Taylor)

who graduated from Harvard Business School and returned to OU to become dean and Fred E. Brown Chair of the Michael F. Price College of Business; Kyle Harper, who earned his PhD from Harvard and returned to become interim senior vice president and provost of the Norman campus; and Jason Sanders, an OU Rhodes Scholar who later earned both MD and MBA degrees from Harvard before returning as associate provost of the OU Health Sciences Center.

Eventually one of those leaders may become OU's next president, but Boren will not choose who will take his place. "I don't see it as my duty to have a hand-picked successor. The most important responsibility a Board of Regents ever has is to pick a president, and I don't think that an outgoing president should usurp the ultimate responsibility of the board," he said frankly. Instead Boren believes his responsibility lies in preparing the university for its future. The hard-earned wisdom of the late OU president George Lynn Cross has influenced that belief.

During the early years of his presidency, Boren spent many hours visiting with Dr. Cross and former OU first lady Cleo Cross. Although both were physically frail and in their late eighties, their minds and memories were razor-sharp. "I had the benefit of their experience," Boren said. Cross told Boren that he had erred by failing to mentor young professionals who would produce OU's next generation of leaders. "He most regretted that when he retired, many of the top leadership were close to his age," Boren said, adding that OU experienced "a tidal wave" of administrative retirements shortly after Cross's departure. "He told me, 'Within three years, the university that I left was almost unrecognizable to me.'"

President Boren does not intend to make the same mistakes. He has spent the past two decades grooming a new generation of leaders who understand the culture of OU and Oklahoma, appreciate the evolution that OU has undergone, and share the university's commitment to progress and excellence.

The potential candidates to succeed Boren as president will have experienced for themselves OU's rise to prominence over the past twenty years, including earning a top ranking by the *Princeton Review* for academic excellence and affordable tuition. They will already know that the university has started more than thirty new programs and spent almost $2 billion in constructing new buildings and renovating existing ones, and that the university's hard work has made it a leader among all American universities in international exchange and study-abroad programs. In 2013 OU's Research Campus received the Oustanding Research Park Award from the National Association of University Research Parks. OU's entrepreneurship program in the Price College of Business ranks in the top two in the nation among all public universities.

person halfway sometimes, and then you wind up with a very strong consensus."

Sometimes putting students first means being willing to change your own ideas. The president said he has surprised everyone he knows by embracing technology as higher education evolves during the digital age. The university is experimenting with digital components that may someday replace textbooks in the classroom and is implementing online resources for home study that will free up precious class time. OU is also exploring ways to reach gifted and nontraditional high school students through technology. Boren's goal is to keep pace with today's rapidly changing educational market while maintaining the treasured sense of community that he has helped foster at OU. "If a university is not moving forward, it is falling backward," he observed.

Boren has helped move the University of Oklahoma forward far beyond what anyone could have imagined and has said that one of his proudest legacies is the administration he has built, person by person. "You want to be sure that you hand on a very strong university with real depth in its academic leaders, its staff, and administrative leaders." Several of the younger leaders Boren brought to campus had attended the university during his presidency, including Daniel Pullin,

As of 2014, OU's students continue to achieve success in numerous areas. For the seventh consecutive year, OU's Drama School team swept the Kennedy Center National Championship awards, and the debate team had won the national championship four of the past eight years, with one debater being named best speaker in the nation. OU continues to rank first in the nation among public universities in the number of enrolled National Merit Scholars, and OU has twice been named a "Character Building College" by the Templeton Foundation for stressing the value of community. In 2013, OU was the only university in America, public or private, whose students earned Rhodes, Marshall, Mitchell, Goldwater, Fulbright, National Security Education Program, and Truman scholarships all in the same year.

One day it will be the next president's job to put students first and help carry the University of Oklahoma—including all that has been shaped and nurtured by David Lyle Boren and the twelve presidents who preceded him—into an even brighter future.

President Boren admits that he is not ready for that day to arrive just yet. "I hope I will know when it's time to retire—that's an important quality in a president," he said with a smile. "But I hope I get to keep doing this for quite a while longer."

INDEX

College of Nursing, 116, 119, 130, 140–41, 192
College of Pharmacy, 119, 130–31, 133, 135, 192
College of Public Health, 90, 192
Collings, Ellsworth, 36, 66, 84
Collings Hall, 84
commencement exercises, 10–11, 17, 119
Communication Workers of America, 161, 163
Communism, fear of. *See* anti-Communism
community colleges and junior colleges, 48, 52, 147, 161
Community Medicine School. *See* School of Community
    Medicine
community service, 180, 199
Confucius Institute, 186
Congregational Church, 20, 49
Conner, Bart, 122, *135*, 137
Conoco/DuPont, 153
conscription, military. *See* military draft
Constitutional Convention of Oklahoma. *See* Oklahoma
    Constitutional Convention
Constitution of the State of Oklahoma. *See* state constitution
continuing education. *See* adult continuing education
Copeland, Fayette, 36
Copeland Hall, 36, 118
Cornell University, 117
Cosier, Richard, 164
Couch, Glenn C., 69, 79, 83, 167
Couch Center, 75, 90–91, 100, 175
Council of Deans, 62–63
Crawford, Jan Marie, 179
Crawford, Richard J., 179
Cross, Cleo, 68–70, *70*, *71*, *72*, 89, 94, 96, 98; Boren relations, 120,
    200; at Boyd House, 82, 93; international scholarships, *95*
Cross, George Lynn, 54, 62–96, 69, *70*, 88, 90, 94, *95*; and Ada
    Lois Sipuel Fisher, 75–76, *75*, *77*, *95*; Boren relations, 93,
    95, 96, 101, 120, 173, 200, *200*; on Brandt, 62, 63, 67; on
    Hollomon, 101, 107; Morris appointment, 167; presidential
    portrait, 80; *Professors, Presidents, and Politicians*, 68, 71,
    75, 79, 85; OU centennial, 161, *162*; OU's ninetieth birthday
    party, 131, *131*; statue dedication, 96, *96*
Cross, Leon, 148
Cross Center, 83–84, 110
Cross Hall. *See* George Lynn Cross Botany and Microbiology
    Hall
Crowe, William J., Jr., 158
Cruce, Lee, 24, 27, 30
Cunningham, Robert, 79
curfews, 91–92
Curtis, Lloyd B., 15
Cwens. *See* Society of Cwens

Dads' Association, 73
Daily Oklahoman, 128, 137, 146, 147, 165
Dale, Edward Everett, 32, 46, 59, 67–68, 90
Dale Hall, 90
Dalton, Deborah, 164
Daly, Charles F., 80
dances and dancing, 9, 11, 19, 32, 34, 48, 82
David, Paul, 86
David Ross Boyd Tree Planting Program, 131, 138
Davies, Kimberlee, 188
Davies, Nancy, 116

Dean, John O., 99
Dean A. McGee Eye Institute, 119
Deans' Council. *See* Council of Deans
death threats, 93, 151, 155
DeBarr, Edwin C., 5, 8, 31, 41
DeBarr Hall, 31, 32, *35*
debate teams, 113, 201
Decker, Charles E., 67–68
DeGolyer, Everette L., 81, *81*
DeGolyer Collection, 81, 88
Democratic Party, 19, 28, 53, 80, 126, 130; gubernatorial role,
    18, 24, 40, 52, 53, 55; in Norman, 4; state constitutional
    convention, 17
demonstrations. *See* protests and demonstrations
Dennis, James L., 90, 99, 110
Dental College. *See* College of Dentistry
Depression, 51–53, 54, 70
diabetes centers, 193
Distinguished Service Citation, 68, 112, 124, 138
divestment, 146
Dodge, Homer L., 35, 63, 64–65, 70
Donald E. Pray Law Library, 182
Donald W. Reynolds Foundation, 184
Donald W. Reynolds Performing Arts Center (Holmberg
    Hall), 8, 33, *34*, *43*, 54, 57, 76, 173, 174
Dorman, Phyllis, 129
dormitories. *See* residence halls
Doty, Ralph, 167
Dowd, Jerome, 29
draft, military. *See* military draft
drama, 52, 54, 75, 103, 104. *See also* School of Drama
Droegemeier, Kelvin, 191, *191*
drinking, 6, 13, 15–16, 82, 89, 92
drugs, 92, 100, 112, 153, 155
due process, 71, 76–77, 86
Duncan, Donnie, 148–49, 153, 154, 155, 164
Dunjee, Roscoe, 75, 76
Dunlap, E. T., 128
Dunlap Clock Tower. *See* E. T. Dunlap Clock Tower
Dunnavant, Keith, *The 50-Year Seduction*, 132
Dupree, Marcus, 136

Earth Observation Satellite Company (EOSAT), 141, 159
Economics Department, 29, 39, 80
Edmondson, Howard, *88*
education program. *See* College of Education; School of
    Education; School of Teaching
Elbert, Arthur J., 129
Elder, Frederick Stanton, 8, 13
Ellison, Gayfree, 28, 35, 53
Ellison Infirmary, 53
endowed deanships, 181
endowed faculty positions, 65, 73, 89, 120, 131, 136, 158, 161;
    cancer research, 192; chemical engineering, 153; Kingfisher
    College, 49; nursing, 141; State Regents Program, 183–84
endowment, university-wide, 165, 183
Energy Center, 130–33, 135, 136, 139, 141, 150, 160, 168
Energy Center Founders, 131–32, 133, 134
Engineering College. *See* College of Engineering
Engineering Research Center for Collaborative Adaptive
    Sensing of the Atmosphere, 191

plane crashes, 86–87, 117

Plans for the Future of the University of Oklahoma (Cross), 73

plays. *See* drama

Plessy v. Ferguson, 75

Plumberg, Diane, 165

police, 89, 103, 106. *See also* campus police

Pollard, Art, *148*

Pope, Tim, 164

Powell, Colin, *188*, 189

pranks and high jinks, 11, 19, 35. *See also* panty raids

Pray, Joseph C., 86

Pray Law Library. *See* Donald E. Pray Law Library

preceptorship programs, 84

prefabricated housing, *74*, 75

Preparing America's Foreign Policy for the Twenty-First Century, 189

prep school, 5–6, 11, 29

Presbyterian Church, 19, 26, 39

Prescott, Maurice, 36, 52

Presidential Faculty Fellows Program, 185

presidential inaugurations, 98–99, *98*, 128, *145*, 160, 171–72, *172*

Presidential International Travel Fellowship, 188

presidential portraits, 80

Presidential Professors Program, 181–82

Presidential Study Abroad Scholarships, 187, 188

President's Associates. *See* University of Oklahoma President's Associates

President's Council, 122, 129

President's Fund, 144, 146, 147

president's home, *11*; Pickard Avenue, 103, 104, 111, 117, *117*, 123, 152. *See also* Boyd House

President's Leadership Class, 89, 100, *142*

presidents' salaries, 4, 52, 60, 61

President's Task Force on Enrollment, 140

President's Trophy, 180

Price, B. Byron, *195*

Price, Michael F., 184

Price College of Business, 29, 186, 187, 191, 200. *See also* Center for Economic and Management Research, 49

Prickett, Kirby, 16

Pride of Oklahoma Marching Band. *See* marching band

Princeton University, 60, 61

Professional Writing Program, 32

Professors, Presidents, and Politicians (Cross), 68, 71, 75, 79, 85

Project Threshold, 167–68

protests and demonstrations, 76–77, 91, 92, 100, *102*, 116; anti-loyalty oath, 79, 85; antiwar, 102–7, 112, 168; by faculty, 93, 100; on racial harassment, 159, 160. *See also* sit-ins

Provost's Office. *See* Office of the Provost

Psychology Department, 20, 166, 167, 168–69

public art, 177, 192. *See also* statues

Public Health College. *See* College of Public Health

Public Information Service, 47–48

Pullin, Daniel, 191, 200

Purcell, Chris, *173*

"Push Class," 6

Race and the University: A Memoir (Henderson), 93, 110, 115–16

racial harassment and violence, 111, 115–16, 159–60, 169

racial segregation and integration, 75–78, 87–88

radicalism, 91, 93–94, 100. *See also* anti-Communism

Rader, Jesse L., 23, 35, 51

radio, 36, 41, 52–53, *52*, 55, 104, 107, 118

Rainy Day Fund (State of Oklahoma), 163, 164

rape, 153

rare books, 81, 88

Ray, David H., 185–86, *185*

Ray, Joseph, 129

Reach for Excellence, 171, 182, 183, 185, 190

reading groups, 185–86, *185*

Reaves, Samuel Watson, 16

recessions, 132–33, 134–35, 139–40

Records, Ralph, 71

recruitment of athletes, 118, 149, 153

recruitment of faculty, 71, 140, 145, 181

recruitment of minorities, 110, 159, 167

recruitment of students, 5, 6, 12, 140, 159, 167, 181

"Red River Bridge War," 53

Red Scare. *See* anti-Communism

Reese, Jim E., 80

Reeves, Samuel Watson, 71

Regents. *See* Board of Regents; Oklahoma State Regents for Higher Education

Regents Professors, 11, 26, 112, 123, 168

religion, 6, 19–20, 49, 92–93, 125. *See also* churches

Religious Studies program, 186

Renfrow, W. C., 4, 7

Republican Party, 4, 17, 19, 28, 126, 127, 130, 134

Research Campus, 190, 191, 200

Research Institute, 65, 70, 81

research professorships, 66, 67–68, 70, 71, 94

Reserve Officers' Training Corps (ROTC), 34, 56, 59, 86–87, 89, 102–7, 168, 194

residence halls, 8, 36, 65–66, 72, 73, 83–84, 90–91; athletes', 153; Faculty in Residence, 175, *175*; fires, 82–84; honors students', 145; Memorial Stadium, 55–56, *55*; policies, 91–92, 175; women's, 41, *43*, 48

residential colleges, 175–76

Retired Faculty Program, 182

retirement benefits, faculty. *See* faculty retirement benefits

Reynolds, Joe Brett, 147

Reynolds Foundation. *See* Donald W. Reynolds Foundation

Reynolds Performing Arts Center. *See* Donald W. Reynolds Performing Arts Center (Holmberg Hall)

Rhodes Scholarship, 32, 53, 95, 118, 172, 173, 186; Brandt's, 50, 59

Rice, William N., 4–5, 8

Rich, Clayton, 142

Richards, Aute, 49

Richards Hall, 49, 73

Riggs, Lynn, 35

Ring Ceremony, 180, *180*

riots, 89, 102, 103, 104, 115, 125

Risinger, Bud, 8

rivalries, intercollege, 35

Roberts, Fred, 12

Robertson, Port, 92

Robertson Hall, 41, *43*, 83

Rock Building, Norman, Okla., 5, 6, 13, 18, *19*

rock concerts, 99, 105

Rogers, John, 46

Rogers, Tammy, 158

Roller, H. Duane, 88

room and board plans, 6, 75